MOVING OUTWARD

A PROPOSAL FOR THE
NEW EVANGELIZATION IN THE
UNITED STATES

4-25-20
Feast of St. Mark

To Caleb —
a great server at the
altar of our God. May
you always serve.

Deacon Vince

MOVING OUTWARD

A PROPOSAL FOR THE
NEW EVANGELIZATION IN THE
UNITED STATES

VINCENT L. BERNARDIN

TO

Two Mary's –

My Heavenly Mother

and

the Mother of our five children

Table of Contents

Prologue

If there is any truth to the aphorism, *"timing is everything"*, this book may be in serious trouble from the outset. I was beginning to write the book in earnest when the sorry business about Theodore McCarrick came out. On the heels of that story, the Pennsylvania Grand Jury released the results of its two-year investigation into clergy sex abuse. The report documented in detail not only the horrible crimes that some of our priests perpetrated against innocent children, but the numerous instances in which bishops facilitated the perpetrators with blithe excuses and convenient transfers and continued life-long security. The whole sorry nightmare of 2002 was replayed in lurid detail and multiplied by the revelation that one of our American cardinals was a longstanding predator of seminarians, using his position of power to compromise idealistic young men.

To make matters worse, the former Vatican nuncio to the United States, Archbishop Carlo Maria Viganò, publicly accused some of the top prelates in the Church – including Pope Francis himself – of knowing about Abp. McCarrick's history of sinful abuses and doing nothing to censure him.

On the heels of Archbishop Viganò's letter, any number of state attorneys general announced the opening of their own grand jury investigations. Shortly thereafter, the U.S. Department of Justice announced a federal investigation. All the while investigative reporters were releasing accusations about possible new cases of priestly abuse and the press examined prelates around the country under a hyperbolic microscope with the aggression of a pack of piranhas.

With the "Summer of Shame" only recently in our past, plus the resignations of more bishops and the prospect of more diocesan bankruptcies looming, conventional wisdom suggests that this is not the time to publish a book that proposes our bishops lead a new, unprecedented era of evangelization. Many American Catholics would rather follow a blind man off a cliff and many bishops would rather go into hiding and hope the world forgets they are still around. If any of the recommendations in this book are ever implemented, secular society will undoubtedly appraise them as a last-ditch, cynical attempt of our bishops to stave off the inevitable demise of the Catholic Church.

My personal feelings are more sanguine. Our Lord has an amazing way of making *all* things work for the good for those who love him (cf. Rom 8:28), even our bishops.

There is also 2 Timothy 4:2: *Proclaim the word; be persistent whether it is convenient or inconvenient; convince, reprimand, encourage through all patience and teaching.* This book may very well come at an "inconvenient" time. But who knows? It may also prove to be providential. I'm willing to put all that in our Lord's hands.

There is never a time when the call to evangelize can be put aside until it is more convenient. As it is, it has been put aside far too long. According to one perspective, there may not be a better time than right now for us to evangelize intelligently, but also with unprecedented passion. Regardless of our feelings of impotence facing a world full of cynicism, we need to remember it is our Lord's strength that will get the job done.

We are probably better off preaching from a position of sin and weakness anyway. When the Apostle Paul begged that the thorn in his flesh be removed, the risen Christ reminded him: *My grace is sufficient for you, for power is made perfect in weakness.* (2 Cor 12:9) All authentic witness is born out of weakness and, at times, even sin.

History has shown that it is just at such times as these when our gracious Father raises up saints to reform the Church and proclaim the Gospel in new ways. *When sin abounds, grace abounds all the more* (Rom 5:20). Despite the sad, humbled position that we find ourselves in, the antidote is not withdrawal or accepting a role of irrelevance. It is one of true apostolic initiative, one that sends us outward, albeit with sincere humility and forthright repentance. The actions that are proposed in this book really are the sort of things that need to be done and if I demurred in saying so, I would not be true to my Lord who loves me and whom I love.

As I date this message, the fact that today is the Solemnity of the Immaculate Conception brings back a memory from five years ago on December 8th when George Witwer and I stood at the altar of the Shrine of Divine Mercy in Stockbridge, MA. Together, we consecrated ourselves and our new ministry, the St. Paul Evangelization Society, to our heavenly Mother. My hope today is that Mary will make use of this book for the greater honor and glory of her Son.

December 9, 2019
Solemnity of the Immaculate Conception

Introduction

This book is about a *Proposal* for "doing better" as evangelizers. When I look at the world today and the Church in the midst of the world, I continuously find myself thinking that we can do better than this... Surely, for the sake of our Lord Jesus, we can present the Gospel with greater fruitfulness. We can do better at retaining our youth. We can bring more people into the community of Faith.

In its essence, the book is a proposal for *what* we should consider doing and *how* we might do it. It is divided into three parts (like Gaul). As the title suggests, Part I – *The Proposal* – presents what the book is all about. Chapter I makes a case for wide-scale evangelization as the single greatest unmet need in the Church and, for that matter, the world. The *Proposal* itself is presented in Chapter II with a minimum of embellishment. It is presented in the form of "resolutions" for all members of the Church. There is a part that applies to the laity, another part for diocesan clergy, a part for religious, one for diocesan bishops and one for the United States Conference of Catholic Bishops. The third chapter takes a "deep dive" into the *Proposal*, describing the ways in which it represents a paradigm shift for evangelization as we know it today.

Scattered throughout the book are short, vignettes in the life of a fictional American bishop, identified simply as Bishop Paul. I think of these brief interludes as "word-pictures" describing the humanity of a bishop as he struggles to become a "fisher of men" and to lead his diocese in the same direction. Chapter IV is the first of these little fictional interludes in which Bishop Paul surprises his presbyterate with a bold Vision for the future.

Part II – *The Challenges* – discusses a variety of hurdles that the Church in America will have to get over in order for the *Proposal* to succeed in really doing better than we are now. Chapter V deals with the importance of understanding and forgiveness, especially in the context of the clergy sex abuse scandal. Specifically, the forgiveness that is proposed is the need to forgive our bishops. I contend that without an understanding of how we got into this mess and without sincerely extending an olive branch to our bishops, the evangelical potential of the Church will be gravely damaged for a long time to come.

At the heart of the Gospel is the recognition that God actually loves. His love is incarnated in Jesus of Nazareth, the "pearl of great price", the longing of every human heart. Chapter VI advocates for a Church that leads with this message, before and above all else. No other message, regardless of how true it may be, has the power to save. Chapter VII is an appeal for ecclesial leaders to step out and really lead their flock. In an era of broad-based accommodation and decision-making by committee, this is one of the biggest challenges facing the Church today.

The second fictional interlude in the life of Bishop Paul is presented in Chapter VIII. In this episode, he is faced with a tough personal decision on how to move forward.

Chapter IX explores two prevalent and opposing attitudes holding us back from sharing our love for Jesus with those around us. In Chapter X, the evidence that we really have been called and are expected to evangelize is presented. This evidence is drawn from Sacred Scripture, the current state of the Church in the United States, and the magisterial message of all the pontiffs from John XXIII through Francis. Chapter XI points out something that is culturally missing within Catholicism, but that exists and enlivens many evangelical churches: a sense of purpose. We have one, but it tends to be a well-hidden secret.

Up to this point, the book has been propositional and expository in tone. In the final part – *On Achieving the Vision* – the emphasis shifts into a more practical mode, focusing on *what* we might do and *how* we need to go about doing it if we hope to achieve widespread, fruitful evangelization in the United States.

Chapter XII proposes a long-range strategy along with sequential steps for evangelizing an entire region (aka, diocese). While recognizing that every diocese is unique, it suggests that there is a common-sense, step-by-step process that needs to undergird the work of any diocese in trying to achieve this ambitious vision.

Of course, *what* we do is only as effective as *how* we go about doing it. Chapter XIII uses a fictional event in the life Bishop Paul to illustrate the power of heroic, holy leadership. The focus of Chapter XIV is on the need to change the culture of the Church to become supportive of evangelization; a change that can only happen through extraordinary transformational leadership and a very un-American willingness to follow.

Finally, Chapter XV takes up the even more ambitious dream of evangelizing the entire country; what national evangelization might look like and how the bishops would need to interact among themselves in order to achieve this dream.

* * *

In summary, this book presents a *grand* proposal. The very ideas seem out of reach, Pollyannaish, maybe even utopian. One thing it is not, however, is triumphalist. You cannot seriously consider the ideas herein without feeling very small and inadequate. But for some reason, I suspect that is exactly the way our Lord wants us to feel, for power is made perfect in weakness.

Regardless, the time has come to have this conversation. Perhaps, under the humbling empowerment of the Holy Spirit, the "sleeping giant" called the Catholic Church can be roused and the world will take notice, eternal destinies changed, and human lives made better. With all that at stake, at least it's a conversation worth having. One thing is sure. In a world dismissive or even antagonistic of the Christian faith, if we don't take conscious steps to elevate our own expectations, it won't happen.

Join me in dreaming big dreams, in being inspired by the possibility that the end of the world is *not* just around the corner; that the Church is still in the business of saving souls and has within her all the power she needs to fulfill that mission.

Won't you pray with me for the achievement of this very big dream? At the very least, we can do better.

Part I
The Proposal

PARACLETE PRESS
PO Box 1568
Orleans, MA 02653

We hope you will enjoy this book and find it useful in enriching your life.

Book title: _____

Your comments: _____

How you learned about this book: _____

Reasons why you bought this book: *(check all that apply)*

☐ SUBJECT   ☐ AUTHOR   ☐ ATTRACTIVE COVER   ☐ ATTRACTIVE INSIDE

☐ RECOMMENDATION OF FRIEND   ☐ RECOMMENDATION OF REVIEWER   ☐ GIFT

If purchased: Bookseller _____ City _____ State _____

Please send me a Paraclete Press catalog. I am particularly interested in: *(check all that apply)*

1. ☐ Spirituality
2. ☐ Spiritual Practices (Which ones?) _____
3. ☐ Theology

4. ☐ Prayer/Worship
5. ☐ Catholic Inspiration
6. ☐ Orthodoxy
7. ☐ Fiction

8. ☐ Religious Traditions (Which ones?) _____
9. ☐ Other _____

Name (PRINT) _____
Street _____ City _____ Phone _____
E-mail _____ State _____ Zip _____

Please send a Paraclete Press catalog to my friend:

Name (PRINT) _____ Phone _____
Street _____ City _____ State _____ Zip _____

PARACLETE PRESS
PO Box 1568 • Orleans, MA 02653 • Tel: 1-800-451-5006 • Fax: 508-255-5705
Available at better booksellers. Visit us online at www.paracletepress.com.

I. The Greatest Unmet Need

Where there is no vision, the people perish.

Proverbs 29:18 (KJV)

Have you ever asked yourself what is the Catholic Church's greatest unmet need at this point in history in the United States? It's a question worth asking. Ask several different people and you'll get several different answers. And yet, it is not simply a matter of opinion. If we were to ask God that question, he would recognize various needs, but in the final analysis, he could and would identify one single greatest unmet need, more important than all the others, because it is *truly* the greatest unmet need. With God, there would be no biasing influences; just the truth.

As committed members of the Church, a difficulty is bound to arise in us trying to answer this question on our own: we are too close to the subject. We can't "see the forest for all the trees". We develop a kind-of spiritual blindness in the midst of all our ecclesial distractions.

I can't speak directly for our Lord, but I believe his gift of discernment is available to us. Moreover, the question of greatest unmet need is so important that we should muster the temerity to offer prospective answers and discuss them and follow them to their logical conclusions. We need to do this simply to please him; to be good stewards. So, at the risk of sounding amazingly arrogant, I am going to posit one possible answer and propose a course of action to address it.

Owning the Truth

I want to be as unambiguous as possible. In my view, the Church's greatest unmet need at this point in history in the United States can be summed up in a single word: *evangelization.*

Since *"evangelization"* means different things to different people, a working definition seems in order; moreover, since this is a book written to Catholics, the definition is to be understood as specific to *Catholic* evangelization.

Working Definition of Catholic Evangelization

Evangelization is an initiative of the Holy Spirit that requires human cooperation. It includes all the formal and informal activities of the organized Church and of her individual members and ecclesial divisions which are aimed at eliciting a personal encounter with Jesus that leads to belief in the Triune God and a committed and mature life of discipleship. Central to the apostolate of evangelization is the verbal and/or written word of faith communicated within the witness of holy lives.

As used in this book, evangelization includes not only the initial work aimed at introducing a person to Christ, but also the important work of pre-evangelization that enables initial belief and the essential post-evangelization work that moves the new believer into mature discipleship.

Clearly this definition needs to be unpacked, which I will attempt to do throughout the book. It also begs the question "how can we evangelize well?" The book also proposes some answers to this question. But, whether or not you agree with the ideas offered here, the cornerstone on which this book is build is the following proposition: the Church in the West needs to re-appropriate the Great Commission in a much more fruitful way than we have in recent centuries. This re-appropriation is needed, in order to give both ourselves and the rest of the world a chance to consciously become disciples of Christ Jesus (cf. Mt 28:16-20). To my way of thinking, this is the uncontestable truth that the Church needs to own. As the reader, if you cannot accept this proposition, there is no point in reading on.

Evangelization is the single greatest unmet need because it is a constitutive element of the Christian life and yet, with notable exceptions, we shy away from doing it

Evangelization is not the single greatest unmet need of the Church because we are losing Catholics, although we are (see Chapter X). It is not the single greatest unmet need because other Christians *are* evangelizing, although they are (thankfully). Evangelization is the single greatest unmet need because it is a constitutive element of the Christian life and yet with notable exceptions, we shy away from doing it.

Every diocese in the United States has an arm of Catholic Charities. Most, parishes have working St. Vincent de Paul conferences and other charitable ministries to assist the poor and visit the lonely. We take up special collections to aid victims of natural disasters and help citizens of the Third World establish businesses. As a people, we are acutely aware of injustices in the world, from protecting the unborn to assisting refugees fleeing persecution. These are just a few of the reasons why I am proud to profess the fact that I am a Catholic. In these areas of Catholicism, there is a concerted effort to align praxis with what we profess. It is not perfect, of course, but we are consistently trying.

Evangelization is a different matter. Praxis and profession do not line up and there is not widespread awareness of this fact. The "average" Catholic in the pews simply is not touched by evangelization, either as

> Few of us have ever spoken of God's love to another human being

the evangelized or the evangelizer. The New Testament is filled with explicit admonitions to proclaim the Good News and the Magisterium teaches it (see Chapter X). A great "cloud of witnesses" throughout the ages affirm it... and yet, with few exceptions, we avoid it. We talk *about* it enough, but few of us ever intentionally set out to look for opportunities to bring the light of Christ into people's lives. Few of us have ever spoken about God's love to another human being. Ask yourself, when was the last time you spoke to anyone about the depth of your own love for Jesus and why you love him?

I am not suggesting that we start tackling people on the street and bashing them over the head with our bibles. In fact, true evangelization avoids coercion and harsh judgment. As Pope Francis has pointed out, such behavior is prosyletism and must be avoided.[1] At its root, true evangelization is a high form of love; of willing the best for the beloved. The point is this: the fact that we do not place a high premium on evangelical love distorts who we are both as individual Christians and as the Church.

Catholicism with a Purpose

What if some of us found that all the many the comforts of life obviated the need to stand upright and walk? So, we sat in our most comfortable ottoman all day. We simply didn't need to walk anymore. Technology and modern modes of transportation could take care of all our reasons for getting up and walking. Despite the fact that we are designed with legs and are meant to walk upright, we just simply stopped. Predictably, we would start putting on weight. We would gradually become overly-dependent and start imposing on others. Given enough time, we would become totally self-centered and would probably wind up bed-ridden. Such passivity and weight gain might even bring on death. Why? Because we are designed with legs and we are meant to use them for our good and that of others.

As walking is to our physical being, evangelizing is to who we are as Christians. By Baptism, it is something we were *designed* to do, even though we seem to exist just fine without it. One might go so far as to say it is the *sine qua non* for everything else we do as Christians. If we do not forthrightly acknowledge the One who commanded us to be peacemakers, to feed the hungry, to celebrate the Eucharist, and to receive absolution from our sins, why should we bother to do any of these things? The original reason for doing them begins to fade and we eventually can lose our faith altogether. The fact is, many of us are *not* doing these things anymore and this is the very reason that we have ceased to believe. We cease to believe because, at least in part, we have ceased to proclaim and defend the lordship of Jesus. To the extent that we allow this to happen, we become deformed, mere caricatures of the winsome Bride of Christ that our Lord desires.

> "… evangelizing all people constitutes the essential mission of the Church… She exists in order to evangelize."
>
> -   *Pope St. Paul VI*
>   *Evangelii nuntiandi*

Pope St. Paul VI was one of the most prescient prophets of the twentieth century. With clear and compelling arguments, he wrote some 40-odd years ago in his encyclical *Evangelii nuntiandi* that the *essential purpose* of the Church is to evangelize.

> …evangelizing all people constitutes the essential mission of the Church. This task and mission are particularly urgent because of the expansive, penetrating changes in present-day society. In

29

fact, evangelizing is the [Church's] utmost identity. She exists in order to evangelize...[2]

Pope Paul wrote this encyclical because he recognized the spirit of missionary zeal slipping out of the Church and, for him, if that missionary zeal did not hold the premiere place in the ministry of the Church, then literally nothing should.

But, is it really true? Is this really the central purpose of the Church?

Creating a medley of Sacred Scripture, the Prologue of the *Catechism of the Catholic Church* begins with the words:

> "FATHER, … this is eternal life, that they may know you, the only true God, and Jesus Christ whom you have sent (Jn 17:3). God desires all men to be saved and to come to the knowledge of the truth." (1 Tim 2:3-4) "There is no other name under heaven given among men by which we must be saved" (Acts 4:12) than the name of JESUS.

The Prologue follows with: "God, infinitely perfect and blessed in himself, in a plan of sheer goodness freely created man to make him share in his own blessed life."[3] There it is. God wants us to experience salvation and it is only through Jesus that salvation is possible. The Prologue continues: "… So that this call should resound throughout the world, Christ sent forth the apostles he had chosen, commissioning them to proclaim the gospel." These words are proclaimed in our *Catechism* before anything else is mentioned. Everything else is subordinate.

Sometimes, the *Catechism* has a way of presenting the truth in a surprising way that seems to contradict common experience. One example is Paragraph 888 as shown below:

> Bishops, with priests as co-workers, have as their first task "to preach the Gospel of Christ to all men," in keeping with the Lord's command (*Presbyterorum ordinis, 4; cf. Mk 15:15*). They are "heralds of faith, who draw new disciples to Christ; they are authentic

teachers" of the apostolic faith "endowed with the authority of Christ." (cf. *Lumen Gentium, 25*)

If one were to ask most Catholics to give a description of a typical twenty-first century bishop in the United States, it is not likely that many would say bishops spend a lot of time "preaching the Gospel of Christ to all men". That doesn't appear to be a high priority for bishops, let alone "their first task". All too often, they simply don't seem to be "heralds of faith, who draw new disciples to Christ."

The same can be said of our priests and deacons, most of whom spend all their waking hours focused on *internal* parish matters and little of that has to do with evangelization (see Chapter XI).

> It is hard to conceive of a greater need within the Church than something that is associated with our salvation that we tend not to do

Of course, the problem does not stop with the clergy. It applies to the laity as well. Paragraph 1270 of the *Catechism* reads:

"Reborn as sons of God, [the baptized] must profess before men the faith they have received from God through the Church" (*Lumen Gentium, 37*) and participate in the apostolic and missionary activity of the People of God.

In other words, by virtue of Baptism *all Christians* are commanded to evangelize. In Paragraph 1816 the *Catechism* even goes a step further and documents the serious consequence of *refusing* to evangelize:

The disciple of Christ must not only keep the faith and live on it, but also profess it, confidently bearing witness to it, and spread it: "All however must be prepared to confess Christ before men and to follow him along the way of the Cross, amidst the persecutions which the Church never lacks." (*Lumen Gentium, 42*) Service of and witness to the faith *are necessary for salvation*: "So everyone who acknowledges me before men, I also will acknowledge before my Father who is in heaven; but whoever denies me before men, I also will deny before my Father who is in heaven." (Mt 10:32-33) (*italics added*)

In short, according to the teachings of our faith, the work of evangelization is absolutely central to what all of us are supposed to be doing; in part, our very salvation rests on it. It is hard to conceive of a greater need within the Church than something that is

> Imagine what it would be like if membership in the Catholic Church clearly denoted the job of bringing others to Christ

associated with our salvation that we tend not to do. We must learn to believe in our hearts what St. Paul the Apostle clearly felt: *Woe to me if I do not proclaim the Gospel* (1 Cor 9:16) .

Despite Pope St. Paul's efforts and those of all his successors since, the spark of evangelical purpose that is beginning to be seen in such outstanding groups as the Fellowship of Catholic University Students (FOCUS) and the Amazing Parish movement has not yet caught fire throughout a broad cross section of the American Church. We are now at a point that only a few recognize the centrality of evangelization. Consequently, as a whole, the Catholic Church is a large, but relatively lethargic contingent of the Christian Faith in North America, despite being the original trunk from which all the other branches sprouted. One can imagine a sleeping giant that is hard to rouse, but fraught with potential strength if ever awakened.

Try to imagine the Catholic Church functioning as if *evangelization really is our central purpose;* our goal, first and foremost, salvation not only for me but for many others as well. Imagine what it would be like if membership in the Catholic Church denoted the job of bringing others to Christ. In fact, as we have just seen, it *does.* The problem is not in our official teachings; it is translating teaching into praxis.

We all seek for meaning in our lives. Evangelizing brings with it great personal meaning. It changes us. Imagine the renewed vigor and enthusiasm, even the excitement, about being part of a world-wide team consciously proclaiming the Truth in all the arenas of our lives. Can you envision the bishops of the United States joining together and calling for prayer and fasting in every diocese and eparchy in our country; prayer and fasting offered for the evangelization, conversion, and salvation of each person in our families, in our dioceses, and in our country?

Can you imagine a time when parishes are filled to overflowing with loving disciples of Jesus who are constantly looking for opportunities to propose the love of Jesus to every child, every friend, every shut-in, and even to strangers?

Can you envision the combined hierarchical and institutional resources of the Church systematically working in concert with the charisms of the ecclesial movements and new apostolates to build up missionary disciples on a large scale?

Imagine a pro-life nation in which everyone recognizes the personal dignity of each child, pre-born or new-born, "normal" or "needy", "perfect" or "imperfect", "convenient" or "ill-timed"? Imagine a society that replaces narcissistic individualism with a new *zeitgeist* based on the inherent dignity of each person made in the image and likeness of God.

Revel in the possibility of a new culture wherein music is beautiful once again and movies inspire audiences with stories of heroic virtue and reverential romance.

Imagine the smile of Our Father.

* * *

Wonderful dreams, but how can we make these dreams a reality? In my view, we need a clear, concrete proposal as a starting place.

Such a proposal can always be modified, but without it there will be nothing around which to build unity and, without unity, there will never be a clear sense of purpose.

Hence, a proposal is offered for the consideration of the Church in the following pages....

II. Be It Resolved

In war: Resolution. In defeat, Defiance.
In victory: Magnanimity. In peace: Good Will

Winston S. Churchill

A fundamental thesis of this book is that the *whole* Church – not just specialized ministries – needs to reclaim its most fundamental purpose. As noted earlier, Pope St. Paul VI identified the apostolate of evangelization as that most central of ecclesial purposes.

If we exist in order to evangelize, if evangelization is our "essential mission", our "utmost identity" as taught by Pope Paul, then we should be able to look each other in the eye and say that we have thrown ourselves into this mission without reservation; that we are giving it our best effort; that evangelization is indeed our highest priority. Despite oceans of ink devoted to the topic, an honest assessment must admit that the New Evangelization has not come into full flower in recent times. Rather than being the central focus of the hierarchical, institutional Church, Catholic evangelization largely remains the domain of specialized apostolates, a few rare parishes and even rarer dioceses. Despite over fifty years since the Second Vatican Council and over forty years of impassioned papal pleas, the work of the New Evangelization is haphazard, at best. The *Proposal* referred to in the sub-title of this book is an appeal to all the faithful to change the status quo as we know it.

PART I: THE PROPOSAL

At the risk of minimizing the problems of clergy sex abuse and episcopal accountability that commandeer the attention of our bishops at this point in history, I have complete faith the Church is on the way to resolving these issues; that – as serious as they are – they will slowly fade and be replaced with new problems in times to come. The fact of the matter is that there is a more long-standing problem than the one that occupies our attention today; and this problem has been largely ignored by the institutional Church: *We simply do not evangelize;* at least, not so as anyone would notice. It is not a part of our religious DNA. This problem was with us before the plague of clergy sex abuse and episcopal prevarication and it will be with us long after *unless* we consciously own up to our *sins of omission* and resolve to change with honest humility.

Crises demand our attention. It is always easier to recognize and deal with a crisis that is starring us in the face than it is to deal with problems we are *not* having for lack of something we *should* have been doing all along. If human health presupposes an appropriate level of physical exercise and yet we never exercise, we will never define the lack of exercise as a problem in our lives. That is, until we have a heart attack.

The *Proposal* places evangelization back at the center of who we are supposed to be as a people. To use an old-fashioned expression, it recognizes that our *central purpose* is to "save souls".

It explicitly places the New Evangelization as the uppermost priority of the Church, both locally and nationally. It recognizes that the diocesan bishop *must* be at the center of this apostolate, demanding both his constant attention and personal involvement. It calls him to new levels of personal holiness and transformational leadership.

But the *Proposal* doesn't stop with the bishops. It calls for a change in the culture of the Church that currently allows the faithful to comfortably ignore our Lord's command to "make disciples of all nations". It makes the transformation of ordinary Catholics into missionary disciples a new, central activity of the institutional Church; as central as the administration of the sacraments and far more central than fund-raising, athletics, and the many other activities that divert our attention and zap our energy.

It calls for the reorientation of the clergy into proclaimers of the *kērygma* in all of their everyday activities and it places all of the institutional and financial resources of the Church at the service of the evangelical apostolate.

Essential to the *Proposal* is the work of *organizing for evangelization.* As boring as "planning" may sound, the development of an explicit long-range diocesan *Vision Achievement Process* is anything but boring. The *Vision Achievement Process* has only one goal, but it is the most exciting goal possible: nothing less than the conversion of every human being living in a region into a Christian who is in love with the Lord. While ignoring none of the other works of the Church, the *Proposal* subsumes them all into a new awareness of the many evangelical moments that stare us in the face on a daily basis. The *Vision Achievement Process* is proposed as both a permanent management tool for guiding and coordinating the work of the local Church and an accountability tool for keeping the bishop and the other leaders of the local Church on task. (More will be said on this subject in Chapters XII and XIV.)

Grounded in intercessory prayer, the *Proposal* would replace ennui and irrelevance with joyful zeal and commitment and hope.

* * *

The *Proposal* borrows the form of a "legal resolution" for the purpose of condensing into just a few pages the essence of a *process* for moving forward in mission and unity. Beginning with our bishops, it is hoped that every baptized Catholic will prayerfully consider "adopting" at a personal level those aspects of the *Proposal* that apply to them as a perpetual resolution for the remainder of his or her life. It is also hoped that the U.S. bishops – as a college – will adopt and implement the collective aspects of the resolution that affect them.

In short, the following text is offered for prayer and discussion within the Church in the United States. It is a special appeal to each diocesan bishop and to all our bishops collegially to lead the faithful in a sustained effort that is unprecedented in modern times, an effort to proclaim the existence of God, the Incarnation, and the *kērygma*. It is an appeal to the faithful to respond in unity and love. May we all resist the urge to pray too long and discuss the *Proposal* until all the fine points are resolved. We do not have the luxury of time. The world needs God *now*.

Resolution for the Lay Faithful

While faithfully supporting all of the Church's legitimate ministries and, in a simultaneous spirit of humble repentance and enthusiastic joy,

BE IT RESOLVED THAT EVERY LAY CATHOLIC IN THE UNITED STATES WHO CLAIMS A COMMITTED RELATIONSHIP WITH JESUS...

† *pray daily for the evangelization and conversion of many people to Jesus in her own parish, throughout the diocese, and the world;*

† *acknowledge that her responsibility to help others love and follow Jesus (cf. Mt 10:32-33, Mk 5:19 et al) is just as constitutive of her identity as a committed Catholic disciple as is her responsibility to perform the corporal works of mercy (cf. Mt 25:31-46 et al);*

38

† commit to personal formation and training as a missionary disciple who is ready to answer the evangelistic calling both in all his personal relationships and in the organized evangelical work of the Church;

† encourage and support her diocesan bishop in his efforts to make evangelization his highest personal priority and the highest priority of the local Church;

† encourage and support his pastor to work in unity with the bishop in the diocesan evangelistic apostolate.

† Make the apostolate of evangelization a cause to which she contributes financially.

* * *

Resolution for Diocesan Priests and Deacons

BE IT FURTHER RESOLVED THAT EVERY DIOCESAN PRIEST AND DEACON IN THE UNITED STATES...

† pray daily for the evangelization and conversion of many people to Jesus in his own parish, throughout the diocese, and the world;

† acknowledge his responsibility to help all people within his parish boundaries love and follow Jesus whether they are parishioners or not (cf. Presbyterorum ordinis (4); Canon 528 §1);

† commit to personal formation and training as an evangelizing priest or deacon;

† teach his parishioners about their own evangelical responsibilities;

† *seek out and participate in formation opportunities to reform his parish into an evangelizing community;*

† *passionately preach every homily in such a way that the personal, life-changing love of God through Jesus is communicated;*

† *recognize and make use of every evangelical opportunity that presents itself in the course of his daily work (e.g., marriage preparation, hospital visits, etc.);*

† *ensure that all parish pastoral staff receive formation and training in how to evangelize in the course of their everyday ministries (e.g., baptismal prep, registration of new parishioners, religious education classes, etc.);*

† *encourage and support his bishop in his evangelical resolutions (see below);*

† *be a voice of unity within the presbyterate and diocesan deacons in support of his bishop.*

* * *

Resolution for Religious Priests, Brothers, and Sisters

BE IT FURTHER RESOLVED THAT EVERY RELIGIOUS IN THE UNITED STATES...

† *pray daily for the evangelization and conversion of many people to Jesus in area of residence;*

† *commit to personal formation and training as an evangelizer to the extent that his religious charisms permit;*

† recognize and make use of every evangelical opportunity that presents itself in the course of her daily work;

† encourage and support his bishop in his evangelical resolutions.

* * *

Resolution for Diocesan Bishops

BE IT FURTHER RESOLVED WITHOUT UNDUE DELAY THAT EVERY DIOCESAN BISHOP IN THE UNITED STATES...

† resolve to live humble, penitential lives of heroic holiness;

† initiate and sustain a permanent diocese-wide prayer movement interceding for the personal conversion and ultimate salvation of every person who lives in the region geographically delineated by his diocesan boundaries;

† widely announce with great clarity that for the duration of his active ministry as the diocesan bishop he is elevating the apostolate of proclaiming the Gospel to the uncommitted and those who are weak in faith to be: 1) his highest personal priority as the bishop, and; 2) the highest priority of the entire particular Church, so as to facilitate widespread personal conversions and ongoing maturation as disciples of Christ in the Church;

† passionately preach every homily in such a way that the personal, life-changing love of God is communicated;

† commit himself to a form of missionary holiness that is ordered to sharing his own personal love for Jesus with all people who live in the diocese – Catholic and uncommitted non-Catholic alike;

41

† *pursue a personally authentic style of leadership that is capable of transforming those around him with love for Jesus and zeal for faithfully living the Gospel;*

† *lead by example by shepherding not only the Catholic faithful, but also those who are far away from the Lord and the Christian faith.*

† *through his every effort, "normalize" evangelization as the highest purpose of individual disciples, parishes and other Catholic institutions that comprise the local Church;*

† *build unity within the diocesan presbyterate and among the faithful around the paramount goal of evangelizing and accompanying those who do not have a deep personal relationship with Jesus;*

† *take personal responsibility for developing and overseeing the implementation of a permanent, regional Vision Achievement Strategy that offers multiple opportunities for every Catholic and uncommitted non-Catholic to hear the kērygma communicated in those ways most appropriate for the particular hearers and that also offers multiple opportunities for ordinary faith-filled Catholics to spread their faith;*

† *in the early years of the Regional Vision Achievement Strategy, concentrate efforts around the two-fold goals of: 1) transforming every parish and Catholic school into fruitful communities, growing both in the number of sincere disciples and in personal holiness, and; 2) forming an ever-growing "army of missionary disciples" – both lay and clerical – who will effectively proclaim the Gospel in every environment in which they live;*

† *hold himself and the other leaders of the local Church accountable for ongoing evangelization by measuring progress against the short-*

and long-term goals of the Regional Evangelization Vision Achievement Strategy;

† cultivate an ethos among the diocesan staff that explicitly recognizes the advancement of the truth of the Gospel as their highest goal; if necessary to achieve this goal, reorganize the diocesan offices;

† strive to put in place significant financial resources committed to the continuation of evangelization throughout the diocesan region, in perpetuity.

* * *

Resolution for the United States Conference of Catholic Bishops

BE IT FURTHER RESOLVED THAT THE UNITED STATES CONFERENCE OF CATHOLIC BISHOPS (USCCB)...

† publicly resolve to lead the Church in a new direction of humbly proclaiming and witnessing to the salvific death and resurrection of Christ Jesus above all other messages;

† elevate the evangelization of the entire United States to its highest collegial priority;

† undertake and sustain a national program of Catholic research to gain understanding of the anthropological and psychological aspects of personal Christian conversion; also undertake market research into evangelistic messaging that resonates with prospective converts;

† undertake those elements of evangelizing society and culture that lend themselves to national action by developing and implementing

a National Evangelization Strategy that makes use of the knowledge gained from the social science and marketing research;

† *systematically implement and monitor the fruitfulness of the National Strategy;*

† *amend and update the National Strategy as appropriate;*

† *establish reasonable norms of mutual accountability among the bishops for the long-range, systematic evangelization of their respective dioceses;*

† *summon all the prayers, institutional and financial resources of the Church in the United States to the joyful mission of proposing the Gospel to society and contemporary culture;*

* * *

Prayer for Our Bishops

Come, Holy Spirit, inspire our bishops as 'fishers of men'. May You guide them in the blessing of the New Evangelization. With their paths lit by tongues of fire, may our bishops lead the faithful in the perfection of the Father's plan for salvation.

May they seek to re-orient their ministry from lesser priorities to that which is most urgently needed at this point in history. Born out of a spirit of repentant humility and fearless conviction, grant them all the wisdom and zeal to lead a New Evangelization that bears great fruit in the changed lives and eternal destinies of the people you have called them to shepherd.

They are the successors of the apostles who were the first to receive the Great Commission to "make disciples of all nations". Following their lead as "fishers of men", may all of the clergy, religious, and faithful participate in this great new surge of evangelization with filial respect and affection for our bishops and with a great increase in the catch.

We ask these things in the name of Jesus, our Savior.

Amen

III. A Paradigm Shift

*"The Christian ideal has not been tried and found wanting.
It has been found difficult; and left untried."*

G.K. Chesterton

Make no doubt that the *Proposal* as encapsulated in the above "Resolutions" is meant to represent a sea change in the way the Church in the United States does business, especially with respect to the apostolate of evangelization and the subsequent accompaniment of reverts and converts. Despite its ostensibly innocuous language, a careful reading of the *Proposal* conveys a radical and urgent paradigm shift. Ironically, this paradigm shift would move the Church into closer conformity with her own teachings. But, as a matter of praxis, the shift would require major changes in our ecclesial spirituality, culture, identity, and evangelistic outreaches. Some of these changes are highlighted in the table on the following page.

In its essence, the *Proposal*, has ten core attributes as listed below. It takes aim at a condition of the Church in which **evangelization would be...**

1. Driven by the vision of a converted society
2. Born out of love and dependent on Grace
3. Culturally constitutive of the institutional Church
4. Culturally constitutive of each individual baptized Catholic
5. Ordered to a "decision for Christ" that is personal and life-long
6. Directed not only to the Church, but to wider society
7. Locally led and unified by the diocesan bishop

47

THE PROPOSAL'S PARADIGM SHIFT

From...

To...

† Evangelization with no particular vision	➔ The Vision of a society converted to Christ
† Evangelization viewed as foreign to Catholic culture	➔ Evangelization viewed as central to a Catholic's identity
† Delegated evangelistic leadership	➔ Fully-committed Bishop leading evangelization
† Bishop's self-understanding as a manager	➔ Bishop's self-understanding as a witnessing leader-saint
† Episcopal decision-making by "group think"	➔ Episcopal decision-making by Purpose and 'Vision'
† Evangelization seen as 'something we talk about'	➔ Evangelization seen as concrete things we say and do
† Ecclesial leadership focused on the Church only	➔ Ecclesial leadership focused on the Church and the World
† Little or no prioritization of diocesan goals	➔ Evangelization as the paramount diocesan goal
† Evangelization as the topic *du jour*	➔ Evangelization as permanently integral to the Church's identity
† Optional and disconnected evangelical apostolates	➔ One, essential, coordinated evangelistic mission
† Evangelization by the individual alone	➔ Evangelization by both the individual and the institution
† Short-range 'program' orientation	➔ Permanent, long-range 'process' orientation
† Evangelization only carried out by specialized ecclesial movements and "gifted" people	➔ Evangelization by "ordinary" Catholics and parishes with help from specialists
† Evangelization at the local level only	➔ Evangelization networked at the local, regional & national levels
† Self-centered adult faith formation	➔ Adult faith formation with a clear "missionary" dimension
† Catholic education focused on academics and athletics	➔ Catholic education focused on personal commitment to Christ

8. Both "charismatic" and "institutional"
9. Trans-diocesan in scope
10. Long-range in expectations and permanent in commitment

The following discussion digs into the *Proposal* and describes it in terms of these ten constitutive elements.

Driven by the Vision of a Converted Society

However improbable as is may appear now, the Church would take on the collective vision of a society in which everyone has heard the Gospel clearly articulated and in which many have accepted it and been baptized. This implies evangelization that is goal-driven and energized by the dream of a future that is difficult to imagine, but worthy of sacrifice. Evangelization would be driven by the very goal which was given to us by our Lord as his last words to the apostles: *Go and make disciples of all nations* (Mt 28:19).

Born out of Love and Dependent on Grace

One of the risks in writing a book like this is the potential to leave the impression that everything is in our hands. If we just do all the "right" things, the Church will be perfected and massive conversions will ensue. That, of course, is patently false. Jesus made it imminently clear: "Without me you can do nothing." (Jn 15:5) No matter what we do or how well we do it, grace is key. No one has ever come into a relationship with our Lord without his specific intervention of grace. He assured us: "No one comes to the Father except through me. If you know me then you will also know my Father. From now on, you do know him and you have seen him." (Jn 14:6)

> The work of evangelization is first-and-foremost an act of love

The work of evangelization is first-and-foremost an act of love. Without honestly caring for the people to whom we witness we become no more than "a noisy gong or clashing cymbal," possibly even driving people away by our misguided zeal. If our motivation is rooted in anything other than love, we are doomed to failure. If our work is born out of a reaction to declining membership numbers or out of fear that society is "going to hell", we have missed the point. In the first instance, the work of evangelization is not about "numbers" or about "society". It is about love for the One who "loved us first" and about love for real people, not abstractions (cf. 1 Jn 4:19-20). Numbers can be useful as a wake-up call and, in some applications, as a measure of progress toward a specific objective. But, headcounts cannot measure the heart of man.

If our hearts remain focused on the Lord and our intentions remain pure, we can be sure that there will be "fruit", even if it does not bloom on our timetable or in the ways that we expect.

Our utter dependence on God is the reason the *Proposal's* first order of business is *a permanent diocese-wide prayer movement interceding for the personal conversion and ultimate salvation of every person who lives in the diocesan region*. Most of the real work of evangelization may be hidden. In his masterful little classic on the life of St. Thérèse of the Child Jesus, Père Raymond de Thomas de Saint-Laurent offered the following thought:

> Perhaps the most surprising aspect of the miracles of our Saint, one which demonstrates their supernatural origin, is their clearly apostolic character. What she dreamed of during her life came to be after her death. Thérèse became a great converter of souls.
>
> Providence thus gives us a lesson of the greatest importance, and how much we need it! In our days, even the best are frequently victims of a deplorable error. They confuse action with agitation. While moved by an indisputable zeal, they want to do good, but in their works they include that trembling note so characteristic of our era; they seem to rely more on their natural action than on divine grace. Is the cause of our few successes, not to mention our failures, not to be found in this practice?

May we have the courage to face the truth. Whatever their fecundity, our "works," although very numerous, never seem to give the fruits corresponding to the immense efforts we make. It is because we too often forget the teachings of the Faith and of history.

What does the Faith tell us? By ourselves, we can do nothing; we haven't the capacity to convert a single soul, to move a single heart. The help of grace is absolutely necessary. We are but little instruments in the hand of God.[4]

It is impossible to emphasize how essential intercessory prayer will be to the success of the *Proposal*. Moreover, the <u>united</u> *prayer offered by the local Church* has the power to change everything. The great first-century, bishop-martyr, St. Ignatius of Antioch, wrote in his epistle to the Ephesians: *"For if the prayer of one or two possesses so much power, how much more that of the bishop and the whole Church!"* Following one of the maxims of another great Ignatius – St. Ignatius of Loyola – may we "pray as if everything depends on God and work as if everything depends on us."

Culturally Constitutive of the Institutional Church

When we think of all worldwide Christian communities, it is obvious that each group has its own distinguishing characteristics. As a Christian community, we Catholics are highly sacramental. On a day-to-day basis, we encounter the living God most especially in the sacraments of the Eucharist and Reconciliation and what a tremendous joy this is for us!

With two thousand years of history, it can also be said that we are an "intellectual" community and a highly juridical people. Our theology is rich and well-developed. We also know who is "in" and who is "out" of the community and that determination is made in terms of the institutional Church. So, when we ask the question, "Is she a Catholic?" we normally answer based on the external requirements for "membership in good-standing". If a man is divorced and civilly remarried without the benefit of an annulment, a common response would be to say, "Well he used to be a Catholic." We might say this even though in good faith and conscience, he still considers himself Catholic. If a woman has ceased coming to Sunday Mass, we might say, "Well, she is a lapsed Catholic." The point is this: Deep in our "cultural DNA", we Catholics are drawn to nice neat categories and, as a result, can be casuistic and hurtful.

As a Christian community, we are also known for our care for the sick, poor and downtrodden. We have a keenly developed sense of justice that drives us to care for and advocate for the weakest and most vulnerable among us: the unborn, refugees, victims of sex trafficking, war, and racism.

> The bishop will widely announce with great clarity... that he is elevating the apostolate of proclaiming the Gospel to the highest priority of the entire local Church

And this compassion exists side-by-side with our "clubbishness", often sparking bouts of cognitive dissonance at the level of the individual and the ecclesial community at large.

There is far more that could be said about our cultural inheritance, mainly good, but also deficient in some ways. The point is this: when we define who we are as a Christian community, we have to admit that we are a mixed bag; saint and sinner all rolled up together in one Church and often in one person. Whatever else we may be in spiritual and ecclesiological terms, speaking anthropologically, these traits are "constitutive" of who we are.

"Evangelistic" is among the characteristics of the Catholic Church in the United States that is *not* currently constitutive of who we are. Not that it will be easy, but the *Proposal* would strive to change that. It states: *"The bishop [will] widely announce with great clarity... that he is elevating the apostolate of proclaiming the Gospel to... the highest priority of the entire local Church."* Among other things, this means that the

52

local institutional Church – with all of her resources and organs of communication – will intentionally and publicly proclaim the lordship of Jesus. By making evangelism the local Church's *highest priority*, with sufficient time, the hope is for it to become a part of our cultural DNA.

Culturally Constitutive of all Baptized Catholics

As a whole, the Proposal seeks to elevate the Lord's commission to "make disciples" to the level of everyday consciousness of the average Catholic mom, dad, student, priest or religious. Rather than understanding evangelization as an apostolate of the few or of merely the official organs of the Church, the Proposal envisions evangelization as constitutive of every Catholic's personal identity. It is "faith with a purpose" that goes beyond one's personal goal of "getting to Heaven" to a goal of bringing others along.

The *Proposal* states that the bishop will initially concentrate the regional evangelization process around forming *"… an ever-growing 'army of missionary disciples' – both lay and clerical – who will effectively proclaim the Gospel in every environment in which they live…"* The idea is "to equip the holy ones for the work of ministry" in every season, place, and phase of human life – from childhood to old age, from the rich to the poor, from the dysfunctional to the healthy, from sin-saturated places to the cathedral (cf. Eph 4:12). This equipping for a day-to-day evangelical lifestyle would take place through an organized process of forming mature Catholics in a missionary spirituality and training for evangelization. The purpose of *"initially concentrating"* on the formation *"of an ever-growing army of missionary disciples"* is a recognition that pervasive, fruitful evangelization is not going to happen by itself. First, the would-be missionary disciple must experience her own inner healing and be prepared spiritually to become a minister herself. Beyond that, as is true of anything worthwhile, practical training is required to prepare the evangelizer to recognize opportunities and to respond confidently with sensitivity, patience, and trust.

Ordered to a Personal, Life-long "Decision for Christ"

The *Proposal* speaks of *"personal conversions"*, *"ultimate salvation"*, and *"ongoing maturation as a disciple in the Church"*. The purpose of evangelization is to elicit an explicit response to God's invitation to love him and commit oneself to him. For many of us, we gave our hearts to Jesus as children because of the day-to-day evangelical witness of our parents and other adults. We simply grew into it. There was no one 'aha moment' we can point

> Why is it then that we never ask them to make a definitive, personal decision to love and faithfully commit themselves to Jesus?

to and say, "That was it." And that's okay. In the best of worlds, this gradual movement into a commitment to Christ would be the norm.

Unfortunately, we are a long way from the best of worlds. At this point in the United States, most are born into families with poorly defined views of God. There may be a very rudimentary "relationship" that comes out during moments of personal crisis; prayers directed to the largely unknown God in the sky. There may be a family history of affiliation with this or that denomination which is more of a tradition than a source of life and truth. Moreover, the "new normal" for many parents is a hands-off approach to questions of faith and religion. While it is fair play to inculcate children into a set of political views, it is considered patronizing and manipulative to help a child embrace revealed truth.

The Need for a Decision Increasingly, individuals "create themselves". In this highly individualized process, decisions are made that were rarely even considered in earlier times. Today, a young person not old enough for a driver's license will make the decision: "I think I will dye my hair green and change my gender this year." Accordingly, more than ever before, evangelization in the present age must evoke a very explicit decision. Much of what we as Catholics have passed off as "evangelization" is not

Explicitly "accepting Christ" may not be everything, but it is a very good place to start

ordered to a decision. All-too-often, we pass off entertainment-oriented youth ministry as evangelization or adult-directed biblical exegesis that rarely, if ever, mentions the central tenets of the Christian faith. Often, even the most basic pre-supposition for Christian faith is ignored; that there really is a God who is responsible for everything in creation.

The young person may go to Mass and eat pizza with the youth group and participate in a summer mission trip. These are all good things, but never in this entire process do we ask them to make a definitive, personal decision to commit their lives to Christ. And then we scratch our heads when we learn that most of them have abandoned the Faith by the time they graduate from college. Young people today are sometimes making irreversible decisions that have the potential to do serious harm to themselves and others (e.g., active sex lives, abortion, obtaining weapons, drug experimentation, sex change, etc.). The new Zeitgeist expects society to honor those decisions; even demands it. Why is it then, that we never ask them to make a definitive decision to love and faithfully commit themselves to Jesus, a decision that can only benefit them?

Consider the workplace or other social settings. Some political subject comes up – say, immigration – and we forthrightly explain the Church's long history of defense and advocacy for refugees. We may even mention that Jesus and his family were refugees; all good stuff and certainly worth saying. But at best, we have shared the *implications* of our faith; we haven't really shared God with them. We may have planted a seed of *pre*-evangelization, but God's immense love, the fact that God became one of us out of mercy for us, the fact that Jesus bridged the gap between God and us and gave us a share in his own resurrected life – the truly good news – has not been mentioned. Perhaps, that particular group and setting simply didn't lend itself to sharing the Incarnation and the *kērygma.* And, that's okay. But, it is important to come to understand that, properly speaking, evangelization has not really happened.

Evangelization is the clear proclamation of the Truth and it is carried out so as to encourage the hearer to accept and commit to the Truth he/she has just heard. A part of the *art* of evangelization is to recognize or even create those moments when the Truth can be spoken clearly and an explicit response solicited.

As Catholics, we do not believe that a person is saved the moment that he accepts or even professes the Truth. But, that moment may very well be the first step toward ratifying his baptism... and eventual salvation. A person does not graduate from college the moment she decides to go, but without that decision, she will never go and do the hard work to get that degree. The point is this: Explicitly *"accepting Christ" may not be everything, but it is a very good place to start.* It can be the "turn-around" moment in a person's life, and we should praise God when we are honored to be a part of that in someone's life.

Can Catholics Be Evangelical? It may be that a part of our reluctance to ask for a "decision for Christ" is rooted in a subtle prejudice against evangelical Protestantism. We may be thinking, "That's the sort of thing *they* do. It's just not very Catholic." It may also be rooted in the sin of resentment over their "raiding" Catholic populations or envy that they have been so successful at it. Regardless of our attitudes toward the evangelical community, we would do well to examine our conscience and ask ourselves if we didn't deserve to be raided. We should also question why we are such an easy target? If we are such a lukewarm contingent of Christians that people feel the need to go elsewhere to find a community with an impassioned love for God, should we expect to be rewarded?

I can hear the objections now. *We* have the Eucharist. *We* have the sacraments and the fullness of faith. True enough, I agree. The validity of the sacraments is beyond question. God always does what he promises to do. As the *Catechism* explains: "The sacraments act *ex opera operato* (literally: by the very fact of the action's being performed)… the power of Christ and his Spirit acts in and through it, independently of the personal holiness of the minister."(para 1128) However, the *personal fruitfulness* of the sacraments is a different matter. Accordingly, the *Catechism* also states: "Nevertheless, the fruits of the sacraments also depend on the disposition of the one who receives them." (para 1128) If the one receiving the sacrament is not *seriously committed* when it comes to loving our Lord and striving to love each other, we cannot expect them to have some magical effect on us. If we haven't *first* given our lives to the Lord, the sublime meaning of receiving Holy Communion will be lost on us. The starting point for personal holiness and virtue is the conscious entry into a personal love relationship. That has to come first. With it, the sacraments and all of the spiritual treasures of the Church can bear immense fruit. Without it, we make a travesty of God's gifts and can even cause scandal.

To many post-modern ears, the whole subject of evangelization sounds like a patronizing form of manipulation. In a world in which absolute truth itself is questioned, such a view is understandable. If in some way, the freedom of the hearer is not respected or an attempt is made to manipulate a decision, evangelization *can* step across the line into the realm of coercion. In his landmark encyclical *Evangelii nuntiandi*, Pope St. Paul VI responded to this very question, making the distinction between heavy-handed proselytism and the proposition of truth made in love:

> It would certainly be an error to impose something on the consciences of our brethren. But to propose to their consciences the truth of the Gospel and salvation in Jesus Christ, with complete charity and with a total respect for the free options which it presents – "without coercion, or dishonorable or unworthy pressure" – far from being an attack on religious liberty is fully to respect that liberty, which is offered the choice of a way that even non-believers consider noble and uplifting. Is it then a crime against others' freedom to proclaim with joy a Good News which one has come to know through the Lord's mercy? And why would only falsehood and error, debasement and pornography have the right to be put before people and often unfortunately imposed on them by the destructive propaganda of the mass media, by the tolerance of legislation, the timidity of the good and the impudence of the wicked? The respectful presentation of Christ and his kingdom is more than the evangelizer's right; it is his duty. It is also the right of his fellow men to receive from him the proclamation of the Good News of salvation. God can accomplish this salvation in whomsoever he wishes by ways He alone knows. And yet, if His Son came, it was precisely in order to reveal to us, by His word and His life, the ordinary paths of salvation. And He commanded us to transmit this revelation to others with His own authority.[5]

So, to the question "can Catholics be evangelical", the answer is "we need to be… especially if we really want all that the Church has to offer." What is more, the Bible, our popes, and the *Catechism* all make it clear: Our Lord has called us to be evangelical. It is a matter of obedience. (See *Sharing Our Faith Openly… Really?*)

Long-Term for Evangelizer / Life-Long for Evangelized The call to evangelize also demands a long-term commitment on the part of the missionary disciple. Consider the teenage girl who decided to go to college. The decision to go to college is a very important moment for many people. But ultimately, if I am the person who helped persuade the young lady that she has the talent to do it and that it is really possible, my hope for her is that she will

> If we really want to stanch the flow of young people leaving the Church, maybe we should expressly ask them to stay

follow through and achieve her dream. What I really want for her is an education and a good life. So, I am going to encourage her every step along the way. When she is a freshman and struggling with calculus, I'm going to encourage her not to give up. When she is a sophomore and her French professor refuses to speak English, I'm going to coach her in conversational French. I will go the distance with her and be there for her commencement.

For us, evangelization must not stop at the point of decision, as important as that may be. The ultimate goal is "eternal life in Christ Jesus our Lord." (Rom 6:23) Throughout our lives, we need to be reminded of our decision to love and follow Him. It is the all-important decision that we have to re-affirm over-and-over again. This is why "evangelization" as it is used in the *Proposal* goes beyond the initial decision. We proclaim the Gospel as... *"the highest priority of the entire local Church so as to bring about widespread personal conversions and ongoing maturation as a disciple in the Church."* The *Proposal* goes beyond Baptism and reception into full communion in the Church. It also includes "the ministry of accompaniment", a long-term commitment of friendship and mentoring to help cement the neophyte or the young person in the ways of faith.

This accompaniment can only happen within the community of the faithful. Accordingly, the Church is not incidental. It is essential that the work of evangelization go on to incorporate the new Christian into the faith community. Too often, we "drop" the new adult Catholic "at the altar" as if our responsibility ends there. Evangelizers must integrate the neophyte in the local church where the Body of Christ is united in the Eucharist and the works of charity and justice. His commitment must truly involve friendship over time.

The same applies to our young people. If we really want to stanch the flow of young people leaving the Church, maybe we should do something unthinkable: *Explicitly ask them to stay.* More than that, we need to take great care to give them *reasons* to stay. They need to hear the witness of older people who can speak from the experience of their own lives as to how the Church kept them faithful over many years or brought them back into a love relationship with Christ. We must be willing to *ask them* to step up and, even more, *take a solemn vow to love and follow our Lord Jesus and never miss Mass on Sunday for the rest of their lives.* Why not make this a condition for receiving the sacrament of Confirmation? Many of our young people go through a year of Confirmation prep and we never think to ask them to make this decision. Either we assume they have, which is unbelievably naïve, or we assume they are just too immature to make that decision. The fact is that even an immature decision to follow Christ can be a beginning. It is the first step toward maturity and it is certainly something they will never regret.

Just as our accompaniment of young people must go beyond Confirmation, it also needs to continue *beyond high school graduation.* Remember what it was like to be a college freshman away from home for the first time and encounter a range of new choices never previously experienced? Now, imagine getting an email from that special person at home who helped you make the first explicit decision to follow Christ; the same person who urged you to commit to weekly Mass participation. Imagine that email conveying how much you are missed, encouraging you to find the Newman Center, and promising to see you when you come home for Fall Break. Then, further imagine getting another email from the director of the Newman Center inviting you to join him and a large group of your fellow students for a get together on Friday night. Then next week, you receive a text from the FOCUS missionaries on campus. That's the kind of accompaniment we need to provide our young people. With a modicum of creativity and commitment, it would be manageable.

Directed to Wider Society as well as the Church

The *Proposal* urges *"that multiple opportunities for every Catholic and uncommitted non-Catholic to hear the kērygma [be] communicated in those ways most appropriate for the particular hearers."* Many today think of the New Evangelization as a "churchy" mission aimed at proclaiming the *kērygma* in homilies to Catholics who "have been baptized but not evangelized". There is no doubt that this is an important area of concern. In dioceses that are predominantly Catholic, converting Catholics may in fact be the primary focus of concern. But, in most places, the call to evangelize doesn't stop there.

When Pope St. John Paul II coined the term "new evangelization", many interpreted it as an initiative to reach out to those parts of the traditionally Christian world (including the United States) where millions of Catholics have lapsed in the practice of the faith. Indeed, as he addressed the Conference of Latin American Bishops (CELAM) in 1983 and again in 1990 with the publication of *Redemptoris missio*, his references to the "new evangelization" were made with the fallen-away Catholic in mind. But the call to evangelize is bigger even than that.

PART I: THE PROPOSAL

In more recent years, the distinction between inactive or former Catholics and anybody else has become blurred to the point of becoming moot. Despite the great diversity of modern society, there exists an increasing amalgamation of belief systems into a syncretistic blend of secularism with an occasional quasi-Christian sentiment thrown into the mix. Entire generations who may have had Christian roots in earlier times have grown up and joined the ranks of secular society. Consequently, the New Evangelization is beginning to look more and more like the mission *ad gentes.* Today, more often than not, we have no idea what the religious background is of our next-door neighbor or the person in the next cubicle over. Points of differentiation are more along the lines of political persuasion and tastes in fashion or entertainment. (These differentiators, however, do provide hints as to where a person "is coming from" and the ways that may be most fruitful for communicating the Christian message.)

> The New Evangelization is beginning to look more and more like the mission *ad gentes*

In any event, our outreach needs to be to the entire world, not just those we know are "Catholic". There are, however, two overarching caveats. The first is to respect the dignity and freedom of each person. The second is to avoid trying to convert the converted. Protestant brothers and sisters who are plainly in love with the same Lord that we are should be treated as brothers and sisters, even to the point of cultivating strong bonds of love and mutual admiration. In many cases, we should be allied in the work of evangelizing together; not masking over our differences, but letting it be known that the Holy Spirit holds us together in a spiritual unity that is far stronger than our differences.

This begs the question of what to do in the case of a lapsed Protestant who *still identifies strongly with a Protestant tradition* and makes a decision to recommit his life to Christ. Even if it feels uncomfortable, our responsibility as the evangelizer should extend to finding him a faithful Protestant community. While we may prefer that he consider Catholicism and while we may hurt over the fact that he will not know the full joy of the transubstantiated Eucharist or the amazing peace of Confession, our faith assures us that he is a member of the Mystical Body of Christ and we are to respect that fact. In these instances, our love and magnanimity should shine through brightly.

At a personal level, evangelization to the whole world means venturing out of the comfortable familiarity of our "Catholic ghettos". At times, it will mean cultivating friendships with people who are "different" and knowing how and when to drop deep-set cultural taboos against "talking about religion". At the level of parish life, it will mean letting go of our "club mentality". The authors of *Rebuilt,* a groundbreaking book on transforming parishes into evangelizing communities, put it very well when they wrote that it will mean "looking beyond the people in the pews to the people who are *not* there, creating a path to help them there, and leading both parishioners and newcomers to grow as disciples of Jesus Christ..."[6]

Led and Unified by the Diocesan Bishop

G.K. Chesterton famously wrote: "The Christian ideal has not been tried and found wanting; it has been found difficult; and left untried." Like the Christian ideal, I would contend that – at least in recent times – the ideals of the *Proposal* have not been tried and found wanting. One if those largely untried ideals has to do with our diocesan bishops stepping up and leading a new movement of evangelization.

The Essential Leadership of the Bishop Hardly anybody has nice things to say about bishops these days. Many people would like to hide them and just pretend they are not there. Accordingly, the idea of elevating their role in the life of Church may seem preposterous. Notwithstanding feelings to the contrary, it is impossible to overemphasize the role of the diocesan bishop in the *Proposal*. Like it or not, we Catholics are generally a passive flock. Ordinary Catholic lay people do not feel they have the authority to initiate significant renewal in the Church. We look to the bishop for leadership on matters of import. As anyone who has ever tried to do anything on a diocese-wide basis knows, the bishop is the lynchpin to the success of the undertaking. Accordingly, an essential component of the *Proposal* is that the ordinary must personally lead the mission of diocesan evangelization. The *Proposal* invites diocesan bishops to involve themselves with verbs such as *"lead"*, *"commit"*, *"pursue"*, *"announce"*, *"initiate"* and *"sustain"*. Evangelization is so central to the purpose of the Church – and thus the bishop himself – that it cannot be delegated away as if it was some insignificant administrative matter. On the contrary, it deserves and requires the diocesan bishop's full attention and personal immersion. This is fundamentally important on both theological and practical grounds.

> In its origin, the most significant aspect of "apostleship" was the missionary function of proclaiming the Gospel

Concerning the theological grounds, for two millennia our faith has held that bishops are the successors of the original twelve apostles. The Second Vatican Council's *Dogmatic Constitution on the Church (Lumen Gentium)* taught:

> In fact, not only had [the apostles] various helpers in their ministry, but in order that the mission trusted to them might be continued after their death, they consigned, by will and testament, as it were, to their immediate collaborators the duty of completing and consolidating the work they had already begun... They accordingly designated such men and then made the ruling that

64

likewise on their death other proven men should take over their ministry.[7]

Lest there be any doubt that these "immediate collaborators" of the apostles were the "bishops" referred to in the New Testament (cf. Acts 20, 2 Tim 4:6), a first-century pope, spoke to this point in his famous epistle to the Corinthians. Reigning from 88-99 A.D. as the third Bishop of Rome following St. Peter, St. Clement wrote:

> The Apostles received the Gospel for us from the Lord Jesus Christ... Having therefore received a charge, and having been fully assured through the resurrection of our Lord Jesus Christ and confirmed in the word of God with full assurance of the Holy Ghost, they went forth with the glad tidings that the kingdom of God should come. So preaching everywhere in country and town, they appointed their first fruits, when they had proved them by the Spirit, to be bishops...[8]

> And our Apostles knew through our Lord Jesus Christ that there would be strife over the name of the bishop's office. For this cause therefore, having received complete foreknowledge, they appointed the aforesaid persons, and afterwards they provided a continuance, that if these should fall asleep, other approved men should succeed to their ministration.[9]

In its origin, *the most significant aspect of "apostleship" was the missionary function of proclaiming the Gospel.* The Greek word *apostoloi* (ἀπόστολος) means *"one who is sent".* (The etymology of *post* office, *postage* stamp, *postal* system, etc. derives from the same word.) To be sure, preaching the Good News was not the *only* responsibility of the apostles. In addition to being sent, they were also charged with celebrating the Eucharist (cf. Lk 22:19), forgiving sins (cf. Jn 20:23), healing the sick (cf. Lk 10:9, Jas 5:14), exorcizing the possessed (cf. Mk 6:7), etc. But, proclaiming the Gospel had a certain primacy of place in their identity (cf. Mt 28:16, Mk 6:7, Jn 20:20). Indeed, before Jesus mentioned any of the other apostolic ministries, he told Simon Peter and Andrew: *Come after me and I will make you fishers of men* (Mt 4:19).

They were to become the chief spokesmen for the Gospel of Christ. Insofar as evangelization was chief among the apostles' tasks, likewise it is chief among the responsibilities of their successors. Again, quoting *Lumen Gentium:*

> The bishops, inasmuch as they are the successors of the apostles, received from the Lord, to whom all power is given in heaven and on earth, the mission of teaching all peoples, and of preaching the Gospel to every creature, so that all men may attain to salvation through faith, baptism, and the observance of the commandments (cf. Mt 28:18, Mk 16:15-16, Acts 26:17 *et seq*).[10]

> Among the more important duties of bishops, that of preaching the Gospel has pride of place. For the bishops and heralds of the faith, who draw new disciples to Christ; they are authentic teachers, that is, teachers endowed with the authority of Christ...[11]

And apostles were indeed fishers of men. Sometime following Pentecost, nearly all of them left Jerusalem and took the Gospel "to all nations".

Tradition holds that Peter preached extensively throughout modern-day Turkey before traveling onto Italy and founding the Church in Rome alongside Paul. Andrew went to Bulgaria and Greece. Paul's missionary pursuits throughout the Mediterranean and on to Rome are well-documented and may have also included a foray to Spain. Headquartered in Ephesus in modern-day Turkey, John spent much time in Asia Minor and died on the Isle of Patmos, Greece. Matthew preached in

> The Proposal is a call for our bishops to re-appropriate the ancient apostolic calling to be 'fishers of men' and to make it their highest ministerial priority

the region of modern-day Iran and was martyred in Ethiopia. Some Catholic communities in India even today trace their origins back to Thomas, who also traveled to Iran and Afghanistan. There are various traditions about Bartholomew, including mission work in

Georgia and possibly India. Matthias (the replacement for Judas) preached in Greece and along the coast of the Caspian Sea (modern Georgia, Azerbaijan, and Turkmenistan). Philip preached in Turkey. Simon the Zealot and Thaddaeus – possibly working as a team – proclaimed the Gospel throughout the Mesopotamian region (modern-day Iran, Iraq, Syria, and Turkey). Both were martyred in Syria near present-day Lebanon. According to one disputed tradition, James the Greater took the Gospel to Spain before returning to Jerusalem to be martyred at the order of Herod Agrippa in 44 A.D. (cf. Acts 12:1-2) Only James the Lesser remained at home in Jerusalem as its first bishop. Indisputably, the apostles were missionaries who passionately proclaimed the Gospel.[12, 13]

So were the early bishops of the Church. There is a long and impressive history of bishop-saints who were noted for their zealous proclamation of the Gospel. Nearly all of the ancient church fathers were bishops who undertook great preaching and teaching ministries – Ignatius of Antioch, Polycarp, Irenaeus, Athanasius, Basil, Cyril, Martin of Tour, Ambrose, John Chrysostom, and on-and-on. Many of the bishop-saints were expressly committed to pushing the geographic boundaries of Christendom, preaching to people who had never heard the name of Jesus – Patrick and Augustine of Canterbury in the British Isles, Boniface in the eighth century pushing northeast into the Germanic territories, and Norbert doing likewise in the twelfth century. As recently as the nineteenth century, Anthony of Claret preached throughout Catalonia, founding an order of missionaries and becoming the first bishop to Cuba. And then there were the great reformers – Peter Damian, Charles Borromeo, Robert Bellarmine, Josaphat, and Francis de Sales. No small number of these bishop-saints gave their lives as martyrs for the Gospel including the most recently canonized among them, St. Oscar Romero. Another twentieth-century bishop, Bl. Fulton J. Sheen is also likely to be canonized in the near future. He was an evangelizer *par excellence.*

The point is this: one of the charisms of the episcopacy has been the apostolic calling to be "fishers of men". It is arguably the most ancient aspect of the episcopacy and there has been a great procession of evangelizing bishop-saints through the ages that have carried on the commission to "make disciples of all nations." The *Proposal* is a call for our bishops to re-appropriate this ancient charism and – given the times in which we live – make it their *highest ministerial priority.*

While there can be no doubt that the office of bishop has evolved over two thousand years, to this day the Church teaches that their prophetic or teaching role commands a certain "pride of place". Moreover, the bishop's preaching and teaching is not to be aimed just at active Catholics.

Now, ask the average Catholic what she thinks the most important role of her bishop is. Although I can't prove this with empirical data, there is little doubt that she would say something like: "Managing the diocese". We might also hear responses like: "Keeping our schools open", "finding new vocations", or "dealing with the sex abuse crisis". A few might say: "Confirming our kids". In other words, the episcopal role of governance would far out shadow anything else, even the role of sanctifying.

It is with these thoughts in mind that the *Proposal* calls for each bishop to adapt *"a form of missionary holiness that is ordered to sharing his own personal love for Jesus."* Personal authenticity is a prerequisite for effective leadership. Not every bishop has the *persona* of Archbishop Fulton Sheen or the winsome appeal of Bishop Robert Barron, but every bishop has a personal relationship with God. The difficulty – and this applies to any preacher – is cultivating a kind of missionary zeal that empowers him to share the singular importance of that relationship with his flock as well as those outside his flock.

Only when the people know how deeply in love with Jesus their bishop is, will they begin to grasp that the Church is more than an impersonal, distant bureaucracy. Only when he can communicate his love and commitment from his heart will people be deeply affected by him. It is only at this point that evangelizing dioceses will become a real possibility. It is this sincere, *transformational* leadership that the *Proposal* has in mind for our bishops.

What a bishop says may not trickle too far away from the source. But as a public person, what a bishop *does* – good or otherwise – is going to be noticed. Accordingly, the bishop's missionary holiness cannot stop with words. It has to be seen through the witness of his life. A bishop who can swing a hammer on a *Habitat* site or pray in front of an abortion clinic communicates the Gospel to the world.

"Running together" with the Bishop As a practical matter, if the diocesan bishop is not the *only* person who can instigate widespread ecclesial culture change, he is by far the most obvious. Moreover, the Church teaches as much. *Lumen Gentium* unabashedly proclaims: "… bishops, in a resplendent and visible manner, take the place of Christ himself, teacher, shepherd, and priest, and act as his representative (*in eius persona*)." (21) It goes on to state: "The individual bishops are the visible source and foundation of unity in their own particular Churches…" (23) Diocesan bishops are uniquely positioned to unify the Church for the work of evangelization.

St. Ignatius of Syrian Antioch (circa 35-108 AD), one of the earliest Church Fathers, taught the same message. While under arrest by Roman authorities, Ignatius dashed off six letters to various churches in the Mediterranean region and one letter to his dear friend, St. Polycarp, while he was being taken to Rome to meet his martyrdom. By my count, in the space of these seven letters, *Ignatius exhorted the churches twenty-seven different times to be united with their bishop.* He even emphasized how important this unity to the bishop was to

Polycarp, who was himself the Bishop of Smyrnæa and he exhorted the faithful in Smyrnæa with the same message: "Wherever the bishop appears, there let the people be; as wherever Jesus Christ is, there is the Catholic Church." (8) To Ignatius, the bishops represented Christ, which is why it was so fundamentally important to be united with him.

On several occasions Ignatius used the expression "run together" as an image of a local church united in action with their bishop.

> I have therefore taken upon myself first to exhort you all to *run together* in accordance with the will of God. For just as Christ Jesus, our inseparable life, is the manifested will of the Father; so also bishops are, settled everywhere to the utmost bound [of the earth] by the will of Jesus Christ... Wherefore, it is important that you should *run together* in accordance with the will of your bishop.[14]

How important it is for our bishops to be the pacesetter and for the rest of us to run along with him! Obviously, this is not the current state-of-affairs. That said, "running together" has *never* been easy. Knowing that there were those who didn't or wouldn't recognize the central role of the bishops, Ignatius wrote:

> It is fitting, then, not only to be called Christians, but to be so in reality: as some indeed give one the title of bishop, but do all things without him. Now such persons seem to me to be not possessed of a good conscience, seeing they are not steadfastly gathered together according to the commandment.[15]

To round out his teachings on local church unity, Ignatius extended his exhortations to the presbyters (i.e., priests) and deacons. He called on them to be in perfect agreement with and in submission to the bishop and with one another. He understood this unity among the ordained in and with their bishop as a "type" of the unity between the Father and the Son to which the faithful were to be gathered.

Ancient tradition has it that both Ignatius and Polycarp were disciples of the apostle John. Thus, the centrality of the bishop and unity with him comes to us from the very first generation of post-apostolic believers. Throughout the history of Christianity, ruptures in this unity have occurred with devastating effects, doing violence to the credibility of the Gospel. In the words of Ignatius, "Give no occasion to the Gentiles, lest by means of a few foolish men the whole multitude [of those that believe] in God be evil spoken of."[16]

> We must find ways to encourage our bishops to take up the mantel of "chief evangelizer" in their dioceses; effectively, to "give them permission" to make evangelization their No. 1 priority

Needless to say, we are today a long way from the ideal of unity portrayed by Ignatius. Many bishops find themselves at odds with their presbyterates for a variety of reasons and many presbyterates' track record of trying to implement episcopal initiatives has left them "gun shy" about any new ones. We have a long way to go. Nevertheless, if there is to be a new wave of evangelization that becomes a normal part of Catholic life, it will only come about with the forthright leadership of diocesan bishops and our willingness to work alongside them. We must find ways to encourage our bishops to take up the mantel of chief evangelizers in their dioceses; effectively, "to give them permission" to make evangelization their No. 1 priority.

Both "Charismatic" and "Institutional"

Gallup, Inc. has been tracking confidence in organized religion annually since 1973. Their findings are very telling. Between 1973 and 2015 the percentage of Americans with a "great deal" or "quite a lot" of confidence in "Church/Organized Religion" has declined from sixty-six to forty-two percent. [17] Moreover, one of the foremost sociologists of religion, Dr. Rodney Stark of Baylor University, contends that a significant portion of the rise of the religiously unaffiliated (aka, 'nones') represents a shift from organized Christian denominations to "nondenominational" Christian churches.[18] While Stark's findings attenuate somewhat the mainstream media's headlines to the effect that Americans are becoming dramatically less Christian, both Gallup's findings and Stark's spell bad news for organized religions, such as the Catholic Church.

One would think that "institution" is a four-letter word. Many Catholics are defensive about belonging to an "institutional" Church. We tend to find ourselves apologizing for it. It goes against the *zeitgeist* of our culture. Especially to Millennials, words often associated with the Catholic Church such as "institution" and "bureaucracy" seem to reflexively evoke adjectives such as "corrupt", "unnecessary", "self-serving", "wasteful", etc.

In some quarters, since bishops lead diocesan "institutions" with (what are perceived to be) large bureaucracies, they are *ipso facto* suspect. I have heard at least one very theologically-minded churchman refer to plans that emanate mainly from episcopal leadership as insensitive to the social justice teaching of subsidiarity! In reference to the Church, an old friend (now deceased) used to quip, "A tree grows from the roots up and dies from the top down." It is almost as if no good idea is *allowed* to come from the "top-down".

This is ironic and something of a Catch-22 since many Catholics use the very institution they disparage as an excuse for avoiding their own responsibilities. In his incisive book, *Strangers in a Strange Land,* Archbishop Charles Chaput observed:

> U.S. Catholics are used to the Church as a large institution. We have big buildings. We run a large network of schools, hospitals, parishes, charities, and ministries. It's easy to

abdicate our personal sense of mission to the official religious machinery.[19]

In any event, the anti-establishment attitude has tempered legitimate leadership impulses in some bishops.

We need to find a place in our hearts and our thinking for the fact that good things *can* come from the top-down. The *Proposal* recognizes that "charism" and "institution" need not be mutually-exclusive Such events as World Youth Day initiated by Pope St. John Paul II stand as clear testimony of this fact. The *Proposal* recognizes that "charism" and "institution" need not be mutually-exclusive. It intentionally seeks to "marry" the spiritual charisms of the Church with the "institutional" Church.

In fact, throughout the history of the Church, what was begun by the extraordinary gifts of the few, frequently blossomed into the great organizational work of the many. Many of the great works of the Church came about precisely because specially-gifted people inspired nascent organizations and large institutions grew out of those seminal efforts. Jesus himself hinted that such might be the case when he said:

> Amen, amen, I say to you, whoever believes in me will do the works that I do, and will do greater ones than these, because I am going to the Father. And whatever you ask in my name, I will do, so that the Father may be glorified in the Son. If you ask anything in my name, I will do it. (Jn 14:12-14)

Throughout the world, we have Catholic institutions to thank for housing the displaced and providing food for the starving (e.g., Catholic Relief Services), preventing single-parent families from becoming homeless (e.g., Catholic Charities), healing countless poor people (e.g., the hospitals of the Daughter of Charity), educating thousands of children without respect to their religion (e.g., the numerous Catholic schools in the Middle East), *et cetera, et cetera.*

Our Father desires the *entirety* of his people to proclaim the Lordship of his Son, not just a few extraordinarily gifted or trained people. If *all* Catholics are called to participate in spreading the Gospel, the only way such a thing is likely to happen is through the initiative of our bishops, who personify the institutional Church. In fact, many of these men are extraordinarily gifted themselves. Therefore, it should come as no surprise when they step up and work to change the culture of the Church and *mainstream* evangelization in every aspect our lives.

> The *Proposal* encourages the institution of the Church to reclaim its original purpose: to boldly proclaim the *kērygma*

The danger will always be there that we lose the charismatic element. This has happened before. But, we must not refuse to work because of the dangers that *may* occur. Besides, the goal is not to build a large bureaucracy, but to take the large institution of the Church and insinuate the spiritual gifts of preaching and teaching, wisdom and courage, zeal and awe throughout; to be the leaven in the dough of the Church and beyond (cf. Lk 13:20-21).

The *Proposal* encourages the institution of the Church to reclaim its original purpose: to boldly proclaim the *kērygma* both "informally" through her many members and "formally" through expanded communications media and other institutional resources. Fed by the united prayer of the diocesan Church, it aims to take the perceived weakness of the *institution* of the Catholic Church and turn it into a strength with all of her authority, organization, liturgical splendor, magisterial teaching, spiritual and educational formation, potential for coordination, and specialized resources working at the disposal of the Gospel. The spirit of hope embedded in the *Proposal* envisions the behemoth of the supposedly *impersonal* institution becoming the organizing principle through which masses of humanity can be led into a *personal* relationship with Jesus in the Church; into a welcoming place where they will encounter disciples who will personally befriend and accompany them for a lifetime.

None of this is meant to suggest that bishops and their associated institutions can ignore the reservations of those who are disenchanted with "organized religion". Bishops and their representatives will have to work hard to overcome the image that many people have – rightly or wrongly – of the organized Church. They will have to embrace forms of leadership that are sincerely transformative.

Vision Achievement Strategy Evangelization on a large-scale is going to require an organized and patient "process-minded approach". As mentioned in Chapter I, "evangelization" is understood herein as shorthand for a **process** (not just a plan) that includes: (1) the cultivation of outward-looking parishes and the formation of missionary disciples on the "front end"; (2) the sustained work of faith-sharing itself, whether that be in the family, on TV and social media, among friends, workers, or even strangers, and;

The *'Vision Achievement Strategy'* involves all the "levels" of the Church: the individual, the parish, ecclesial movements, evangelistic ministries, formal and informal communities, the diocese, and the "national Church"

(3) long-term accompaniment of converts/reverts on the "back end". The goal of this process is nothing less than facilitating the achievement of the vision of a fully-converted society over the long haul.

As envisioned by the *Proposal*, this organized process needs to involve all the "levels" of the Church: the individual, the parish, ecclesial movements, evangelistic ministries, formal and informal communities, the diocese, and the "national church". Nearly all discussions of evangelization that are current today apply to either the individual disciple or the parish or both. The farther away from the individual, the less discussion there is. Accordingly, the diocese receives very little attention and the national Church even less. The *Vision Achievement Strategy* must involve *all* levels of the Church.

Chapter XII goes into to this subject in considerable detail. Let it suffice to say for now, the process borrows some practices from the business world that can be more than a little helpful. Well-conceived "process planning" and project management have the potential to build unity and accountability, even excitement and a sense of purpose within the presbyterate and the faithful at large.

Trans-Diocesan in Scope

In 1964, the urban designer Melvin Webber wrote a paper entitled *Explorations into Urban Structure* in which he observed a new phenomenon, something that he called "community without propinquity".[20] Throughout the history of humanity, "community" had almost always been experienced by people in close proximity to one another. Increasingly, Webber observed that this need for physically localized communities was diminishing as personal modes of transportation overcame distance bringing people of like mind together. For better or for worse, Webber saw this trend as obviating the historic need for neighborhood communities. Today, we would react to such an observation with a big, "Duh"; our social relationships are no longer constrained to the people in our immediate environs. In the period of a half-century, megalopolises have expanded in such a way that once distinct cities now blur together into one gigantic urban space. We have come to take this reality for granted.

Of course, what the automobile, commercial air travel, and television did in the mid-twentieth century to "shrink" human society, the Internet and its many forms of social media are doing now. Increasingly, corporations employ talent from across the globe without a care to where their people live geographically. Meetings take place in virtual space as if everyone was sitting around the same table.

In addition to its interpersonal and organized local dimensions, the *Proposal* envisions evangelization as a social movement that transcends geographic boundaries

Geographically-anchored professional and organizational structures are becoming less and less important as well. If a surgeon faces a rare surgery, super-specialized knowledge from another surgeon across the country can guide her hands and direct her techniques. Without respect to historically necessary geographic boundaries, social movements operate in the same way.

Circumstances are a bit different within the Church. Apart from the subject of ecumenical dialogue, the goal of unity in the Catholic Church has generally been understood as something that applies to relatively small geographically circumscribed areas and relationships (read families, parishes, and in rare cases, dioceses). We then jump to universal unity at the level of the entire Roman Catholic Church. At least for the ordinary Catholic, unity is not an ideal that seems to be relevant at any level in between the local and the universal.

Getting Beyond Episcopal Autonomy Throughout most of Christendom, episcopal sees were fiercely independent of each other. Collaboration and negotiation with worldly lords was of far greater concern than collegiality among bishops. There were no permanent structures within the Church to encourage collegiality except the occasional regional synod that might be called to address a heresy or some other common threat. Especially after the fall of the Roman Empire and the accompanying deterioration of its renowned roadway infrastructure, the means for long-distance communication reverted to a very primitive and dangerous undertaking making peer consultation among bishops exceedingly difficult. Accordingly, within their individual sees, bishops held absolute sway over their flocks. With the important exception of papal primacy, local autonomy was virtually imprinted into the DNA of the Church.

Other events served to reinforce episcopal autonomy. The social justice principle of "subsidiarity" developed in the late nineteenth century is a good example. First articulated at the papal level by Leo XIII in 1891 (see *Rerum novarum*) and later bolstered by Pius XI in 1931 (see *Quadragesimo anno*), the Gospel principle of subsidiarity emphasized inter-personal and local problem-solving in contrast to the monolithic "national solutions" of Marxist Communism or Nazism.

Accordingly, throughout most of the twentieth century united initiatives across diocesan boundaries remained the exception rather than the rule. The ethos of episcopal autonomy continues right up to the present time. In fact, it is partially responsible for the sex abuse scandal. Bishops are well-known for "staying out of each other's hair". Thus, the reticence of some otherwise wonderful prelates to call Archbishop Theodore McCarrick to account, even though they were aware of credible evidence that he was engaging in mortally sinful behavior.

Inter-Diocesan Cooperation While the walls that protected morally wayward bishops from censure may be starting to crumble, mechanisms to identify and help inept or ineffective bishops are still in the future. That said, the 20th Century saw the advent of a new spirit of inter-diocesan cooperation. Indeed, the "distance" among episcopal sees has been closing. Increasingly, the Church has recognized the need for unity at intermediate levels that bridge the gap between Rome and individual bishops. In 1917, the Catholic War Council (CWC) was created in the United States as a means for bishops to cooperatively provide relief and spiritual care to servicemen and their families. Forty-nine years later, Pope St. Paul VI issued guidelines for the establishment of national episcopal councils which had been authorized during the Second Vatican Council. In the new spirit of collegiality, the National Conference of Catholic Bishops was created as the institutional heir of the CWC. Later, it was renamed the current United States Conference of Catholic Bishops (USCCB).

While the prerogative for disciplining individual bishops remains the sole province of the pope (with limited exceptions), the USCCB has provided bishops with a forum for discussing common problems and taking common action. Notably, in recent years the bishops have taken outstanding collegial action on religious freedom and the protection of human life.

The USCCB has also placed its stamp of approval on evangelization in America. Three documents are noteworthy:

- *Go and Make Disciples: A National Plan and Strategy for Catholic Evangelization in the United States* (1992)
- *A Time to Listen... A Time to Heal: A Resource Directory for Reaching Out to Inactive Catholics* (1999)
- *Disciples Called to Witness: The New Evangelization* (2012)

Collectively, these actions of the USCCB Committee on Evangelization and Catechesis (or its predecessor) represent a serious national commitment to evangelization. However, they lack two important dimensions: (1) all of the recommendations in these documents are aimed at parish and diocesan activities only, and; (2) there is no accountability for their implementation.

Regarding the first issue, a positive step would be for the bishops to begin thinking in terms of the contributions that multi-province or national cooperation could bring to the case of evangelizing society at large. This is not meant to imply in any way some sort of reduction in emphasis on the parish or diocese. Rather, in addition to the essential local work of evangelization, the *Proposal* recommends *undertaking those elements of evangelizing society and culture that lend themselves to national action rather than the work of individual dioceses or provinces.*

For example, in addition to evangelization being understood exclusively in terms of inter-personal, parochial, and diocesan initiatives, there would be great value in also conceiving of evangelization *as a social movement transcending geographic boundaries.* Especially with the advent of the Internet, "communities without propinquity" have become the norm. Social movements have powerful influences on people, particularly on Millennials and Generation Z. These "communities" tend to feed on the entertainment industry and social media. Trans-diocesan email blasts, pop-ups, chat rooms, etc. managed by the USCCB offer the possibility of huge economies of scale for reaching thousands of young people. Moreover, this national effort could be designed in such a way as to connect back to the local diocesan evangelization office when individuals show a sincere interest in Jesus and/or Catholicism. At the very least, the work of *pre-evangelization* would take a giant leap forward.

Another possible illustration of trans-diocesan cooperation: Recent research has shown that many young people in "Generation Z" are rejecting belief in God because of the grossly mistaken notions that the Church is at odds with science and that science disproves the existence of God.[21] Moreover, youth are embracing this worldview at a very young age. A recent study of people who are now between 15 to 25 revealed that the median age when they decided to leave the Church was 13 years old![22]

Where did our youth get such patently false ideas? No doubt, some of it derives from slanted science courses tainted with an ideological agenda; another part of it from social media propagated in part by the new breed of aggressive atheists. Rather than parishes and individual dioceses trying to challenge this amorphous monster, the most fruitful way of debunking these myths is united action at the national level. Perhaps under the direction of the bishops acting collegially, new, first-class history curricula and science courses could be developed that point out the historic role of the Church in the sciences and the theistic implications of the Big Bang, the "anthropic principle", and other scientific evidence that points to God. Moreover, a national, all-out, multi-media campaign could quickly counter these deceptions. If linked with expert scientists trained in good communications who can respond to challenges and questions in online chat rooms, talk shows, and the like, many people could be turned around on this issue, reestablishing the intellectual prerequisites for even being open to the possibility of the *kērygma*.

At the sub-national level, new provincial and/or regional collegial actions could also be taken to advance the cause of the Gospel. As an example, the evangelistic organization known as *Catholics Come Home* has conducted numerous TV ad campaigns that have been seen by many across the country. But, better use can be made of this tremendous apostolic resource. More often than not, television market areas do not conform to diocesan or provincial boundaries. Accordingly, individual dioceses sometimes feel that broadcast media is not a very good investment. Moreover, some have observed the fact that, while the TV spots are effective at increasing short-term Mass attendance, the effects may be short-lived. Greater cooperation among contiguous dioceses could overcome both of these objections. Working together, multiple dioceses can more frequently share the cost, rather than one shouldering the whole burden by itself. Moreover, if the same cluster of dioceses worked together to form missionary disciples and companions for those who do respond to the ad campaign, the short-lived benefit would have the potential to turn into (re)commitments to Jesus that last a lifetime.

Regarding the issue of episcopal accountability, the USCCB does not have the authority to require individual bishops to make evangelization or anything else their *highest priority*. Each bishop is *expected to make his own decisions* with respect to everything that is not expressly covered by Canon Law or mutual agreement. Voluntary action, however, is another matter. In *Go and Make Disciples*, the USCCB's 1992 "national plan and strategy for Catholic evangelization in the United States" the bishops clearly stated: *"Because this plan must involve everyone of us, we bishops first of all pledge to implement it ourselves."*[23] Almost thirty years later, an objective assessment would have to admit that many of our bishops have not followed through very well on this pledge. In fact, with the normal turnover of bishops and the passage of years, many of our newer bishops may not even be aware of this "pledge".

The same USCCB document states:

> As pastors of local churches, we realize that individuals and parishes also need support at the diocesan level. Each bishop will seriously consider establishing a diocesan office and an evangelization committee or otherwise assign staff to give the ministry of evangelization proper visibility and attention, as well as provide resources for evangelization to his people. Parishes will be looking to these offices for direction and materials.[24]

I believe that most bishops have, in fact, seriously considered this organizational proposal. More than a few have created diocesan offices of evangelization in the past thirty years. Many others – especially those who shepherd poor mission dioceses – have not been able to find the funding. Others have simply added the apostolate of evangelization to the job description of their offices of religious education, where it is deprived of the "visibility and attention" (not to mention, the "resources") it deserves. The point is this: Too often there is no accountability for evangelization ever really happening. The open-ended nature of such a proposal makes no provision for larger and wealthier sees coming to the aid of their poorer brethren. Moreover, the bishops are so independent of each other that they are generally not well-informed about what is happening outside of their own province and sometimes, not even there. In this respect, meaningful collegiality still has a long way to go.

It should not be too much of an overreach to ask diocesan bishops to submit periodic reports of what they are doing to advance the cause of the Gospel within their sees and to submit themselves to fraternal counsel when little or no progress is taking place. Accordingly, the *Proposal* advocates the USCCB *establish reasonable norms of mutual accountability among the bishops for the long-range, systematic evangelization of their respective dioceses.*

Long-Range in Expectations and Permanent in Commitment

It takes a long runway Have you ever sat in a Boeing 747 at the end of a long runway getting ready for takeoff? If so, you'll remember that the thought inevitably crosses your mind: Can this thing really get off the ground? I mean, how can a three hundred-ton vehicle overcome the inertia of sitting at a standstill and pushing through the friction of a thick atmosphere with massive tires grinding against concrete fighting its way into the air? You hear the low rumble of the giant Rolls-Royce engines as they throttle up. The behemoth starts off painfully slowly. You glance out the window twenty feet away from where you're seated and it looks like you're barely moving. That's a little disconcerting, so you utter a quick prayer, tell yourself to stop being so silly, and close your eyes. A half-minute later, you're still rolling, so you take another quick peak. You guess you're speeding over 100 mph and you estimate you must have travelled over a mile since your last look, but... you're still on the ground. Fortunately, before you panic, you sense the comforting feeling of the plane beginning to rotate and in another few seconds, wheels off. The giant is actually in the air. A few minutes later, you're soaring through a far thinner atmosphere at 30,000' and speeding along over 500 mph. Amazing! It took a very long runway and a lot of energy, but the "impossible" actually happened.

Sitting at a metaphorical dead stop, the prospect of evangelizing and converting a whole region can seem at least as daunting as a soaring 747 to a cave man. What's more, unlike the known principles of physics that determine the time and space needed to get a 747 off the ground, no one knows how long it will take to convert an entire population. It takes a leap of faith to believe it is possible and a bigger leap of faith to commit to such a bold idea as one's highest aspiration.

And yet, in the power of the Holy Spirit the apostles set out to do just that. A late-comer – Saul of Tarsus – expanded the other apostles' mission by preaching to the Gentiles. According to Professor Rodney Stark, by the year 350 A.D., almost 34 million people, or fifty-six percent of the population of the Roman Empire, had converted to Christianity. This represents a staggering growth rate of forty percent per decade sustained for over three hundred years![25] The *Proposal* asks for this kind of single-minded commitment *for the duration of (each bishop's) active ministry*.

It is one thing to agree to this type of long-range commitment. It is another to live it out unflaggingly over years or even decades. In the best case, time will be needed to form the faithful in a mature missionary spirituality and commitment. It will take yet more time to equip them with the knowledge and skills to witness their faith in a range of different circumstances. Priests and pastoral ministers will also need to be formed. Money will be needed to hire support staff to assist parishes. Special evangelistic apostolates such as St. Paul Street Evangelization and campus FOCUS ministers may need to be invited and organized at the local level.

> The Gospel has its own 'stickiness factor', but a few committed individuals must create situations whereby large numbers of people can experience the stickiness

After all these and other initiatives, it is likely to take years for the new generation of missionary disciples to bear visible fruit. Friendships that lead to conversions usually take lots of time and lots of love to cultivate. A new generation will have to grow up before the fruits of their parents' prayers, teaching, and example can be recognized. Only after all this, is it likely that a diocese will begin to discern the visible fruits of their evangelical commitment: a discernably higher percentage of youth practicing their faith, increased Mass attendance and Confessions, more Catholic marriages and infant baptisms, an increase in inquiries, more baptisms and receptions into full communion, etc. Eventually, one might expect an acceleration in the growth rates of these metrics, but only after patient, prayerful experimentation and trial-and-error.

In his now-classic best-seller *The Tipping Point,* Malcolm Gladwell observed that social change often happens in a manner very similar to the outbreak of epidemics. Gladwell makes the point that a very small number of people can create an epidemic. However, two other conditions must be conducive to the outbreak. The viral agent must have a highly infectious component, and the lives of the few carriers must put them into social contexts that encourage the spread of the disease. Gladwell calls these conditions the "Three Rules of

Epidemics": The Law of the Few, the Stickiness Factor, and the Power of Context.[26]

Fortunately, not all epidemics are bad. Consciously or not, every marketer is on the lookout for the unique combination of these three factors to ignite an explosion in the demand for her product. Often, all it takes is a small adjustment in one of the factors to create the right conditions for the epidemic to "go viral". The Gospel has its own "stickiness factor", but a few committed individuals must create situations (perhaps, a network of communities?) whereby large numbers of people can experience the stickiness. Patience, prayer, time, and commitment are the seedbed in which the epidemic can spread.

We live in an age that is not conducive to patience and long-term commitments. New fads and distractions pop up with the rapidity of a machine gun. Crises divert our attention and deplete our resources. Every kind of resistance will come against us, both from outside and within the Church. We will need to "[r]un the race so as to win." (1 Cor 9:24b)

Permanent in Commitment Where we are headed is an entirely new destination, not a slight course change. What can be accomplished by any given bishop is limited. In my own Diocese of Evansville, we have had six bishops since the See was created in 1944 (not counting our current bishop who was just installed in late 2017). That works out to an average of about twelve years-per-bishop. At that rate, about every twelfth year there is likely to be new episcopal leadership. Most bishops are honorable, humble men who respect the policies and general priorities of their immediate predecessor. Still, as time passes, commitments can change.

Given the long-term nature of "winning souls", the most vexing aspect of the *Proposal* is finding a way to ensure that a *permanent commitment* is made to the apostolate of diocesan evangelization. This concern may seem exaggerated insofar as evangelization is *so*

> It is sadly telling that there are so few endowments dedicated expressly to proclaiming the Gospel

foundational to the Christian Faith that one might expect it to become a permanent priority with very little effort. In theory, maybe so. But reality can be a different matter. As of this writing, legal settlements for sex abuse cases has sent sixteen U.S. dioceses into bankruptcy.[27] It is not a stretch to imagine the pressure on a bishop to lay off "non-essential" diocesan staff. Unfortunately, nothing in Canon Law requires that there be an episcopal vicar for evangelization, let alone a support staff.

One can imagine another situation in which a diocese experiences an economic boom setting off the enviable problem of major growth. The bishop is short on priests and doing his best to keep up with the booming demand for new parishes and schools to accommodate the new workers and their families. He is forced to focus his energies on finding missionary priests and raising money. When he gets a chance to breath, his priorities instinctively go to fostering indigenous priestly and religious vocations. For years, he hardly gives a thought to bringing more people into the fold. From his perspective, he has enough on his plate already.

Leaving aside real-life circumstances such as these, the fact is that many dioceses have not placed a high priority on evangelization. Accordingly, funding the staff to support it never takes place. Due to a culture of episcopal autonomy and no mechanisms for accountability to ensure the spread of the Gospel, all-too-often it doesn't happen.

Any culture has many aspects and one of these aspects is financial. A sure indicator of what we value is how we invest our money. For example, the U.S. Church has traditionally invested substantial financial resources into general and religious education.[28] We have also raised money to build and maintain our places of worship. In many instances, dioceses have established foundations to assist in the creation and growth of endowments to ensure that a committed stream of income will be available for a wide range of purposes. Endowments, in particular, are a good indicator of what we value. It is sadly telling that there are so few endowments dedicated to proclaiming the Gospel.

In order for long-lasting cultural change to happen, bishops will need to establish and build permanent funds to assist in living out the Great Commission in their own dioceses. This is not to suggest that operating budgets should not include a strong evangelization component. Clearly, they should. However, as bishops come and go, and priorities change, every diocese should have a _permanent_ source of funding reserved for unambiguously evangelistic purposes, which, in accordance with Canon 1267 §3, cannot be easily diverted to other purposes.[29] Ultimately, such a source of funding is one of the ways of changing the culture to ensure that evangelization becomes a critical part of the culture of the Church as we move forward into the future. Accordingly, the _Proposal_ recommends that bishops _strive to put in place_ significant financial resources _committed to the continuation of evangelization throughout the diocesan region_, in perpetuity.

IV. Interlude: *A Bishop's Dream*

The future belongs to those who
believe in the beauty of their dreams

Eleanor Roosevelt

Monsignor Mike, Vicar General (once removed)
DATE: October 22, 2051.

He was a sleeper during the seminary. I don't mean he slept through class. In fact, he was quite bright. What I mean is, hardly anybody knew it. He did his best *not* to stand out. Guys used to call him "the Monk".

On the gridiron, he was something else though. There, he was a Beast. I'm sure you've heard stories about his career at Alabama before he joined the seminary. When he was downfield and had the ball in his hands, nothing could stop him. As short as he was, his strength and sheer grit could either outmaneuver or runover anybody who was dumb enough to get between him and the goal line.

Of course, when I met him, we were both in Theology. But, once in a while, somebody would get a flag football game going. Flag or not, everybody just sort of stayed out of his way. As far as the rest of us were concerned, Paul was the whole Crimson Tide packed into one powerful creature. As you can guess, the scores were pretty one-sided. Anyway, once the game was over, he would revert to his quiet self and, within a half-hour be back at the books.

PART I: THE PROPOSAL

The one I really knew back then was his predecessor, Bishop Tom. Tom and I were inseparable... especially when it came to our passions: golf and beer. Golf was a rare treat. Beer was a lot more often. But, when it came to golf, we had to plan it in advance since the seminary schedule didn't allow much time for that. But, until the summer we were ordained deacons, vacations were always spent either at my house or his, three hundred miles away. For a few years there, Mom and Dad called us the "twins". We were a package deal. But wherever we were, you could be sure we were golfing. Public golf courses, of course, and beer afterwards. Bishop Tom used to say that golf was the most practical preparation for his priesthood that he ever got in the seminary. Same after we were ordained. Of course, we were in different dioceses, but we sure planned our vacations together and we always chose a destination with great golf courses.

Yeah, Tom was a great guy and a great priest. I still miss him to this day. He's the one who gave me this neat title, you know, *monsignor*... the *very reverend, monsignor*. When he was made bishop, one his first official acts was to petition Rome for me. No big deal really, but I appreciated it....

I'm sorry... It was Bishop Paul you really wanted to talk about. This is what happens when you get old: You run off at the mouth.

I'll have to make this brief, since I could talk about Paul forever. And, I'm expected downtown early tomorrow for his funeral. He specifically asked me to preach. Guess he knew at least my mouth still works.

Actually, I resented Paul for a long time. Guess I still thought of him as that quiet, young beast on the gridiron. And I just assumed everything was going to stay the same as it had under Bishop Tom, minus our golf outings, of course. Tom died so unexpectedly. I probably would have resented anybody following him. But Bishop Paul was so... well, so *unepiscopal*. He was still quiet when he arrived here. As brilliant as he was, he had trouble with names and was always asking me who was who. I wasn't the greatest at that either. I loved my parishioners with all my heart, but it took me years to learn some of their names. I was a darn good administrator, a good analytical mind, but always had trouble with names. Anyway, Bishop Paul seemed afraid of his shadow in those early days. He spent a heck of a lot of time in the chapel. After Mass, he would snag a piece of toast and cup of coffee, then disappear back in the chapel and wouldn't come out for at least two hours. That used to upset people, cause a lot of us liked our meetings early in the day. Not Bishop Paul. I really don't think he liked meetings at all... Just not your usual bishop.

Anyway, at first, things did stay the same. No staff changes. No new appointments. In fairness, he did tell everyone to expect that possibility. But, for a long time, nothing happened.

Oh, except the *Prayer Apostolate*. That was his first change. It was a couple years after he was installed. He announced to the consultors one day in the fall of 2020 that he wanted to get an intercessory prayer movement going throughout the diocese. He didn't care what it looked like. He just wanted *everybody* praying. And not just praying, but praying for a great awakening in our diocese... a New Evangelization. He quoted John Paul, *"new in its ardor, new in its methods, new in its expression."* One of the guys after his announcement had the temerity to admit what several of us were feeling. It felt almost Protestant.... and evangelical Protestant, at that. But there was no point in arguing. How could any of us argue against united prayer? Even so, we all knew it was going to create practical problems in our parishes. He made it clear that no proposal was to be denied. If people wanted to respond to his request by creating perpetual adoration chapels, so be it. It was *not* to be denied, despite the difficulties, not to mention the costs of getting something like that up and running. I could just see it now: 3 a.m. phone calls from the security system that an outside door has been left open. Anyway, it could be rosary groups among the quilters, charismatic prayer meetings; it could be whatever people wanted.... *provided* the constant focus was on "the evangelization, conversion, and ultimate salvation of every man, woman, and child in our local church." That phrase became a mantra for him.

He often reminded us that all those people were *his responsibility*, not just the faithful in the pews. He felt the weight of that responsibility. And, then in his own gentle way, he would share some of the weight with us. He'd remind us that, as pastors, all those people out there *were our responsibility*, too. For the skeptical, he'd even quote chapter and verse from the Code of Canon Law.[30] We were responsible for everybody, not just our own registered people. I guess we all knew that, but we had never really thought about it much. It was certainly a different way of thinking and a little intimidating.

Another interesting thing about Bishop Paul was that he hated to call the diocese, "the diocese". To him, it was always "the regional church". I'll never forget the first time he made that point in public. It was over at St. Bonaventure where Father Charlie used to reign supreme. We used to call him the "King of the Southside". Anyway, on one of his pastoral visits plugging the *Prayer Apostolate*, he got in front of the people and asked them: "What 'particular church' are you sitting in right now?" Sensing a trick question, only a few brave souls raised their hands and ventured: "St. Bonaventure?"

Father Charlie seemed happy with that response, but then Bishop said, "No, that's not exactly true. The parish is just a very local subdivision of what the *Catechism* and Canon Law calls the 'particular church'. Sometimes, it's referred to as the 'local church'. I like to call it the 'regional church'. One of my personal goals is to become more of a pastor of this rather big, local church. And, my greatest hope is that we can all really *be* the local church that we're intended to be... *one* church throughout all these counties, working for the same all-important goal: "the evangelization and conversion and ultimate salvation of every soul who lives here." Message delivered... to Father Charlie, anyway.

I remember that evening well, because that was the night our sainted bishop sacked me. Here's what happened. After we left St. Bonaventure, he asked if he could buy me a beer. Far be it from me to tell my bishop I wouldn't have a beer with him and there was a nice little watering hole a couple blocks away, so we pulled in there and got a booth. After we placed our order, he said, "You know, Mike, I've been thinking. The two of us are too much alike." That one caught me off-guard. I didn't think of us as being alike at all.

He went on, "We both love our people, but neither one of can remember names worth a darn. We're both serious-minded and analytical."

All I could say was "uh, huh", wondering where this was going.

After a little pause, he says, "What I need is someone who knows everyone in the local church. I mean *everyone*. I need a 'people specialist', someone who not only knows everyone, but also knows everything about them; who is good at what, who is related to whom. That kind of stuff. Mike, you're as good as they come, but I need someone who'll complement me... and even talk back when he knows I'm about to do or say something stupid."

I was getting ready to talk back, but this gentle man put his hand on my arm and cut me off. "Msgr. Mike, I've been thinking of Larry Godfrey. If ever there was a people person, it's Larry." I couldn't argue with him there. Father Larry knew everyone and everyone knew and loved him. "So, I'm going to accept the resignation you tendered back when I was installed, but not before we have a send-off for you that'll be second-to-none."

And, that was that. I was out and Father Larry was in. At least, that's how I felt back then. A little jilted. But time is a great palliative. And, the bottom line is that he was right. It was a great call. Father Larry could always put the right combination of people together to get a job done. Any job. In some respects, he became a good life coach for Bishop Paul, too. He showed him how he could let go of the numbers (something Bishop actually enjoyed) and to find the time to personally lead the New Evangelization he cared so much about... and did so much for.

You know, Bishop Paul meant that when he said he wanted us "to pray every day for the evangelization, conversion, and salvation of everyone in our local church." He did it himself. If we had five spare minutes waiting for somebody, he'd whip out his beads and lead whoever was there in a Chaplet of Mercy. His little catechesis there at St. Bonaventure wasn't just a message sent to Father Charlie. It was the beginning of what eventually became a *vision* or a *dream* that I can only attribute to the hours he spent in that chapel in front of our Lord.

In fact, after a few years, that's what we started calling it – *The Dream*. That's even what *he* started calling it. Maybe you've heard it or read it. It came out back in the early 20s. Providentially, young Father George Smith recorded and transcribed it. As I recall, he had just been ordained and it was his first Priests Convocation. I remember it was a good turn out that year. Nearly the whole presbyterate was there.

Actually, I have a copy of it here somewhere. Let me dig it out... Here, got it. It *still* inspires me. Listen to this...

Brothers,

I think it's important for us at the beginning of these couple days together to spend some quality time dreaming together. I know, dreaming is a solitary phenomenon, but who says it has to be. Quoting the Prophet Joel, St. Peter at Pentecost reminded the crowd that in the days to come God would pour out the Holy Spirit upon all humankind. He told them:

> *"Your sons and daughter will prophesy,*
> *your old men will dream dreams, and*
> *your young men will see visions."*

Well, guys, there are plenty old men here. So, let's ask the Holy Spirit to help us dream big dreams together. And, young men, ask for a grand vision of what our local Church could look like in the future. I believe in my heart that the Lord hasn't abandoned us. I believe that there is yet the possibility for a better world, even here where we have seen so many disappointments and setbacks; I believe that we can have a world that is very different from what we see around us today. A future that defies the trends we have come to take for granted. These trends, this "new normal" need not portend the future.

So, indulge me. For a few minutes, let's dream together. Let's pray for and envision what really is possible right here in our fallen world. This may seem a little strange, but let's dream that it's thirty years from now – some years after my time as bishop is over... but a time that some of us will probably live to experience. Father George, God willing, you'll be there and most of you younger men.

Let's imagine that the date is 2050 and our country is very different from the crisis-riddled society we live in today. Imagine a society where school shootings are a thing of the past. Imagine the percentage of Catholics who celebrate Mass every week is 90 percent instead of 25 percent; a society in which the "average Catholic" celebrates the Eucharist because that is the highlight of his week. This is a world in which soccer moms can't wait to go to Mass because that – more than any place else – is where she consciously encounters the God who loves her. In fact, she now hates missing even a single day. Life is different now than it once was.

You serve in an incredibly amazing parish now, but the same thing is going on at every parish in our local church; in fact, something similar is happening at every parish in the country because – years before – lovers of the Lord saw the Vision and said 'yes' to it. The Holy Spirit showed us that the future did not have to be a continuation of the present.

It all started back in the '20s. In a moment of clarity that could have only come from our Lord, a few bishops began to recognize that their lives consisted of endless activity and no discernible fruit. Tired of fatigue and hopelessness, these bishops began to stand up and inspire their people with a zeal for souls that hadn't been seen since the evangelization of the British Isles in the 6th Century or the mass baptisms of millions of Aztecs in the 16th century. Bishops became ignited with the same passion as the great bishops of old - Patrick, and Boniface, and Augustine of Canterbury, and Josaphat, and Stanislaus, and John Fisher and so many others. In a surprisingly short period of time, the model of the episcopacy re-captured its apostolic missionary roots and the people followed their lead.

In their inspiring faith, these apostles called on miracles from heaven and got them. They spoke with a clear focus about the hope of ordinary Catholics winning their families, and friends – and even strangers – to the divine heart of Love and Mercy and the people responded.

And, after a little time, it was not just us Catholics, but our other brothers and sisters got a glimpse of the Vision, too. Right here in our own city, the biggest complaint you hear from your people now is accompanied by a wink and a smile that they all have to leave for Mass on Sunday twenty minutes earlier than they used to, because of all the Sunday morning traffic.

The new normal for preaching now was unheard of back in 2020: twenty-five-minute homilies. That was the hardest part for us: preparing for the higher standard that the people asked of us; their expectation that every *homily comes from heart and speaks with passion of what our Lord has done for us and is now doing in our midst.*

You reflect on how just last week, one of your men related that as he went to work the morning before, he was praying about his newest client who is still a dedicated 'none'; praying about when and how to share his own story of conversion; of his now-constant love for Jesus, who "loved him first".

Now, as you look around at the same city you grew up in, you reflect back on how much things have changed in the last few decades. You remember the beginning of the change when we made a serious, long-term commitment to the formation of "missionary disciples"; lay-saints to witness to the Truth in all of their environments, but especially in their homes; and priest-saints to work with their lay counterparts in reforming their parishes into evangelizing communities. There had been no blueprint, no single program; just the intercessions of the Prayer Apostolate and our work and reliance on the Holy Spirit. You remember the months of commitment on the part of the missionary disciple "candidates"; a commitment that culminated on their Commissioning Day when I sent them "out" and "back" to their families and friends and parishes, and workplaces; even into restaurants and bars, bowling alleys and playing fields; into counseling centers and jails and 12-step programs and shelters.

Slowly, our world began to change and all this became our new normal, not just a flash in the pan that happened once, but an experience that continues to this day as our missionary disciples grow into a huge community serving as "leaven" not only in our parishes, but everywhere.

From the vantage point of thirty years from now, think back with me, Brothers, on the day when you and I stood together in the sports arena and led a huge gathering of men and boys in a solemn vow before God to honor his wife or future wife by never again using pornography. And in that world of the future, once- dysfunctional families are becoming healthy and loving again. Many more marriages are staying together now rather than ending with brokenness, recrimination, and wounded children. Amazingly, it is beginning to show in the statistics: fewer single-parent households and poverty rates that are edging downward.

You realize that young couples are now getting married again as they recognize that marriage and family is God's vocation for their lives, a thought that was almost unheard of when you were a young man. And, this is happening because, from the time these young people were children, their parents told them about the (in)credible love that our Savior has for them. Their parents had <u>asked them</u> to give their hearts to Jesus… and they <u>had</u>. Those missionary parents had asked the new generation – <u>even in their youth</u> – to make a firm decision… and they <u>did</u>. And they still are… every day.

The world we know is a different place now, a long way from perfect but moving in the right direction. Our parishes have changed profoundly. You look back on those dreaded evenings when your finance council met so many years ago. You remember those horrible budget meetings when the only question was what and how much to cut, not whether. Now, you have so much money that a third of the parish income is going overseas to parishes in the Third World.

Back in those days, the average age in our parishes was 58 years old. All but a few of the GenXers and Millennials were 'missing in action'. But, that turned around as a new cohort of "missionary" Catholic couples began to bear a new – and growing – generation of children. Indeed, the law of compounding growth has begun to kick in. As a result of all this, our schools and home-schooling families are both thriving. Enrollments are up for the first time in 60 years and with a growing number of parishioners, we can now afford to send our children tuition-free and many others are being admitted at steeply discounted tuitions.

Teen youth groups, which had only served to segregate our young people from mature adult mentors were gradually phased out and replaced by integration into the growing community of Catholic families meeting in homes and backyards; places where they learned to pray and play and serve together; places where they encountered mature men and women of deep faith, many of whom had been commissioned as our missionary disciples.

In response to these encounters, young men started joining the seminary. They had caught "the vision" and wanted to become pastors just like their own pastors – compassionate and passionate, kind but firm, inspired but collaborative. Similarly, a growing number of our young women started applying as postulants in convents that are now bursting at the seams.

There has been serious change on our streets, too. Now, so many of the societal problems we used to have due to drug addiction and broken families are gradually dissipating. As we look back, our old city seems like a very different place; another world that was impossibly sad, bereft of hope, clinging to a few scraps of soul-killing, mindless "entertainment" wherever they could be found. That was a world where there were signs of hopelessness and addiction standing under every overpass. There were belligerent faces squatting to keep warm on sidewalk grates every winter and gun fire was a common-place occurrence. Even our police officers lived in fear.

What a world it was, but now things are changing. Now, old parishes of a past era are being re-opened by our growing number of young priests shepherding some very unlikely flocks. It started years ago, in an effort to respond to Pope Francis' call to "go to the peripheries". You may remember that some of our earliest missionary disciples began playing cards with clients from our soup kitchens. Some improbable, but genuine friendships formed out of these card games and, before too long, food for the soul was being served too. It was a tricky business and continues to be. A few of the men have been baptized, but mostly they just come to church to receive big hugs and coffee and offer loud "amen's". Along with all this, now we have communities of young sisters wearing long white habits and beaming smiles taking over long-abandoned inner-city schools with low-income children coming by the busloads... largely underwritten by our growing suburban parishes. And there are bald, full-bearded friars clad in grey denim changing the lives and the culture of our teens.

Most of the people in those neighborhoods had only known a distorted caricature of the Church in the past, whatever Hollywood served up. Now, they are experiencing first-hand the kingdom of God on earth.

Brothers, this is my vision. Can I prove to you that this will happen? Of course not. But, there have been many times in history when Christians could have simply given up; when the enemy arrayed against us seemed overwhelming... But, we will not give up. I am asking you to join me in this great battle...

My brothers, do you believe we can have this future? There is much we can't control, but there is so much we can, because we have the Holy Spirit as the first fruits of our redemption.

Let's spend some time laboring over how we can make this Vision a reality? And then, let's do it, with the fervor of the apostles.

When Bishop Paul finished, you could hear a pin drop. None of us knew how to respond. It was embarrassing, actually. We had never heard anything like that from *any* bishop. Gone were the erudite insights and humorous anecdotes so characteristic of episcopal speeches. Instead, we just heard a man's passion... and his vision that seemed almost childish in its naiveté. Despite the ridiculousness of it all, something inside us began to respond. No, Some One inside us. Despite the "odds", we all knew that this vision represented a future that *could* happen. In any event, it was worth spending the rest of our lives working and fighting and loving for. One at a time, men began to stand and applaud.

It all changed that day; first, tentatively. We had some false starts. There was a lot of healing that had to take place before we were able to come together as a team. But, gradually it did happen. Over time, our sense of excitement grew as Bishop Paul continued to lead and reassure us that it wasn't a pipedream. It was the kind of dream that God Himself bestows....

Well, it's time for me to go to bed now. Early day tomorrow.

Part II
The Challenges

V. Finding Forgiveness

Then Jesus said, "Father, forgive them,
they know not what they do."

Luke 23:34

How Could It Have Happened?

We live in dark times, perhaps among the darkest days in the history of Christianity. Surely, among the most serious challenges to evangelization at the present time is the clergy sex abuse crisis. It seems every week we learn more about the full scope of priests who have used their positions of trust to abuse innocent souls. All the while, no small number of bishops have concealed these heinous sins hidden right in the heart of the Church.

At this point in history, many Catholics – not to mention broader society – would say that our bishops have lost their standing to lead. R.R. Reno, editor of *First Things* put it this way:

> We are moving toward an anti-establishment ecclesiastical culture, one in which the bishops have a less important role. Their canonical authority will remain intact. They are and will always be the governing authority in their dioceses. But they will lose their moral and spiritual authority. They already have.[31]

Disappointment, hurt, and anger are all legitimate responses to the revelations of the summer of 2018 when the former cardinal-archbishop of Washington, D.C., Theodore McCarrick, was credibly accused of sexually predatory behavior and legal investigations brought to light the full scope of long-standing mismanagement of sexually abusive priests by the hierarchy. As mentioned earlier, the primary purpose of this book is to propose that the Church should make evangelization its highest priority not only in its teaching, but in its praxis, as well. How can we possibly do that if the primary spokesmen for our faith – the bishops – have lost their credibility?

Our bishops have a critical role in making the New Evangelization truly fruitful; perhaps, the pivotal role. It is only the diocesan bishop who can create a culture that initiates and fosters widespread evangelical action among the laity. Without the bishops calling this forth from their people, it is not likely to happen. So far, when it comes to sparking a new era of evangelical proclamation, with a few notable exceptions, they have been missing in action.

But, wouldn't it be a disaster if our bishops – experiencing a powerful grace of repentance and *metanoia* – reordered their priorities and called us into what could be a new era and, out of anger over their past mistakes, we refused to follow them? Judging from the statements I have heard and read from influential Catholics in the recent past, this strikes me as a very real eventuality.

Regardless of the anger we may feel toward our bishops, our response should *not* be to disown them and wander off on our own. To do that would be to lose our Catholicity. Moreover, we *need* our bishops to evangelize in ways that *only a bishop* can by virtue of his anointing as the leader of the local Church. This is not merely a credal assertion. It is also a natural one. As our legitimate leaders, bishops are the face of the Church to the public in the same way that the opinions of the world toward the United States are formed by President of the United States. Regardless of one's feelings toward a bishop (or a president for that matter), his official capacity *establishes* what it is others think we stand for. So, like it or not, we cannot abandon them. If we want them to be other than who they have been, then we have to help them make that transformation. This will require a new season of hope in the face of despair and a new willingness to forgive when forgiveness is very difficult. But, hope does not disappoint and forgiveness is the very heart of the Good News we proclaim (cf. Rom 5:5).

* * *

My mother had more "sayings" than anyone I have ever known. But, they stuck. To this day, when I'm together with my siblings, one of us will recall one of Mom's famous sayings. That always kicks off a string of aphorisms that leaves us in paroxysms of laughter and affectionate memories. One such was this: "The middle of the road is the best place to be, but the hardest place to stay." She was right, of course. It's a lot easier to get in the flow of traffic going one way or the other than to hold to the middle of the road and risk getting hit by both sides.

An "issue", by definition is "a point in question or a matter that is in dispute." Regardless of what side of the road we may occupy with respect to any issue, there is almost always some element of truth to the countervailing argument. With respect to the controversies roiling the Church these days, we must seek this middle ground in a spirit of humility regardless of our personal leanings.

The secular narrative looks at the sex abuse crisis and portrays every perpetrator as the most heinous of characters dedicated solely to using the Church as a cover for the horrors he inflicted on children. For their part, the bishops are seen as being complicit in the "good ol' boy" system, covering for the perps without a thought given to the harm they inflicted. As a basically conservative person, I *must* struggle with this perspective and admit that there is at least some degree of truth in it. The fact that the liberal *Boston Globe* unveiled this problem back in 2002 and the fact that the liberal media seems to relish continuing to drag up every allegation and describe it in the most salacious of terms does not remove that part of their rendition of the facts that is true. The truth, regardless of its source, must be accepted. If we perceive nothing but attack on the Church, we are burying some element of the truth. If we perceive nothing but a just cause on the part of the secular media, we are doing exactly the same thing. Judicious balance will get us both the compassionate forgiveness as well as the moral outrage the situation dictates.

It is true that our bishops have let us down. Yes, sometimes they did close their eyes to grave damage inflicted by the powerful on the powerless. That said, as a group, our bishops were thrust into "no win" situations that were not of their own making. When all is said and done, they had to struggle for the prudential judgment to unearth the truth in each situation and apply justice as best they could.

The secular attitude toward the priest sex abuse crisis is made up of equal or unequal parts genuine concern for the victims, antagonism toward the Church, and the bourgeois pleasure of watching the "mighty" fall. As Christians, however, we cannot uncritically adopt the mentality of the secular world. Our basis for approaching any issue comes from a more definitive authority. First Timothy 5:19-21 offers a two-edged sword to apply to such matters. Verse 19 states: *"Do not accept an accusation against a presbyter unless it is supported by two or three witnesses."* Looking back, it is easy to see how our bishops rightly brought this scripture-based skepticism to the accusations. They knew full well how a false accusation has the potential to ruin a person. Notwithstanding, they *should* have heeded the next two verses with equal vigor: *"Reprimand publicly those who do sin, so that the rest also will be afraid. I charge you before God and Christ Jesus and the elect angels to keep these rules without prejudice, doing nothing out of favoritism."* Based on these scriptural mandates alone, the cover-up of those found guilty should never have happened. Moreover, the knowledge that any dark abuse of power by a member of the clergy will unfailingly be brought to the light of day is the best assurance that future instances will be dramatically reduced.

In any event, it is fair to ask why only half of St. Paul's admonition to Timothy made it into the episcopal mentality? In my view, there are several factors...

The Times In 2004, the U.S. bishops commissioned the John Jay College of Criminal Justice to study the sexual abuse of minor by priests. This study covered the period from 1950 through 2002. Among the many findings of the *John Jay Study,* it seems to me that the timing of the phenomenon is very significant. Summarizing the major finding, Wikipedia reports:

> The incidence of reported abuse increased by several orders of magnitude in the 1960s and 1970s. There was, for example, a more than sixfold increase in the number of reported acts of abuse of males aged 11 to 17 between the 1950s and the 1970s. After peaking in the 1970s, the number of incidents in the report decreased through the 1980s and 1990s even more sharply than the incidence rate had increased in the 1960s and 1970s.[32]

Having lived out my teen years in the 1960s, I believe much can be explained by revisiting the Zeitgeist of that era. This was the decade of Vatican II, the Beatles, the Pill, the Vietnam War, "free sex", the mainstreaming of illegal drugs, and the impeachment of Richard Nixon. The huge cohort of Baby Boomers were beginning to come of age, unleashing a cultural revolution hitherto unheard of in American history. Virtually everything was called into question: traditional authority, long-held social mores, patriotism, etc. It is not an exaggeration to say that young people actually believed the maxim: "Don't trust anyone over thirty." Even within the Church, the notion that widely available artificial contraception actually changed the teleological nature of human sexuality was widely held. In an era of "anything goes", all sex was considered good. In 1970 Stephen Still's song *Love the One You're With* seemed to replace the Seventh Commandment. I recall as an eighth grader a parish priest telling us boys: "God would never condemn anyone to hell for a sexual sin. It is just too natural." In other words, masturbation and the phantasmagoric objectification of women that went along with it was just find-and-dandy.

Of course, it did not end there. This was the era of Hugh Heffner's "playboy philosophy" with monthly installments that could be found in his new genre of pornographic magazines. Even worse followed. The North American Man-Boy Love Association was founded in 1979, with a now-defrocked Catholic priest in supportive attendance at is founding meeting.[33] And on and on it went. Those were the truly revolutionary times we lived in.

A Culture of Scandal Avoidance and Confidentiality In addition to the turbulent and permissive period of history when most of the sex abuse that is still being reported actually occurred, there are other factors that combined to bring about the crisis we know today.

One factor might be described as the ecclesial culture of professional confidentiality. As is true of other professions – particularly medicine, law, and counseling – priests have been trained to treat anything that is said in confidence as sacrosanct. Only, a priest's sense of confidentiality is multiplied many times over. The seal of Confession is absolute. If broken for any reason, automatic excommunication occurs. Naturally, seminarians come to understand secrecy as part of what it means to be a priest. The norm is never to bring to the light of day anything of a sensitive nature. As a practical matter, after having heard thousands of confessions, the memory or whether or not you heard "it" while administering the sacrament can be very fuzzy. To err on the side of caution makes perfect sense. Clearly, this culture of confidentiality sets up an automatic clash with the secular media which holds that "the people's 'right' to know" eclipses all other concerns.

The Church also has a long history of avoiding *even the semblance of scandal* for fear of damaging the cause of the Gospel. Hence, since 2002 we now have policies that prohibit any adult associated with the Church from being alone with a minor. This policy applies to everyone – priest, teacher, employee, volunteer coach. Many priests will not close the door of their office when counseling a woman to ensure that no one might assume the worst and spark a rumor. The intent is good. No serious Christian wants to damage the cause of the Gospel, inadvertently or otherwise. Unfortunately, there is more to consider than "protecting the cause of the Gospel". The fact is that the Gospel does not need protecting. We have allowed this concern to become a mask for protecting *appearances*.

The *Catechism* never speaks about *appearances* that might bring scandal, and for good reason; Jesus never cared about appearances and he went about causing scandals all the time, eating with sinners and prostitutes, speaking alone with an adulteress, etc. For Jesus, the concern was always for the individual who was being exposed to sin due to the sinful acts of others. Consider what the *Catechism* has to say about scandal:

> Scandal is an attitude or behavior which leads another to do evil. The person who gives scandal becomes his neighbor's tempter... Scandal is a grave offense if by deed or omission another is deliberately led into a grave offense. (2284)
>
> Scandal takes on a particular gravity by reason of the authority of those who cause it or the weakness of those who are scandalized.

It prompted our Lord to utter this curse: "Whoever causes one of these little ones who believe in me to sin, it would be better for him to have a great millstone fastened around his neck and to be drowned in the depths of the sea." (cf. Mt 18:6) Scandal is grave when given by those who by nature or office are obliged to teach and educate others. Jesus reproaches the scribes and Pharisees on this account: he likens them to wolves in sheep's clothing (cf. Mt 7:15). (2285)

Anyone who uses the power at his disposal in such a way that it leads others to do wrong becomes guilty of scandal and responsible for the evil that he had directly or indirectly encouraged. (2287)

This description of scandal, of course, is the very definition of what Theodore McCarrick did when he induced seminarians to sleep with him. It is what predatory priests do when they seduce young men and sodomize little boys. It is these sins that are scandalous. Yet, ironically the "avoidance of scandal" was at the heart of our bishops' secretive response to the sexual abuse crisis. The best way to avoid the real scandal would have been to come down hard on the perpetrators, who were living gravely sinful lives and leading others into the same lifestyle.

Still, it is understandable that many a bishop did not want to be complicit in taking a terrible situation and "making it worse" by bringing it to light. They had the assurance of Jesus that everything would be brought to the light in the fullness of time, but they didn't see it as their responsibility to deter potential sinners by openly inviting the derision of existing sinners. This was wrong-headed to be sure. The ancient Church was hard on serious sinners, demanding severe and very public penance.[34] Hopefully, with God's grace, we will return to a greater dread of sin, but at the time most of the abuses were occurring all the emphasis was on forgiveness. This brings me to the last factor that may help to explain the sex abuse crisis and the bishops' typical response to it.

An Ethos of Forgiveness At least one contributing factor is as noble as the Gospel itself. A central tenet of our faith is *forgiveness.* Anyone who has ever experienced the grace of personal conversion understands the tender power of God's forgiveness. Many a man who has sought ordination did so out of a profound desire to be a minister of Christ's forgiveness. In the seminary, they were formed in it. In their ministries, they dispense it sacramentally. Forgiveness flows in the veins of any good priest. What's more, it is codified in the teachings of the Church in specific ways. For example, the Second Vatican Council's Decree on the Pastoral Office of Bishops states: "A bishop should be compassionate and helpful to those priests who are in any kind of danger or who have failed in some respect."[35]

Now, imagine yourself as a bishop in the late 1970s and a phone call comes in from a concerned mother. She states that her thirteen-year-old son came home from a swimming party for altar servers deeply upset claiming that Father Tim had tried to molest him. You thank the distressed mom and promise to deal with the matter immediately. So, you do just that and the next morning Father Tim shows up at the chancery office visibly upset and ostensibly contrite. He claims he has been struggling with these urges for a long time and tearfully promises never to act on them again. He asks for you to hear his confession. You do so and you are moved by the apparent sincerity of his contrition. Tim is still a young man. You feel a certain sense of paternal protection for him. After all, there isn't a dad on earth who trumpets the transgressions of his son to the world. Every instinct you have is compelling you to handle this matter with great discretion and understanding. You think of Jesus protecting the woman caught in adultery from being stoned (cf. Jn 8:1-11). You remember the words of your own confessor who once reminded you that gossip – even though it may be true – is still the sin of slander; that its truthfulness does not remove the fact that it remains a sin against charity. Conscious of the desire to avoid scandal and the seal of Confession, you call your diocesan attorney and rather elliptically describe "a hypothetical case" to him. In the final analysis, you trust your own instincts and accept the advice of the lawyer to keep the matter out of the legal system. So, you decide to give Father Tim a fresh start. You grant him a "medical" leave of absence and send him off to the Servants of the Paraclete.

Some months later, they report back that Father Tim has been an exemplary resident and is fit for priestly ministry. You re-assign him to a new parish without restrictions. In the meantime, you have talked to the boy and his parents. You offered to pay for counseling plus an extra consideration for their discretion. They assure you the last thing they want is to drag the whole affair into the public spotlight. They want to protect their son's privacy.

It is important to answer the following question truthfully: Placed in the same set of circumstances, would I have made the same mistakes?

Done. It's over… until the next time. Only this time, the matter involves a different priest and the allegation is outright rape. Without hearing the priest's confession, you consult with your vicar general. It turns out this new perpetrator had been in trouble before under the previous bishop. You inquire how he had handled the problem. Like yourself, he had sent the priest off for counseling. Reassured, you repeat your last decision. By now, you think you know how to handle the problem. After all, a precedent of "forgiveness" has been established.

"There, but for the Grace of God…"

I am not arguing that the bishops did not make serious mistakes in covering up the malfeasance of priests who used their positions of trust to harm young people. My point is simply that we need to extend as much understanding and forgiveness to our bishops as we do to others who find themselves in difficult situations that were not of their own making. The fact that they often opted for the easy way out attests only to their humanness, not wickedness. For our part, when we are particularly down on our bishops, it is important to answer the following question truthfully: Placed in the same set of circumstances at the same point in history, would I have made the same mistakes? Answering for myself, I can only say that I would have made exactly the same mistakes? It is easy for us to become blindly self-righteous when the ethos of "the world" has become self-righteous. As Christians, we need to recognize this tendency in ourselves (if it exists), lest we become the hypocritical Pharisees of our own times.

Among his last words as he hung on the Cross, Jesus cried out, *Father, forgive them, for they know not what they do* (Lk 23:34). I have often wondered why He didn't say, "Father, forgive them their many sins." He *could* have. But, as egregious as the sins of the executioners and the temple priests were objectively, the fact is that they really didn't grasp the import of what they were doing. That's the way I think it is with a great deal of behavior that is objectively sinful. If you took all the unintentional sin in the world and compared it with the deeply evil, premeditated kind, I believe the former would vastly outweigh the latter. Perhaps that's why Jesus emphasized the importance of forgiveness throughout his public ministry. Throughout my life, most of the emotional pain inflicted on me by others - maybe even all of it - was never intended to hurt me. The people who hurt me never gave it a second thought at the time, even though some of it was objectively sinful. In fact, in some cases, they probably thought they were doing or saying the right thing. I pray that the same can be said of me in regard to those whom I have hurt.

PART II: THE CHALLENGES

The secular world is very antagonistic toward the Church and, by association, her episcopal leadership. They view the Church as a restraint on freedom of thought and the prevailing zeitgeist. Too often, they are willing to portray decent people in the worst possible light, if it helps to achieve their aim. Living as people "in the world", it is easy to appropriate the world's perspective as our own. But, as people who are "not *of* the world", we need to be on guard not to embrace all of the secular narrative uncritically (cf. Jn 17:16).

The post-modern secular ideal is a form of libertarian individualism that prizes "self-creation" as the path to one's identity and fulfillment. By contrast, as Christians, we are not our own. We *have been bought at a price* (1 Cor 6:20). Christianity has always held that our identity was established for us at our Baptism, the highest identity possible for a human being. Whatever else I may be, it is only an adjective that describes my ontological essence as an adopted child of God. Self-fulfillment comes from trying to be the best son I can be. Among many things, that includes extending forgiveness and encouragement.

At this moment of pain and anger at the missteps of our bishops, it is critical for us to understand that they are hurting, too. It is not an exaggeration to say that the present moment is the most painful many of them have ever lived through. They know they are hated by mainstream media, the entertainment elites, and many others. They realize that to many Catholics, they are merely a figurehead. But, the truly crushing blow is that many of us seem to have turned on them as well. As I think of them, the words of St. Paul echo in my ears: *"God has exhibited us apostles as the last of all, like people sentenced to death, since we have become a spectacle to the world, to angels and human beings alike... When ridiculed, we bless; when persecuted, we endure; when slandered, we respond gently. We have become like the world's rubbish, the scum of all, to this very moment."* (cf. 1 Cor 4:9-10, 13)

114

The best gift we priests, deacons, and laity can give our bishops is forgiveness and friendship. Without these, the Church cannot move forward. The great fourth-century bishop and doctor of the Church, St. John Chrysostom once said:

> Distance separates us, but love unites us, and death itself cannot divide us. For though my body die, my soul will live and be mindful of my people. You are fellow citizens, my fathers, my brothers, my sons, my limbs, my body. You are my light, sweeter to me than the visible light. For what can the rays of the sun bestow on me that is comparable to your love. The sun's light is useful in my earthly life, but your love is fashioning a crown for me in the life to come.[36]

Bishops still yearn for the affection of their people; perhaps now, more than ever. We are their family. May we be a good family.

Is Change Possible?

All of this begs the question: Can our bishops change? After all, they are products of an ecclesiastical culture that, by modern standards, has been slow to change; some would say, even hidebound.

Having said that, the vast, vast majority of bishops are good men. They do what is right based on their understanding of what is right at the time. The bishop's fast action in adopting the 2002 *Dallas Charter for the Protection of Young People* attests to that fact; so does their transparent implementation of the *Charter* ever since. The steps they are taking right now to hold themselves accountable for investigating accusations against wayward bishops and elevating the role of the laity in the investigative process also attests to their willingness to change.

On numerous occasions in history, when serious reforms were needed, bishops rose to the challenge. The Gregorian reforms of the eleventh century came about precisely because simony, clerical immorality, and lay investiture were the rule of the day. Backed by the support of ordinary Christians, numerous holy bishops found common cause with the likes of Saints Peter Damien, Leo IX, and Gregory VII. The net result was a vastly more faithful Church. The point is this: Meaningful reforms grew out of the worst of times, not the best. And that has been the pattern throughout the checkered history of the people of God.

In regard to the New Evangelization, bishops have an important role to play, a role that most of them have not yet recognized. Notwithstanding, there is good reason for hope. In my dealings with bishops around the country, the proverbial lights are beginning to come on. There is an increasing awareness that the maintenance mentality which has characterized the Church for so many years, no longer works. There is also an openness to discuss what needs to change. At this very moment, several bishops and archbishops are beginning to take unprecedented steps to normalize evangelization throughout their dioceses. These are steps of faith. The future is not very clear. All that is known is that it will take at least a generation for widespread fruit to become evident. In these small beginnings, we need to encourage our bishops; effectively, "to give them permission" to lead and to "be there" to help them make it happen.

Evangelical Weakness

Evangelizing out of brokenness and vulnerability is far more powerful than preaching out of a spirit of triumphalist pride. Far too often, we have preached to win over peoples' heads, rather than their hearts. Speaking out of sincere brokenness touches peoples' hearts. I have witnessed this many times on *Cursillo* weekends and Jesuit retreats. After all, the self-righteous cannot speak with sincerity about their own need for a Savior.

As suggested back in the Prologue, this may have been the reason for our Lord's words to St. Paul: *My grace is sufficient for you, for power is made perfect in weakness* (2 Cor 12:9a). Paul went on to respond: *"Therefore, I am content with weaknesses, for the sake of Christ; for when I am weak, then I am strong."* This is the irony of the Cross.

In January 2019, Pope Francis asked all the U.S. bishops to gather at Mundelein Seminary outside Chicago for a seven-day retreat. The retreat master was none other than the preacher to the papal household himself, Father Raniero Cantalamessa, OFM Cap. In his second meditation delivered to the bishops, Father Cantalamessa said:

> We are overwhelmed nowadays by the moral scandals involving the clergy, and rightly so; but we fail to see how much more gospel-like and humble the Church of Christ has become, how more free from worldly power. I would even say that, in some respects, this is a "golden age" compared to past centuries when many bishops were more concerned about governing their territory than caring for their flock. In the past, to be a bishop was an honor; today it is a burden.[37]

Life is now different than it has been in the past and, in some respects, that is a good thing. Along with the present crisis has come a new spirit of repentance and open penance among our bishops. Many of them around the country have called their people to fasting and prayer.

Evangelizing out of brokenness and vulnerability is far more powerful than preaching out of a spirit of triumphalist pride.

Numerous bishops have led public repentance services, often prostrating themselves on sanctuary floors in front of their people. We need to understand this as a sign of good things to come and the advent of a great opportunity for the cause of the Gospel.

Let us encourage our bishops to continue these practices of humble repentance; to very publicly and repetitively let the world know that they are turning over a new leaf that is one of transparent, human brokenness. In his First Letter to the Corinthians, St. Paul wrote the following words:

> When I came to you, brothers, proclaiming the mystery of God, I did not come with sublimity of words or of wisdom. For I resolved to know nothing while I was with you except Jesus Christ, and him crucified. I came to you in weakness and fear and much trembling, and my message and my proclamation were not with the persuasive words of wisdom, but with a demonstration of spirit and power, so that your faith may rest not on human wisdom but on the power of God. (2:1-6)

May we forgive our bishops any wrong-doings they have committed, pray for them, and encourage them to move forward with new forthrightness and single-mindedness of purpose.

VI. Rediscovering the Pearl of Great Price

For God did not send his Son
into the world to condemn the world,
but that the world might be saved through Him.

John 3:17

At the first meeting of RCIA gatherings, it is a common practice to hand out reading material. Among these materials are two gigantic books – one a Catholic Study Bible. So far so good. Most people expect that. But, then they look at the second book, an 800-page tome called the *Catechism of the Catholic Church*. All of a sudden it dawns on the inquirers that their leaders might actually ask them to read it. As they start thumbing through it, words like "Christian Mystery", "theological virtues", "Viaticum", and "integrality" start leaping off the pages. You can just see the wheels turning in their heads and their thoughts might just as well be plastered on the white board: Lord, what did I get myself into?

Let's face it. The Catholic Church is a big, intimidating institution that comes with a doctrinal handbook ranging from the elementary foundations of the Christian Faith to the esoteric. We are the largest and oldest surviving institution in the world. Through our universal reach, we feed, clothe, educate, and heal more people than any other organization on earth. And that is all good.

But, to many people – especially those who don't deal with us on a daily basis – we are all about a huge, inscrutable system of theology and do's-and-don'ts. In the Western world, we are failing as a vehicle for inviting people into an intimate relationship with Jesus. In Jesus, the face of God is revealed. Without Him at the center of all we do and say, we become nothing more than a very busy NGO with a long list of accompanying do's-and-don'ts. We have become like Martha, to whom our Lord said with great affection, *you are anxious and worried about many things. There is need of only one thing* (cf. Lk 10:41).

Our single greatest challenge is to get back to the "one thing", the Love of our Life, the Pearl of Great Price – to Jesus.

A Simple Story

My own story started back in 1950. I was privileged to be born into a family where Mom and Dad were serious about their faith. Among my early memories were daily Mass at the St. Joseph side altar in St. Benedict Church in Evansville, Indiana (now, the cathedral parish). There were all kinds of Catholic devotions: nightly family rosaries kneeling around Mom and Dad's humongous bed, the annual family nativity play, and Dad's sprinkling the Christmas tree with holy water (always with a twinkle in his eye and a little splash on us). There were the cuddles before bedtime with Mom and her impromptu stories about my friend Jesus who lived down the dusty lane in Nazareth and would come to play with me. Sometimes, I would even get invited to his house and Mary would treat us with milk and cookies.

And, in those early days there was the witness of Dad slipping away every Monday evening after dinner for the ministry and meeting of the St. Vincent de Paul Society. Dad was a leader in so many ways. When I was older, he introduced my brothers and me to the "White House" (aka, Jesuit House of Retreats) in St. Louis. Each year with great fanfare, on a specific Thursday afternoon in December, the 'pied piper' would gather us together and along with some fifty other men from the Evansville area, he would lead a caravan to St. Louis for our annual silent Ignatian retreat. (Usually, there was a stop at the Chase Park Plaza bar beforehand just to fortify us for the long weekend ahead.) Dad did that every year until he physically no longer could. And, long after my brothers and I could afford to pay for the retreat ourselves, he insisted on treating us. To him, that's just what a good dad did.

God knows, Mom and Dad were not perfect. Dad had to fight a powerful attraction to alcohol (a problem I've inherited) and most of his waking hours he had either a pipe or a stogie in his mouth. Even after the health effects became well-known, he managed to rationalize the habit with the mantra: "Yeah, but I never inhale." (The rest of us in the same room did all the inhaling.) A few years before his death at 88, he did manage to kick the habit. For all Mom's deep

> "Anyone who loves God in the depths of his heart has already been loved by God. In fact, the measure of a man's love for God depends on how deeply aware he is of God's love for him."
>
> *- Diadochus of Photice, Fifth-Century Bishop*

spirituality and maternal love, she was a bit of a latter-day Jansenist. Diminutive in stature, she was a paragon of discipline and any hint of a venial sin among us was called out and dealt with rigorously. (Not surprisingly, I've had to fight the same judgmental attitude, especially when it involves someone *else's* sin.)

But, all-in-all, we had a wonderful family life. I suppose that's what prepared me for the great "aha moment" in my life. Like many good Catholic boys of that era, I was an altar server and loved every minute of it, serving with near-military precision. In any event, when I was 11 or 12, I was scheduled to serve the Mass of the Lord's Supper on Holy Thursday. I remember it was Holy Thursday specifically because there were 12 of us altar boys all lined up at chairs just inside the communion rail. (In those days the priest would wash the feet of the 12 servers instead of the common practice today of inviting 12 people from the assembly.) As our pastor, Father Gabriel Verkamp, OSB was delivering his sermon (that was before they were "homilies"), he said something that literally changed my life. At the very least, he affirmed the most fundamental of truths and I have never forgotten it. First, it should be mentioned that Father Gabriel was not a particularly powerful preacher. He was aging and going blind and spoke with the hint of a German accent that he must have picked up from his parents. But, Father Gabriel was a holy man and he spoke with the certainty of deep faith that night.

This is what hit me: He said that it had been the constant teaching of the Church down through the ages that "if I was the only person on earth who was in need of salvation, the Son of God would have come and died on the Cross just for me." The truth of that statement hit me with a force I had never felt before. In fact, it brought me to tears (which is a little awkward when you're 12 years old and surrounded by buddies). In any event, there was no fancy talk; no impassioned oratory. There weren't any angelic choirs singing softly in the background (at least that I could hear). It was just the simple Truth. He loves me... He really loves me! The Holy Spirit used Father Gabriel's simple words to give me a special experience of his grace that night. The bottom line: I knew that I knew that I knew I had just heard **the** Truth.

That's the timeless power of the *kērygma,* the core of our Christian faith. God loved us enough to become one of us and give his very life for us. The message didn't have to be dressed up. Spoken plainly and with the strength of simple conviction, it had an amazing power of its own.

Did this event really change my life? Indeed, it did. Fifty-seven plus years later, there is a hardly a day that goes by when I don't think about it. Sometimes, it still moves me. Did it make me perfect? Not by a long shot. But, from that moment on, I knew who I was. I was a Christian, who to this day stand in awe of the love of my Lord. I know I am not my own. I have been purchased at a high price and, for a God like that, I am *all in*.

The Pearl

The kingdom of heaven is like a merchant searching for fine pearls. When he finds a pearl of great price, he goes and sells all he has and buys it (Mt 13:45). This famous parable is usually interpreted as the joy of a person when he experiences the priceless, infinite love of Jesus. The value of this particular "jewel" is like none other. He is willing to give up everything for his beloved. While I value this interpretation, Curtis Martin, the founder of the Fellowship of Catholic University Students (FOCUS), offers a parallel interpretation – an alternative way of looking at the same thing. In this interpretation, the merchant is the Son of God who finds <u>us</u>. He is so in love with us that he freely chooses to "sell everything" to have us, including his own human life. [38] This unmeasurable love is the central truth of our very existence.

Another friend told me a true story about a women's Bible study she was once a part of. In one the discussions, a woman (let's call her Heather) expressed the belief that she was unlovable. She had done some awful things and consequently felt she was worthless. My friend then recounts how another woman in the group told Heather how totally wrong she was; that she was a beautiful human being, beyond priceless. She went on to say with passionate conviction, "Heather, God is crazy about you. He is crazy in love with you."

Wow! God is crazy in love.

In a sense that's true. In his self-giving he goes way beyond what any "sane" person would do. He even loved us before we became "beautiful", before we were lovable, as Scripture says, *while we were still sinners* (cf. Rom 5:8). The abused, rejected, lonely Son of God even begged his Father to forgive us as he approached his final mortal moment hanging on the Cross. He offered that prayer for all of us who helped put him on that Cross. Those Roman soldiers and Temple officials were at their absolute worst during those hours as our Lord hung on the Cross. The truth is, however, they were only *representative* of the entire human family. Only an unreasonable person would love another when he is at his worst, only a "crazy" person.

There is a sad side of the story of the women's Bible study. Heather said to the woman who told her about God's crazy love for her: "I've never heard a Catholic say those things before."

With great sadness, my experience as a cradle Catholic forces me to affirm Heather's reaction.

If we want to understand why our youth are leaving the Church, it is because we Catholics stopped talking about the Pearl of Great Price. We have a treasure and have buried it in a field and forgotten how to find it. At the risk of stretching the allegory beyond its usefulness, we Catholic leaders should consider how it is that we lost the Pearl; how it is that we speak of our great patrimony as if it was all of equal value and we neglect to talk about our Beloved from whom everything came.

I think it may be because we have two thousand years of accumulated wealth. Ours is "old money". That special treasure that contains the Pearl of Great Price is only one of several treasures we own. We know we own an incalculable fortune, but we have had it so long we've forgotten that 99 plus percent of our net worth is the Pearl. By comparison, all those other treasures do not amount to much. All the merits of the martyrs, all the heroic virtue of our saints, all the wisdom of the doctors of the Church derive whatever value they have – and they *are* valuable – from the central truths of the Faith. May we once again come to say along with St. Paul, *I even consider everything as a loss because of the supreme good of knowing Christ Jesus my Lord* (Phil 3:8).

A Hierarchy of Truths

The Second Vatican Council's Decree on Ecumenism *Unitatis redintegratio* stated: "When comparing doctrines with one another, (we) should remember that in Catholic doctrine there exists an order or 'hierarchy' of truths, since they vary in their relation to the foundation of the Christian faith." [39] In *Evangelii Gaudium* Pope Francis reminded us of this teaching and stated:

> Pastoral ministry in a missionary style is not obsessed with the disjointed transmission of a multitude of doctrines to be insistently imposed. When we adopt a pastoral goal and a missionary style which would actually reach everyone without exception or exclusion, the message has to concentrate on the essentials, on what is most beautiful, most appealing and at the same time most necessary. The message is simplified, while losing none of its depth and truth, and thus becomes all the more forceful and convincing. [40]

Perhaps the first challenge facing the Church is to rediscover ways to speak "in a missionary style"; to work in a way expressly aimed at proclaiming those doctrines that are most central "to the *foundation* of the Christian faith". My suspicion is that we tend to *think* we are operating in a missionary mode when we speak out on issues such as religious freedom or even the right to life. While it is absolutely vital for the world to hear our position on these issues, we need to realize that they do not constitute evangelization. Those who will be influenced by the Church's public policy pronouncements are people who already have at least some degree of respect for the Catholic Church. For some, these public positions may serve as a form of *pre*-evangelization, but the truth is, as important as they may be to the social justice doctrine of the Church, they are not "central to the *foundation* of the Christian faith"; rather, they flow *from* the foundation. You would be hard pressed to find anyone more pro-life than I am, but I am pro-life because of my relationship with God; not the other way around.

If we want to reach "everyone without exception or exclusion", we need to go back to the central tenets of Christianity, those truths that we so often *assume* everyone embraces, but increasingly do not.

God exists. While God is not dependent on anything, God loves me and every other 'me' in the world in a very personal way, so much so that he actually became one of us. His love for us was so strong that he allowed himself to be executed for us in the most horrible way possible so that we might live with Him. At least thirty-six hours after his death, He came back to physical life affirming to his followers that all he had taught them was true.

Obviously, there is more to the story than this. But, this by itself has the power to change the trajectory of human lives. His existence, his incarnation, the *kērygma* of his execution and resurrection – these are the foundation of the Christian faith. It is essential we get back to "proclaim(ing) the word, be(ing) persistent whether it is convenient or inconvenient". (cf. 2 Tim 4:2)

There is a fine, but important, distinction between *evangelization* and *catechesis.* The former must precede the latter. Let us put first things first.

VII. Servants Who Will Lead

You are the light of the world.
A city set on a hill cannot be hidden.

Matthew 5:14

When we consider the New Evangelization as it is practiced in the United States, it is clear to the most casual of observers that Catholics as a whole are not a very "evangelical" group. For all our talk about evangelization, we have very little to show for it. To the extent that it takes place at all, it is by and large the province of specialized apostolates and ecclesial movements. Even a generous assessment is forced to concede that evangelization has not been "normalized" into the lives of average Catholics, either as the evangelized or the evangelizers. By and large, it has not touched our lives.

And, for many Catholics, it would be just fine to leave it that way. In fact, the "E-word" is a dangerous subject, because if we ever got serious about actually doing it on a large scale, the Church would have to change... and many of us like the Church just the way she is, thank you very much.

Yet, we need to be evangelized and in turn to become evangelizers, whether it is comfortable or not, whether convenient or not. While perhaps threatening, this is *not* a change that would introduce some new, bizarre form of heresy and it is *not* change without precedent in Church history. But, it is change nonetheless and change nearly always involves pain, if for no other reason than

127

it affects the way we live – both personally and communally; it is not unlike the change that cardiac patients have to make in their lifestyle. After the pain of open-heart surgery, they are the healthier for it. After the changes required of us as Catholics, we will be the holier for it.

But how do we make these changes?

The Call for Leader-Servants

This section title is not a misprint. It really says "Leader-Servants" rather than the other way around. In order to "mainstream" the ministry of evangelization throughout the Church, our leaders will have to act more like leaders in what they prioritize and in how they lead. That does not mean pushy or aggressive; just the steadfast, holy pursuit of a clear-sighted vision for the future of a Church that wins converts to Christ.

This vision cannot become reality without leaders. As a divinely-sanctioned, hierarchical institution, our ordained leaders *must* lead the way. There is no alternative. In his insightful book, *Church, Faith, Future* Father Louis Cameli asserts that the visible, structured leadership of the Catholic Church "is both necessary and helpful, and its roots are in the Gospel." However, then he goes on to point out the downside of our leadership model.

> It also comes with a cost. Historically, it has fostered a tendency among Catholics at large to defer to that leadership and become passive. Catholics at large would generally not perceive themselves as the active agent of renewal and mission, although it is what we hope for and need.[41]

Whether we like it or not, ours is a hierarchical culture. We believe that this model was intentionally established by our Lord. But, as is true of every human system, it is not perfect. Who we are as a people, what we stand for is derived to a large degree from our leaders, especially the *ordained* leaders. If ecclesial leaders hope for a culture in which rank-and-file Catholics assume their rightful roles as envisioned in the Second Vatican Council's *Decree on the Apostolate of Lay People*, there is no practical way it can happen unless our leaders become personally intent on making it happen. If our bishops expect to develop a culture in which evangelization is an accepted part of how the Church lives, then *they* have to evangelize. No number of platitudes and exhortations delivered from the ambo can achieve this. Frankly, our leaders will have to lead more forthrightly than they have.

As Christians, we take comfort in the notion that Jesus exhorted his leaders to be "servants of all". No one can deny the veracity of that commandment. Our Lord wants his leaders to be servants. Humble, disinterested service is truly holy and it cannot be misunderstood or misinterpreted by the one who is served.

But we tend to react differently to the prospect of leading. The very word – leader – is fraught with intimidating connotations that many of us would rather not deal with. In one sense, the servanthood aspect of servant-leadership involves very few risks. In a world where it is easier to keep our heads down and avoid getting shot, those with any pretense to leadership too often use the servanthood part of this hybrid as a rationalization for accommodation and maintenance of the status quo.

One very popular pastor once told me that his parish never did anything unless the idea originated from "the community". For him, the *sensus fidei* was the *only* sense there is. For this priest, a shepherd who actually leads his sheep does not conform to his notion of what a pastor is supposed to do. As a result, problematic things happened in that parish; popular, to an extent, but, Christian, sometimes not.

Leadership – carried out either by an individual or a Christian community – can be an invitation for trouble. *Missionary* leadership is even more dangerous. In post-modern society, the proposition that Jesus is the world's one and only Savior; that He is each individual's one and only Savior; that his truth is the *real* Truth and his ways are superior to other ways are viewed as dubious propositions, at best. Often, they are rejected outright. Even when it is done well, evangelization will be viewed in the sight of some as hypocritical, disrespectful of human freedom, manipulative, condescending and arrogant. Even when motivated out of the purest love, evangelizers face the possibility of rejection. Too often this risk becomes an excuse for servant-leaders to opt out of the cost of prophetic leadership. It is easy to avoid the whole messy business, especially when there doesn't seem to be much excitement about it in the first place.

If outright avoidance is not acceptable, procrastination almost always is. After all, evangelization is a long-range project and we all have pressing matters we have to do *today*; or, at least we think we do. "My life is just too complicated right now, so I'll tackle evangelization next year." We kick the ball down the road. Sometimes, we'll get a committee together and talk about it. However, by and large, it remains something we just talk about, but avoid doing. The leadership required to inspire, to teach, reorganize an entire local church (read "diocese") for mission is daunting and so easy to put off.

> If being a Christian leader involves servanthood, it also involves the frightening prospect of personal risk-taking; of venturing out

Make no mistake, it isn't that our Lord does not want his leaders to be servants. He does! But, at the same time, Jesus spent a substantial amount of time training and forming his disciples to be leaders, precisely for the task of mission. *He summoned the Twelve and began to send them out... He gave them authority... He instructed them... So they went out and preached repentance...* (Mk 6:7-13). *After this the Lord appointed seventy-two others whom he sent ahead of him in pairs... He said to them... "Carry no money bag, no sack, no sandals... cure the sick and say to them, 'The kingdom of God is at hand for you'."* (Lk 10:1 et seq) *Jesus said to them again, "Peace be with you. As the Father has sent me, so I send you."* (cf. Jn 20:21) If being a Christian leader involves servanthood, it also involves the frightening reality of having been sent; of personal risk-taking; of venturing out. It means taking the same risks our Lord took, which nearly always involved misunderstandings. How often Catholic leaders think not as God does, but rely on conventional wisdom. Isn't this what prompted Jesus' words to Peter: *Get behind me, Satan! You are an obstacle to me. You are not thinking as God does, but as human beings do* (Mt 16:22-23).

Evangelistic leadership requires breaking out of the safe and comfortable ecclesiastical *modus operandi* we are so used to. *Why does he eat with tax collectors and sinners* (Mk 2:16)? It may involve the perception that we have "gone over the edge", even by those who may be close to us. *As a result of this, many of his disciples returned to their former way of life and no longer accompanied him* (Jn 6:66).

These are the costs of being like Jesus...

These costs may not allow us the time to eat properly and may provoke misunderstandings even with our families (cf. Mk 3:21, Mt 10:34-39). These costs may prevent us from getting enough sleep or spending the time at home that we dearly desire (cf. Lk 9:57). They may require the proclamation of inconvenient truths that challenge some of the philosophical underpinnings of contemporary culture (cf. Lk 12:11). And all the while, we can fall into the trap of thinking that these costs excuse us from the other universal demands of the Gospel (e.g., the corporal works of mercy), because we are so busy *proclaiming* the Gospel. Whatever the "costs" may be, the challenges of true leader-servanthood will often involve risk-taking and they will *always* involve the Cross (cf. Mt 16:24). But with these risks, come the promise: *Everyone who acknowledges Me before others, I will acknowledge before my heavenly Father* (cf. Mt 10:32).

* * *

Dad's Back Scratches

When our family was young, we had a daily ritual for getting the kids out of bed in the morning. There was a popular Christian children's song back in the day with the refrain *"Rise and shine and give God your glory."* So, every morning I would enter each child's room intoning this song as a cheerful admonition to get out of bed. All I ever got in response were groans. No one was *ever* ready to "rise and shine". In fact, all that moaning and groaning became part of the ritual. It was really an invitation to complete the rest of the process. So, I would move to each child's bed and administer my very own Dad's Back Scratch. They may not have liked the prospect of rolling out from under their nice, toasty covers. But they always wanted Dad's Back Scratch. It was a gentle back scratch, but thorough. And, that usually got the job done. What they really wanted was Dad's touch; nothing else would do. This remains a happy memory for me.

The call to action in the Church is often met with the same moans and groans as my call to get out of bed. Something has to be awakened deep in the soul of God's people and a call is rarely enough. The Church needs the touch of her dad, something personal and loving. The touch is the promise of good things to come and the demonstration that Dad is already doing what the children are being called to do. Dad is already up. Dad is awake and dressed and ready to start the new day.

The Church throughout the world needs the touch of her spiritual fathers, the leadership, the inspiration, even the example. If our bishops are so engaged in "running the Church" that we rarely see them or even hear them, their ability to influence us – either as a leader *or* as a servant – is severely compromised. People need their bishops up close and personal if there is much hope of them coaxing us out from our cozy places. It is easy to cluck and remonstrate that evangelization is the province of the laity; that *they* should be doing it. Okay, well then, be a "father" and teach them how. With that leadership, in time, things will change.

Figurehead, Functionary, or Father

A few years ago, I spent a couple days in an extended meeting with a small group of fairly influential Catholic leaders. The purpose of this little "retreat" was to brainstorm the topic of "diocesan evangelization". No bishops and only one priest was present. Frankly, I was taken aback by some of the feelings that these faithful Catholics whom I admire voiced about our bishops. I remember one of the participants saying (to paraphrase), "If you want to do anything for the Church, don't ask the bishop for permission. All you'll get is a thousand reasons why it won't work or isn't permitted. Just go do it and ask for forgiveness later." This seemed to be the consensus opinion. When the idea of raising funds for diocesan evangelization was floated, the response was completely negative. Typical comments included: "Bishops mis-spend the money they already have." Or, "they wouldn't know what to do with it, if you gave it to them." Or, "they'd spend it on leaky roofs, and call it evangelization."

Admittedly, there was a lot of hyperbole flying around the room. However, there was more than a grain of truth in these observations. I had to admit that – absent a humble episcopal leader who is open to candid advise from trusted friends (both lay and clerical) – real transformative leadership might be a long time in coming.

* * *

It is in a spirit of tongue-in-cheek humor that the following unscientific (and unsolicited) taxonomy of caricaturized "bishop-types" is offered. Hopefully, it will provoke a tiny bit of episcopal soul-searching and/or a good dose of improved public relations...

(Note from the author: I recant in advance! Please don't excommunicate me.)

'Chief Executive Oligarch' This bishop is fully aware of his responsibility to lead, but hasn't a clue as to how to do it. He is well-known by his presbyterate as one who is prone to issue directives which translate into more work for the priests, but little help and little or no results. He is inclined to place more trust in a canned "program" than in the hard work of listening and discerning the promptings of the Holy Spirit. With a load of pent-up frustration, the presbyterate quietly hopes for a replacement who will love them and listen to them. In the meantime, they hope that his excellency will not come up with another idea.

'Avuncular Functionary' This bishop is universally loved by the priests and the people alike... but he is completely irrelevant to their lives. If he were to show up at "Mr. Average Catholic's" front door, the odds are pretty good, he wouldn't be recognized without his miter and crozier. This bishop is everybody's favorite uncle. They all want him at their annual dinners and he loves nothing more than to come. The problem is that he just doesn't have anything of substance to say. He genuinely loves his flock and they love him. He is a people-pleaser *par excellence.* The little one's love to do "high-fives" with him and their parents line up to exchange a joke or just give him a hug. No one wants him to retire, ever. But, in the intervening years... nothing happens. The little hand-slappers grow up, graduate from high school, and immediately graduate from the Faith. All "the numbers" slowly dwindle and he retires with the world's greatest party.

'Chief Operations Officer' Like the good engineer that he is, this bishop knows how to fix everything. Or, at least he thinks he does. He is a micromanager forever getting into the minutiae of everyone else's jobs. This eminently bright bishop insists on doing it all, because he knows he can do it better than anyone else. A lot of the time, he's right. He is amazingly competent. His idea of a good day is "doing it all" and still being able to get home by 7. It's all nice and tidy. He is a master tactician, knowing exactly how to accomplish his aims, but he rarely stops to think about what his aims should be. When it comes to "big picture questions", he chairs great committee meetings and can usually achieve consensus. All the while, the bureaucratic machinery runs smoothly, but "the people perish for lack of vision." (Proverbs 29:18 KJV) When he retires, all accounts balance to the penny, but few seem any closer to God than the day he started.

*   *   *

These caricatures could go on and on... Chief Executive Fundraiser, Monk in the Making, Theologian *du Jour*, Pontificating Populist, Perpetual Thinker, *et cetera et cetera*. The fact is, our leaders are overwhelmingly good men with very difficult jobs. However, to the extent that they settle into lives of glossing over the tough challenges of being a transformational leader in the context of their own particular proclivities, may they consider the words of St. Augustine:

> I must distinguish carefully between two aspects of the role the Lord has given me, a role that demands a rigorous accountability, a role based on the Lord's greatness rather than on my own merit. The first aspect is that I am a Christian; the second, that I am a leader. I

135

am a Christian for my own sake, whereas I am a leader for your sake; the fact that I am a Christian is to my own advantage, but I am a leader for your advantage.

Many persons come to God as Christians but not as leaders. Perhaps they travel by an easier road and are less hindered since they bear a lighter burden. In addition to the fact that I am a Christian and must give an account of my life, I as a leader must give an account of my stewardship as well.[42]

May we pray for our bishops and encourage them to strive to be the "best versions of themselves" – strong but tender, open but prophetic, servant-leaders and leader-servants, deeply spiritual but "shrewd as serpents" (cf. Mt 10:16), fathers to a rebellious household; in a word, saints.

VIII. Interlude: *Rebooting*

Even after [your brother] has thus sold his services
he still has the right of redemption;
he may be redeemed by one of his own brothers.

Leviticus 25:48

"Morning, Ann."

"Go on in, Father Godfrey. Bishop's ready for you."

"Thanks, Ann," he replied to the woman who had been a fixture in that very spot since the creation.

"Hey, Larry. Come on in."

"Thanks, Bishop." Father Godfrey liked this place. He had been there many times. The thought crossed his mind how warm and comfortable Bishop Paul's office is, a lot like its occupant. Still, he hadn't been looking forward to this meeting. As the new vicar general got himself settled on the sofa, all he could think of was how he was dreading the next few minutes. This was going to be a tough one.

As if sensing his edginess Bishop suggested they begin with a little prayer. All Father Larry could think of was how much he needed it.

"Lord, thank you for this beautiful morning and thank you for my brother, Larry. Please be with us as you promised you would whenever two or three are gathered in your name... Well, Father Larry and I make two. Please be the Third and grant us your wisdom and love and all we need to

serve you. Lord Jesus, may we be so bold as to offer this prayer and all we do today in your name to our Father in the unity of the Holy Spirit, now and forever."

"Amen and Amen."

Long pause.

"So… I gather this meeting has to do with your visits with 'the brethren'. I appreciate your update. You know them so much better than I do."

Sensing an opening, Father Larry took a deep breath and jumped in. "Well, Bishop. That's sort of the problem… I don't know how to say this. At the risk of sounding a little dramatic, our presbyterate is broken. Some of them are sick. Others are tired and just waiting to retire. A lot of guys are disenchanted. I even think a couple of them have lost their faith completely. They're just going through the motions. You need to get to know them better. A lot of them feel forgotten, like you wouldn't recognize them if you saw them walking down the street."

"Okay… That *does* sound a bit dramatic."

Thinking he needed to back off a little, Father Larry decided to take the long way around. "Let me back up. You know where I'm coming from on this. Bishop Tom was a great guy. But, with all due respect, I think he loved his golf and his scotch a little more than his priests. Twenty years ago, Bill Jackson tried to talk to him about the stuff he was struggling with. He came right out and asked for help, but according to Bill, Bishop Tom just gave him a pat on the back and told him to keep up the good work. Anyway, over the years, the guys just became estranged from him. Yeah, we had our convocation once a year and he had his summer golf outing for us, but it was all pretty superficial. No one ever really felt that they *knew* him. And with him, we never really got any sense as to where we were going."

"Well, with me at least everyone knows where we're going," Bishop Paul ventured.

"Fair enough, but they haven't got a clue how we're going to get there. They love the vision, Bishop. They really do. I mean, what a goal! But to be honest, they're skeptical. Especially, the older guys have seen a lot of things come and go that never made it to first base. It all amounted to a lot of work for nothing. Back in 2000, Bishop Tom got us all together and asked our opinions about diocesan priorities. The men were all over the ballpark. There was no unity at all. Some wanted liturgical reforms. Some made a pretty good case about improving religious ed, maybe getting catechists certified and training our school religion teachers. A couple of guys developed this big, formal proposal for a "Catholic Help Center" in Frogtown where volunteers could come and freely offer their services to all comers at whatever they were good at: as tax preparers, coaches for household budgeting, whatever. They wanted to recruit *pro bono* help from the Family Counseling Center and get a free dental clinic in there. It was pretty good stuff, really."

"Yes, I heard about that."

"So, anyway, Bishop Tom wanted to please everybody. So, we had "hearings" all over the diocese and eventually developed the *New Millennium* pastoral plan. Well, you know where *that* went. The plan had something like fifteen goals and four or five action steps under each goal and we were all supposed jump right in and make it happen in three years. It was like there was no connection to the real world. Of course, it didn't last long. After a couple plan implementation meetings, it all fizzled. That left a lot of people with a bad taste in their mouths about diocesan initiatives. In the end we wound up with nothing.

"Then came the *REAL* plan. I guess all this planning finally got him thinking about where we were *really* headed. With only six guys in the seminary and our Baby-Boom pastors beginning to retire, all of a sudden it was like, 'Oh, no. We're going to have to downsize.' So, out came the computers and the forecasts and the new round of town hall meetings. You know how that ended. Lots of parishes closed and lots more merged. It seems like overnight, the warm, comfy Church people had known for generations didn't exist anymore. Lots of anger and resentment. Some of it still out there.

"Of course, along with all this, some lifestyles had to change too. All those guys who had gotten used to having the privacy of big rectories all to themselves were now being asked to consider sharing quarters with someone else.

"I know. That went over like a led balloon," offered Bishop Paul.

"Don't get me wrong. Painful as it was, it revealed just how sick some of our guys had become. Of course, we've still got some sick men out there. Have you ever been inside the rectory at St. Thomas Aquinas?"

The bishop slowly shook his head.

"Father Ken is downright weird. I think he has every newspaper since the 80s stacked up in there. All he needs is some cats and he'd be certifiable. How do you expect him to transform St. Thomas into an evangelistic powerhouse? It's only by the grace of God that he can find his way to the sacristy in the morning. Yeah, I know he's known for logging more hours in the confessional than anyone else, but truth be known, I think he's hiding in there."

"Okay, Larry, I get it. We've got some sick men out there. A few people are still angry about the reorganization. Our priests are suspicious about diocesan initiatives that sound good, but never produce anything... See, I've been taking notes... So, what do you think we should do about it?"

"Oh, now it's *we*. I don't know. 'You the man.' They pay *you* the big bucks to figure this stuff out. I'm just the messenger."

A smile and a chuckle. Then, "Really. Father Larry, I need your help."

"I don't know, Bishop. I really don't. I just sense it may be time for a fresh start. Enough stuff has accumulated over the years, it's almost like we need to reboot the system. For starters, why don't you let them know you're going to spend this next year doing nothing but just getting to know them better. I don't mean bishop-to-presbyterate, but man-to-man, one-on-one, father-to-son, brother-to-brother. Get to know their first names."

"Nice idea, Larry, but where do you think I'm going to get all this time for making house calls?"

"Okay, candidly, here's one idea: Stay home! I know everybody out there wants a piece of you, but are all these conference speaking engagements really necessary? This is your flock right here."

"Ouch!"

"I'm sorry, Bishop, but somebody's got to tell you. Hear their heartaches and disappointments and aspirations. Pray with them. No, let them pray with you. Ask their forgiveness for your absences and let them know how much you need them and appreciate the long, hidden hours they put in. Be a father and feed them. *Then*, and only if they're ready, share with them *your* heart. I know you did that at the convocation and it was powerful. But, imagine how much more powerful it could be over a cup of coffee one-on-one. You have that fire in you, Bishop. You have the passion and I really think they want to follow you. They've just known so much small thinking their whole lives, they really can't imagine anything different.

141

"One more thing... Use me. You don't have to go to every blasted committee meeting. I don't especially like them, but that's what I'm here for; to cover for you. So, let me. You've got a pretty big dream and you're going to have to get used to working on it or nothing's going to happen. Only, more disappointment."

This time, a long pause...

Starting slowly, "Father, you know me pretty well. Deep down, I'm an introvert. I do better in front of a crowd than doing what we're doing right now. I hate being vulnerable. Everyone expects a bishop to be strong and the truth is I'm not. I don't know if I can do it, but I know you're right. I can see the truth in your observations and the wisdom in your counsel.

Short hesitation.

"Will you pray for me?"

"Sure, Bishop, I'd be happy to."

"No, I mean right now. Right here."

"Oh... okay... Why don't you kneel down and ask our Lord for his mercy and strength?"

The big man got out of his chair and went right down in front of his friend.

Father in Heaven... I marvel at the confidence you place in us. I marvel at how you use us broken vessels to carry the most precious of treasures to one another... You yourself. Father, hear the heart of my friend and your son, Bishop Paul. He is now feeling the weight of responsibility. He needs your strength. You promised that your burden would be light and your yoke easy. Help him carry the burden, Lord, and yoke yourself to him so that you may move forward together in leadership and service to your people.

Lord, heal his spiritual blindness so that he can see clearly how to lead and how to serve. Deliver him from the deceptions of the enemy who seeks to destroy the dream you have given him; the vision of salvation and mature holiness for the flock you have placed in his care.

May this be a new beginning, a fresh start not only for him but for all the people, a Year of Jubilee in which all is forgiven and all things become possible once again. We ask these things through your Son, our Lord Jesus Christ who lives and reigns with you in the unity of the Holy Spirit, God forever and ever.

Shaky voice: "Father, may I have your blessing?"

"Dear Friend, may the blessing of almighty God – Father, Son, and Holy Spirit – descend on you and remain with you forever."

"Thank you, Father."

"Thank *you*, Bishop."

IX. Attitudes about Evangelization

Weakness of attitude becomes
weakness of character

Albert Einstein

There are many in the Church who are puzzled that evangelization is getting any attention at all. At the risk of oversimplification, I believe that a great deal of this puzzlement can be attributed to two widespread and opposite misconceptions, to wit...

"We just don't do that"

The first misconception is that the ministry of evangelization is totally unnecessary. In fact, it may even be an illegitimate, ill-advised undertaking; it is something that we Catholics just don't do. It's not unusual to hear comments like the following: "Why do we need to evangelize? That's something Fundamentalists and Evangelicals do, but not us. What's the point, really? There are lots of roads to heaven." While things are changing now, I would venture to say this statement summarized the majority attitude of Catholics in the United States until quite recently – and still does for many. Sociological research demonstrates just how widespread this notion has been. As recently as 2005, it was reported that only six percent of Catholic parishes in the U.S. valued spreading the faith as a high priority and only three percent sponsored local evangelistic activities.[43] In the rare case that a parish has an active evangelistic outreach, it is not uncommon for "*that* parish" to be dismissed by its neighboring parishes as an aberration. This is one reason why it is so critical for the diocesan bishop who serves as the main teacher of the Catholic Faith in his diocese to legitimize the ministry of evangelization by his personal leadership.

Here's another common statement that I believe expresses the same underlying sentiment: "I can't believe God would condemn anyone to Hell. God is so good, I don't have to worry if I am on the right path or not. Actually, I'm not sure there *is* a 'right path'. God just wants us to be happy, so why would God ever condemn anyone to Hell? I don't know… Maybe Genghis Khan and Hitler."

The Sin of Presumption In a nutshell, this is one version of the sin of presumption (cf. *Catechism of the Catholic Church,* 2092). I would venture to say that this form of presumption is the soteriological view of a vast swath of Americans, including many professed Christians. Here's the problem: Jesus left us with a strong impression that there *may be many* people in Hell. *Lord, will only a few be saved?* Without directly answering this question, Jesus responded: *Strive to enter through the narrow gate, for many I tell you will attempt to enter but will not be strong enough* (cf. Lk 13:23-24). While God is all merciful, we have it on the word of Christ himself that there is a hell and we can willfully *put ourselves there*, despite his desires otherwise.

Moreover, presumption slips effortlessly into the sin of *ingratitude* and even *indifference* toward our Lord. If God loves us, surely he wants us to love him. The *Catechism* puts it this way:

> Faith in God's love encompasses the call and the obligation to respond with sincere love to divine charity. The first commandment enjoins us to love God above everything and all creatures for him and because of him.[44]

So, the question is: Do we love God or are we indifferent toward him? We now live in an era when only a few approach the Sacrament of Reconciliation. For many who still consider themselves to be "good Catholics", their last confession was literally decades ago. According to the reasoning of presumption, "I don't need to go to confession. God loves me." Never is a thought given to the fact that staying away from such a poignant sacrament doesn't show much love in return. Or, you will hear: "Why do I need a priest? God can forgive me himself." True enough, God can and he does. But, for his own reasons, he set up a sacramental means through which forgiveness was to be mediated by duly deputized human beings (cf. John 20:22-23). It is very doubtful that Jesus would have granted authority to his apostle to forgive or retain sins, if he didn't intend for them to exercise that authority and for us to make use of it. The avoidance of confession is one of many ways the sin of presumption is played out.

In the final analysis, it all comes down to whether or not we recognize that faith in God is more than a cerebral assent to the truth that God exists. Faith in God entails at least the beginning of a *personal love relationship*. In a love relationship, *both* people – not just one – give themselves to one another. Unrequited love – good as it may be – is not a love *relationship*. God can and does love me, but if I don't love him back, a love relationship does not exist. If I don't make a serious effort to love God while I am living here on this earth, can I seriously expect to love him when I die? Or, will it even occur to me to think of him? If I have lived my life *without* him, why should I expect to die *with* him?

One might counter that the "good thief" crucified alongside Jesus, proves otherwise. But the reality is that St. Dismas *recognized* his sins and asked for Jesus' mercy. In the vernacular, he knew he had been a jerk and he regretted it. At a minimum, that is the beginning of a love relationship. He knew he didn't deserve God's mercy. Presumption is often characterized by nonchalance, and apathy toward the whole subject of God and eternity. Clearly, Dismas was not apathetic.

The ultimate problem with *presumption* is that the individual may never get to the point of caring about God at all. The Book of Sirach warns:

> Say not: "I have sinned, yet what has befallen me?" for the Lord bides his time. Of forgiveness be not overconfident, adding sin upon sin. Say not: "Great is his mercy; my many sins he will forgive." For mercy and anger alike are with him; upon the wicked alights his wrath. Delay not your conversion to the Lord, put it not off from day to day. For suddenly his wrath flames forth; at the time of vengeance, you will be destroyed. (Sirach 5:4-9)

The presumptuous "Christian" reasons that God's love is so unconditional, how he or she responds to that love is of no great import. God is simply "above all that". So, I can live my life without any real reference to God. God is treated as a factoid; no more relevant to my life than the fact that Timbuktu is a city in the nation of Mali.

This attitude is further encouraged in our times by the widespread *non*-Christian view that God is an *It*. In other words, God is not a Person at all. Western culture in recent years has been subtly but significantly influenced by Eastern religious philosophies, most notably of the Hindu variety. In these lines of thinking, when we die, we are reincarnated until such time as our lives reach karmic perfection. When that happens, we lose our individuality and are absorbed into Brahma, an ethereal, impersonal cosmic force. According to the *2014 Religious Landscape Study* conducted by the Pew Research Center, amazingly enough only 61 percent of Catholic adults in the United States believe in a personal God and fully 31percent characterize God as an "impersonal force".[45] Whether they realize it or not, Christian theology recognizes the one God as a Loving Family of three divine *Persons*.

VIII. Interlude: Rebooting

As I look back at theology courses I took in college, a common refrain of (Catholic) professors was that one needed to exercise great care against the "tendency" to anthropomorphize or attribute human characteristics to God. This was even a theme that I heard occasionally during my studies to become a Catholic deacon. The human attributes in question during those classes were *self-awareness* and *feelings*. Could God experience love, or excitement, or even anger? The academic admonition would go something like this: "Be careful not to make over God in our image." Fair enough, God is far above petty human feelings. But, the opposite side of the metaphorical coin is the tacit rejection of God's self-revelation throughout sacred Scripture; revelation in which God's "feelings" are on full display (cf. Lk 5:11-32, Lk 19:41-42, Jn 2:13-17, Jn 11:33-36).

Again, looking back, I cannot remember any professor ever mentioning that *we were made in God's image* (cf. Gen 1:27). Where did we receive our capacity for selfless giving, even to the point of dying for the beloved? Where does our capacity for creativity come from? Why can every human being recognize and experience beauty? How is it we all understand what it feels like to be offended by another human being?

The point is this: there can be no such thing as a personal – let alone, *love* – relationship with a *non*-personal god. If the divine *Thing* is some totally foreign and transcendent being that is completely disconnected from us, then there is no way we can offend It. Accordingly, It cannot extend mercy and there is no need for salvation. Interaction with a divine *Thing* versus a divine *Person* entails far fewer demands.

In Eastern religions, the adherent is perfectly free to pick and choose a self-styled religion of one's own making. In Japan it is very common for people to adhere to both Buddhism and Shintoism at the same time; religions with different conceptions of God. Increasingly, here in America, a sincere search for the Truth often gets discombobulated in the same way. Many Millennials (and those younger), in particular, tend toward extreme individualism, "self-creation", and post-modern subjectivism. They often feel the need to establish their own very eclectic identity; sort of, a personalized signature writ large that conforms to no one else's expectation.

In any event, many people today wind up with a disembodied form of spirituality that is disconnected from objective truth claims and asks very little of us. Pope Francis warned about this cultural phenomenon when he wrote:

> [A] new form of Gnosticism puts forward a model of salvation that is merely interior, closed off in its own subjectivism. In this model, salvation consists in elevating oneself with the intellect beyond "the flesh of Jesus towards the mysteries of the unknown divinity."[46]

In the Final Judgment described in Matthew's Gospel, the separation of the sheep from the goats is based on our response of love *toward Him*. The glorious Christ makes the disturbing accusation, "When *I* was hungry, you did not feed me…", to which the guilty reply, "We did not see *You* hungry or thirsty or naked or in prison." In the disturbing disguise of needy people, we encounter God himself (cf. Mt 25:31-46). Christian faith is inextricably intertwined with his desire for a response of love from us. When I make an assent of faith in God, I necessarily open myself to receive his love, which overflows onto many other people, even the least attractive. Conversely, my love for them overflows to Jesus. They are inseparable and demanding, leaving no room for presumption and its inevitable result: indifference.

* * *

Interlude: Parable of the Young Couple Evangelization in the modern world needs to prioritize God's desire for a *love relationship* while recognizing the human tendency toward presumption and ultimate indifference. The following parable is offered to help make the point...

They were a beautiful young couple "in love". Jessie and Troy were crazy about each other. At first, they were inseparable. You'd see them together at the grocery store or even pulling weeds together in the front yard.

Truth be told, it was really *her* yard. Jessie was the industrious one. Even before they met, Jessie worked hard, saved her pennies, and scraped together enough for a down payment on a cute little Cape Cod. She was "only" a secretary, but she was so reliable, resourceful, and thoughtful that her boss gave her a big bonus at Christmas every year, which is how she could afford the house. She poured herself into that little place. She sanded and stained the old hard wood floors, stripped the old wall paper, painted every room, furnished the place with cool antiques, and landscaped the yard all herself. She used to say, "Someday, I'll have someone to share this with."

Well, Troy was the lucky guy! A lot of people speculated that Troy was initially attracted to her because she had done all that stuff. You know what they say: "Opposites attract." I think there may be something to it. Jessie is definitely attractive, but she's more of a classical beauty, if you know what I mean. That's why the two of them becoming a couple sort of caught me by surprise. Troy usually went for sheer sex appeal.

Anyway, the wedding itself was a blow-out; a party for the record books. Don't remember much about the service, except that Jessie cried when she said her vows. But that party – even though it went on all night, Jessie looked radiant the whole time. Troy was doing okay too for the first couple hours, but then he got sloshed. I doubt that he can remember much.

I think at first, Troy kind of liked the idea of playing house. Just being married seemed cool. As I said, they shared all the chores and stuff like that. But the honeymoon didn't last long. At first, Troy would just stop by the tavern after work for a beer with "the boys". No big deal, really. Jessie was a little hurt that he didn't want to rush home to spend every last minute with her. But she understood that he needed friends and she was determined not to be a nag, so she let it go.

Of course, it didn't stop there. That after-work beer turned into two or three. When Jessie finally said something, she got a big surprise by his answer. *"Look"*, he said, *"you promised to love me no matter what. So, love me. I don't have to be your little slave."* I mean, what do you say to that? All she could think to say was, "I guess I'll just plan on dinner a little later, so the food's not cold next time."

Too bad it didn't stop there, but things just kept getting worse. That's about when Troy lost his job on account of always coming in late and calling in sick. Jessie just doubled-down and got a second job three nights a week at CVS. This was like giving Troy permission to turn into a first-class jerk. The second night on the job at CVS, Jess got home around 11:15 only to find an empty house. The lights and TV were still on and the dishes were stacked in the sink. But, no Troy. I remember that night, because Jessie called me in tears. "Where could he be?" She still hadn't caught on that he was playing her.

It went from bad to worse. As I said, Jessie was a "homemaker" through and through. She loved Troy so much she'd do practically anything for him. The Monday after they got married, she actually agreed to put his name on both of her bank accounts – checking and savings. She wanted to share *everything* in their lives.... including their finances. Sounds good on paper, but you can guess what

152

happened. One night she came home wondering who was visiting, since there was this brand-new Harley-Davidson Heritage Classic parked in the breezeway. It took about ten seconds to realize that was *Troy's* brand-new Harley-Davidson Heritage Classic. You can imagine the conversation that took place next. Believe it or not, Troy actually said to her, "Hey, you said a long time ago, 'What's mine is yours.' So, suck it up, girl. We're gonna have some great rides on this dude."

Well, the *"we"* part sorta got forgotten in a hurry. It didn't take long for Jessie's life to get real lonely. Now that he had a set of fast wheels, Troy spent every minute riding them. Coming home to an empty house became the "new normal" for Jess. One night, she came home tired, just wanting to be with him. I can't understand why, since he was such a !@#$. Well, miracles never cease, 'cause there he was lying on the sofa, beer in hand, watching something really raw on the tube. She couldn't stand to watch that garbage with him, so she started to clean up around him. Imagine her surprise when she swept under the couch and came out a piece of apparel she wouldn't wear on a dare.

There he was, caught red-handed. You know, any reasonable person would at least start to make excuses. Troy just sat there and asked her to get him another beer...

* * *

A Nonchalant Catholicism In this little vignette, Troy came to take Jessie's love for granted. She loved him so much, he came to a point where loving her back really wasn't very important. He committed the sin of presumption against her. We do the same thing with God as well. So, what happened? How did we come to this place where the sin of presumption is so dominant in what should be our love relationship with God?

PART II: THE CHALLENGES

At the risk of oversimplification, I believe the current state of affairs is at least in part the result of a distortion of German theologian Karl Rahner's concept of "Anonymous Christianity".[47] It was not that Father Rahner denied a Christological understanding of salvation; he was clear that it is only through Christ than anyone can come to salvation. Notwithstanding, he had difficulty accepting the notion that a good man who, through no fault of his own, did not profess belief in Christ would spend eternity in Hell. While "Baptism of Desire" had been a long-standing teaching of the Church, the person who had never even heard the name of Jesus, but followed the dictates of her conscience in good faith remained something of an enigma. Moreover, Rahner went beyond this specific case and allowed that there are numerous cultural circumstances in which the freedom of a non-Christian to accept the Faith and receive baptism is effectively curtailed leaving them in a state of "inculpable ignorance". Rahner contended that such people had access to grace and could be saved. Accordingly, there could be many "Christians" who literally do not know they are Christian. Whence, came the term "Anonymous Christianity".

In 1964, the Second Vatican Council adopted this reasoning (if not the expression) and promulgated it in the *Dogmatic Constitution on the Church (Lumen gentium)*. The following excerpt from paragraph 16 articulates this truth:

> Nor is God remote from those who in shadows and images seek the unknown God, since he gives to all men life and breath and all things (cf. Act 17:25-28), and since the Savior wills all men to be saved (cf. 1 Tim. 2:4). Those who, through no fault of their own, do not know the Gospel of Christ or his Church, but who nevertheless seek God with a sincere heart, and, moved by grace, try in their actions to do his will as they know it through the dictates of their conscience – those too may achieve eternal salvation.[48]

In his outstanding books, *Will Many Be Saved?* and *The Urgency of the New Evangelization,* Ralph Martin makes the point that this legitimate teaching of the Church *has become distorted* in the minds of many people. In brief, Dr. Martin observes that *the possibility* of salvation for non-believers has morphed into the *near certainty.* The phrase "through no fault of their own" has been broadened to embrace almost any form of personal irresponsibility. But Dr. Martin's greatest accomplishment is his painstaking, scholarly demonstration that this point of view is totally contrary to 2,000 years of Catholic teaching.

He makes the point that – while the previous excerpt from *Lumen Gentium* is frequently quoted, very few mention the remainder of paragraph 16, which reads in part:

> But very often, deceived by the Evil One, men have become vain in their reasonings, have exchanged the truth of God for a lie and served the world rather than the Creator (cf. Romans 1:21 and 25). Or else, living and dying in this world without God, they are exposed to ultimate despair. Hence to procure the glory of God and the salvation of all these, the Church, mindful of the Lord's command, 'preach the Gospel to every creature' (Mk 16:16) takes zealous care to foster the missions.[49]

In short, the problem is not with Anonymous Christianity properly understood, nor the teachings of the Second Vatican Council. Rather, the problem is that the teaching has been distorted into the *presumption* that virtually all are saved. This presumption of *universalism* has effectively eviscerated the missionary impulse to proclaim the truth of Christ to the world and has seriously limited the ability of the New Evangelization to excite the average faithful Catholic. After all, if nearly everyone is heaven-bound, what difference does evangelization make?

It all comes back to loving God in return; to entering into a love relationship that lasts beyond the feel-good phase and grows into a deep, reliable love that weathers all life can throw at us.

Emerging Signs of Hope As society has become increasingly secularized and social mores increasingly relativized, there is at least some evidence to suggest that rank-and-file Catholics are changing their opinion about the importance of evangelization. In a 2013 survey of registered parishioners in the Diocese of Evansville, Indiana, fully 84 percent responded that in comparison to other needs in the Catholic Church in the U.S., reaching out to inactive Catholics was either "important" or "very important." Similarly, 71 percent maintained that it is either "important" or "very important" that the Church should "reach out to those with no church affiliation". Admittedly, this represents the opinions of only one Midwest diocese. Even so, these numbers are a far cry from the 6 percent in 2005 who felt that spreading the Faith was a high priority.

When asked how well the Catholic Church in the Evansville Diocese actually does in reaching out to inactive Catholics, only 16 percent expressed the opinion that we are doing "well" or "very well". Only 10 percent felt that we are reaching out "well" or "very well" to 'nones'.

2013 Survey of Catholic Parishioners: Importance and Fruitfulness of Evangelization

Percent responding...	Question:	...Inactive Catholics?	... 'Nones' (Unaffiliated)?
"Important" or "Very Important"	How important is outreach to...	84	71
"Well" or "Very Well"	How well are we doing reaching out to...	16	10

High importance – low fruitfulness summarizes the views of many ordinary Catholics in southwestern Indiana. Based on these numbers it seems very likely that quite a few of us who are engaged in "professional" parish ministry would be "voted off the island" if the people in the pews could vote.[50] But, the fact that they realize there are problems is a small sign of hope for the future.

Other significant signs of hope include the growth of new ecclesial movements and ministries in the Church. Within a matter of a few years, the Fellowship of Catholic University Students (FOCUS) has grown from nothing to a major powerful missionary force on major secular campuses around the country and now abroad. FOCUS trains and places committed recent college graduates on campuses who befriend other students and lead them into explicit relationships with Jesus. I recently had the pleasure of attending SEEK2019, a recent national conference of FOCUS held at the Indiana Convention Center in Indianapolis. Incredibly, there were some 17,000 college-aged young people in attendance. Virtually all of them were on-fire for their Lord. There was hardly a time day or night when there were not a thousand young people in front of Jesus in the Conference's perpetual adoration chapel. The beautiful daily liturgies – concelebrated by upwards of five hundred priests – routinely took two hours due to the thousands of young communicants.

Other movements are taking the Gospel wherever they can find people to talk to. St. Paul Street Evangelization (SPSE) trains Catholic evangelizers to witness the Faith wherever there is significant pedestrian traffic: downtown commercial districts, street festivals, college campuses, etc. Armed with sincere smiles and Miraculous Medals, they are getting the Catholic story out to people. Their work is accompanied by remarkable testimonies of conversions, reversions, and even physical healings taking place right on the spot.

PART II: THE CHALLENGES

In July 2017, the USCCB sponsored the first-ever Convocation of Catholic Leaders, a major national gathering of ordained, lay, and religious leaders in Orlando, Florida. Led by over a hundred bishops in attendance and accompanied by key diocesan leaders, major speakers and panelists focused on the New Evangelization.

The Amazing Parish organization headquartered in Denver, Colorado is bringing together large conferences for pastors and parish lay leaders for visioning, training, and strategic planning. Like SEEK2019 and the Convocation of Catholic Leaders, Amazing Parish conferences are centered around the Holy Sacrifice of the Mass, Confessions, and praise and worship. These conferences include the practical advice of the pastors from two of the fastest-growing parishes in the western hemisphere – Father James Mallon (formerly) of St. Benedict in Halifax, Nova Scotia and Father Michael White of Nativity Church in Timonium, Maryland. They also incorporate roundtable sessions for pastors and their pastoral teams to evaluate their own organizational health and to plan for parish evangelization.

For decades now, wherever there is zeal for Jesus, you can usually find ecclesial movements such as Communion and Liberation, *Opus Dei*, *Cursillo*, *Focolare*, and/or the Charismatic Renewal. These movements are all loci for serious Catholic communities through which many a secular humanist has found welcoming friendships that brought about deep personal conversions. But despite these wonderful reasons for hope. evangelization is still not *mainstreamed* as a part of the culture in ordinary parish life. This is the direction we must now move to become all that our Lord wants us to be.

To all those who would assert that evangelization is just not "Catholic", it takes a great deal of culpable ignorance to hide from the movements just described and even more intellectual contortionism to explain away the last recorded words of Jesus: *All power in heaven and on earth has been given to me. Go, therefore and make disciples of all nations, baptizing them in the name of the Father, and of the Son, and of the Holy Spirit, teaching them to observe all that I have commanded you* (Mt 28:18b-20a). These words have echoed down through the ages and served as the motivation for thousands of martyrs, right up to our own times. *All* ministry derives its initial impetus from the will of Jesus and the Spirit-empowered impulse of the apostles to share the news of their crucified, yet risen Lord with all peoples.

"It's the work of the Church. We're doing it all the time"

At the beginning of this chapter, I suggested that there are two widespread misconceptions about evangelization in the Church today. The first misconception posits that evangelization is unnecessary, because God is largely indifferent to us.

The second misconception regarding evangelization is virtually the exact opposite of the first, to wit: *everything* the Church does is evangelization. Therefore, it is asserted that if we just do everything well, there is no need to speak of an apostolate of evangelization, *per se*.

In a perfect Church, that might be true. If everything we did were carried out with an eye to the evangelical possibilities they presented, we might not need apostolates of evangelization. Unfortunately, we are not a perfect Church. It is for this very same reason that we need explicit ministries of charity and justice. If everything we did was carried out with an eye to the charitable and just possibilities they presented, one might just as well say that everything we do is charity and justice and we, therefore, do not *per se* need them either.

Getting back to the notion that we are evangelizing in everything we do, the argument asserts that people will be so drawn to Jesus and the Church just by the way we live our lives that we never really have to *talk* about Him.

PART II: THE CHALLENGES

When Pope St. Paul VI penned the words In *Evangelii nuntiandi* "… the Church exists in order to evangelize", he was *not* referring to evangelization as a kind of shorthand for "everything the Church does". His specific intention was to rekindle a burning zeal for unambiguously proclaiming the Gospel in the modern world. Pope St. John Paul II put it this way: "We must revive in ourselves the burning conviction of Paul the apostle, who cried out: *Woe to me if I do not preach the Gospel* (1 Cor 9:16).[51]

The *kērygma* attests that *the incarnate Word of God – Jesus of Nazareth – achieved the possibility of eternal salvation for each of us by his sacrificial death for our sins and he proved it by his subsequent resurrection from death.* Throughout the history of Christendom, the *direct purpose* of unambiguously proclaiming the *kērygma* has been to evoke a *response of personal faith in Jesus* and *conversion of life* born out of gratitude (not to mention a deepening of conversion on the part of the evangelizer). This is not a need that has disappeared in contemporary times. At the beginning of Chapter Three of *Evangelii Gaudium*, Pope Francis quotes and comments on Pope St. John Paul II, as follows:

> "… I would now like to speak of the tasks which bear upon us in every age and place, for 'there can be no true evangelization without the explicit proclamation of Jesus as Lord,' and without 'the primacy of the proclamation of Jesus Christ in all evangelizing work.' Acknowledging the concerns of the Asian bishops, John Paul II told them that if the Church 'is to fulfill its providential destiny, evangelization as the joyful, patient, and progressive preaching of the saving death and resurrection of Jesus Christ must be your absolute priority.' These words hold true for all of us."[52]

Clearly, this *kērygmatic* proclamation is *not* everything the Church does. In fact, it is rarely done at all in the western world today, unless it is vaguely mediated through some other work of the Church, such as pastoral, charitable, justice, and catechetical ministries. In their origins, all of these necessary ministries came about as the result of disciples who had heard the *kērygma* and believed. Without that initial belief, nothing else would have happened. The primary purpose of pastoral, charitable, and justice ministries is to serve human needs, not to evoke initial belief. This service of human needs is an essential part of the mission of believers, but it has come about because people believed in Jesus in the first place. If personal conversion comes about as the result of these ministries – as sometimes happens – it is a happy *byproduct* of the ministry, but not its primary intention.

Similarly, the primary purpose of catechesis is to promote growth in knowledge and understanding of the teachings of Christ and the Church. It may very well deepen one's conversion, but it presupposes that at least some degree of personal conversion and discipleship has already taken place. By contrast, the primary purpose of proclaiming the *kērygma* is to bring about the *starting point* in one's lifelong conversion to Jesus, so that the hearer desires to enter the catechumenate or return to the community of faith and soak up everything she can learn; so that the hearer, in fact, enters the Church where she grows into an even more intimate personal relationship with Jesus in the Eucharist and the sacraments.

That said, even the Eucharist is limited in its efficaciousness to those who have not <u>first</u> believed deeply in the risen Lord. The observation that there are many who have been "sacramentalized, but not evangelized" is a theme that was developed in Pope St. Paul VI's *Evangelii nuntiandi* and was reiterated by Pope Emeritus Benedict XVI when he said: "Many of our brothers and sisters are 'baptized, but insufficiently evangelized.'"[53]

None of this is to suggest that non-evangelistic ministries are somehow illegitimate. However, maintaining that evangelization is merely the sum total of all these ministries and we, therefore, don't need to do anything else is foolishness.

161

One of the dangers of this view is that we can so easily "wriggle off the hook" and never explicitly proclaim that the God of the universe actually became one of us and loved us to the point of dying for us. Unfortunately, at this place and time in the history of the Church, what is *most lacking* is a fruitful proclamation of this truth. We tend to lose our voices as soon as we walk out of the safety of our churches. As Ralph Martin has pointed out:

> This proclamation of the *kerygma*... is precisely the step that Catholics often tend to skip. When the primary focus on the *kerygma* becomes obscured, the risk is that "evangelization" becomes a vague and diffused term that means nothing more than "everything we are already doing," and new evangelization means "more of the same".[54]

Of course, absent the witness of sincere love, simply proclaiming the *kērygma* indiscriminately accomplishes nothing and can even do harm. But the point is: evangelization does not take place in everything a Christian does. I do not fulfill my missionary obligation just by going about my life, even if it is a *good* life. Most of what the Church does is good. But, most of what the Church does is not so holy that it is grabbing the attention of our neighbors and inspiring them to ask why we are so different. Stated bluntly, ordinary living and even many fine ministries are not bringing people into a conscious, loving relationship with Jesus and, all too often, we fail to sustain people in that relationship once it has started.

What is needed most in this world of confusion and disbelief is a Church that places the highest premium on clearly proclaiming the Truth about our God in ways that people can "hear" above all the noise and distractions of everyday life; a Church that facilitates explicit love relationships with our God, and; a Church that helps those love relationships grow in holiness and virtue over time. This is conscious, intentional work. It is neither unnecessary nor redundant. In fact, it is the ultimate "purpose of the Church.

X. Sharing Our Faith Openly... Really?

I have come to set the earth on fire,
and how I wish it were already blazing.

Luke 12:49

The Witness of Sacred Scripture

"Do we really need to share our faith openly? I know I have faith, but it's deeply personal and I have no idea how to talk about it." In *Evangelii gaudium*, Pope Francis flipped this dilemma on its head when he wrote: "What kind of love would *not* feel the need to speak of the beloved, to point him out, to make him known?[55] (italics added) When we're in love, when we're excited about someone, the most natural thing in the world is to talk about her. I believe this is the nub of the issue, whether that love is brand new or seventy years old.

This is the reason why the apostles and first missionaries went to "the ends of the earth" to proclaim the Good News. *They were in love with God.* The unimaginable was true. God Himself loved them and He loved them enough to personally close the gap between his transcendent existence outside of space and time and us mere human beings. St. John put it this way:

What was from the beginning, what we have heard, what we have seen with our own eyes, what we have looked upon and touched with our own hands concerns the Word of life – for the life was made visible; we have seen it and testify to it and proclaim to you the eternal life that was with the Father and made visible to us – what we have seen and heard we proclaim now to you… We are writing this so that our joy may be complete. (1 Jn 1:1-4)

Of course, it didn't end with the eyewitnesses and it was never intended to. That was the whole point of the *evangelion*. Everyone needed to know the unthinkable: that the true God *loves us*. When our Lord appeared to the skeptical Thomas who, having seen with his own eyes and touched with his own hands, professed, *My Lord and my God,* Jesus said to him, *Have you come to believe because you have seen me? Blessed are those who have not seen and believed* (cf. Jn 21:28-29). From his perspective as the risen One, He was referring to *us* who have believed from that time until now. Thus, we have it from his own lips: We are to continue the eternal proclamation of truth both privately to our families (cf. Mk 5:19) and to the whole world (cf. Mt 10:27).

There is *so much* in the way of direct New Testament instruction that it is our Lord's desire for us to evangelize, it is a wonder to me that many Catholics seem to think Jesus only spoke of the need for charity and never made any reference to proclaiming the Truth. In addition to the Great Commission (cf. Mt 28:16-20, Mk 16:14-16), the following sampling of the words of the Master himself should help us answer the question: *Do we really need to share our faith openly?*

> *Therefore do not be afraid of them. Nothing is concealed that will not be revealed, nor secret that will not be known. What I say in the darkness, speak in the light; what you hear whispered, proclaim on the housetops. (Mt 10:26-27)*

> *Everyone who acknowledges me before others I will acknowledge before my heavenly Father. But whoever denies me before others, I will deny before my heavenly Father. (Mt 10:32-33)*

> *Go out into the main roads, therefore, and invite to the feast whomever you find. (Mt 22:9)*

> *"Go home to your family and announce to them all that the Lord in his pity has done for you." (Mk 5:19)*

164

He summoned the Twelve and began to send them out two by two and gave them authority over unclean spirits. So, they went out and preached repentance. (Mk 6:7, 12)

After this the Lord appointed seventy-two others whom he sent ahead of him in pairs to every town and place he intended to visit. He said to them, "The harvest is abundant but the laborers are few; so ask the master of the harvest to send out laborers for the harvest. Go on your way; behold, I am sending you like lambs among wolves." (Lk 10:1-3)

I have come to set the earth on fire, and how I wish it were already blazing. (Lk 12:49)

When Simon Peter saw this, he fell at the knees of Jesus and said: "Depart from me, Lord, for I am a sinful man." For astonishment at the catch of fish they had made seized him and all those with him, and likewise, James and John, the sons of Zebedee, who were partners of Simon. Jesus said to Simon, "Do not be afraid; from now on you will be catching men." When they brought their boats to the shore, they left everything and followed him. (Lk 5:8-11)

When Jesus had said this, he raised his eyes to heaven and said, "Father, the hour has come. Give glory to your Son, so that your Son may glorify you, just as you gave him authority over all people, so that he may give eternal life to all you gave him. Now this is eternal life, that they should know you, the only true God, and the one whom you sent, Jesus Christ. (Jn 17:1-3)

On the evening of the first day of the week, when the doors were locked, where the disciples were, for fear of the Jews, Jesus came and stood in their midst and said to them, "Peace be with you." When he had said this, he showed them his hands and his side. The disciples rejoiced when they saw the Lord. Jesus said to them again, "Peace be with you. As the Father has sent me, so I send you. (Jn 20:19-21)

And they went. And thus began the story of the early Church, as the remainder of the New Testament attests over and over again…

"You will receive power when the Holy Spirit comes upon you, and you will be my witnesses in Jerusalem, throughout Judea and Samaria, and to the ends of the earth." When he had said this, as they were looking on, he was lifted up, and a cloud took him from their sight. (Acts 1:8-9)

PART II: THE CHALLENGES

*Then Peter stood up with the Eleven, raised his voice and proclaimed to
them, "You who are Jews, indeed all of you staying in Jerusalem. Let this
be known to you and listen to my words... You who are Israelites, hear
these words. Jesus of Nazareth was a man commended to you by God
with mighty deeds, wonders, and signs, which God worked through him
in your midst, as you yourselves know. This man, delivered up by the set
plan and foreknowledge of God, you killed, using lawless men to crucify
him. But God raised him up, releasing him from the throes of death,
because it was impossible for him to be held by it... Now when they heard
this, they were cut to the heart, and they asked Peter and the other
apostles, "What are we to do, my brothers?" Peter said to them, "Repent
and be baptized, every one of you, in the name of Jesus Christ for the
forgiveness of your sins; and you will receive the gift of the Holy Spirit.
For the promise is made to you and to your children and to all those far
off, whomever the Lord our God will call." He testified with many other
arguments, and was exhorting them, "Save yourselves from this corrupt
generation." Those who accepted this message were baptized, and about
three thousand persons were added that day. (Acts 2:14, 22-24, 37-41)*

*He commanded us to preach to the people and to testify that he is the one
ordained by God as judge of the living and the dead. All the prophets
testify about him that everyone who believes in him receives forgiveness
of sins through his name. (Acts 10:42-43)*

*But what does it say? "The word is near you, in your mouth and in your
heart" (that is, the word of faith that we preach). For, if you confess with
your mouth that Jesus is Lord and believe in your heart that God raised
him from the dead, you will be saved. For one believes with the heart and
so is justified and one confesses with the mouth and so is saved. For the
scripture says, "Not one who believes in him will be put to shame."
(Rom 10:8-11)*

*For "everyone who calls on the name of the Lord will be saved.' But, how
can they call on him in whom they have not believed? And how can they
believe in him of whom they have not heard? And how can they hear
without someone to preach? And how can people preach unless they are
sent? As it is written, "How beautiful are the feet of him who brings good
news!" (Is 52:7) (Rom 10:13-15)*

*Thus faith comes from what is heard, and what is heard comes from the
word of Christ. (Rom 10:17)*

*If I preach the Gospel, this is no reason for me to boast, for an obligation
has been imposed on me, and woe to me if I do not preach it! If I do so
willingly, I have a recompense, but if unwillingly, then I have been
entrusted with a stewardship. (1 Cor 9:16-17)*

*Although I am free in regard to all, I have made myself a slave to all so as
to win over as many as possible. To the Jews, I became a Jew to win over
Jews; to those under the law, I became like one under the law – though I
am not under the law – to win over those under the law. To those outside
the law, I became like one outside the law. To the weak I became weak, to
win over the weak. I became all things to all, to save at least some. All
this I do for the sake of the Gospel, so that I too may have a share in it.
(1 Cor 9:19-23)*

There are many other such passages, not to mention the parables
and the witness of the first believers not cited above. Yet, I suspect
that most "typical" Catholics would be hard pressed to cite any
biblical evidence that we are called to evangelize; that evangelizing
is a matter of obedience for a Christian just as much as almsgiving
and works of service. Love can be exemplified in many ways, but can
there be a higher form of love than introducing a friend to Love
Himself?

Why is it that so few of us Catholics "get this"? In part, I suspect
it is because we rarely or never hear a homily on the subject. In
making this statement, I indict myself along with most members of
the clergy. We may use the vague language of homiletics to exhort
the faithful to "proclaim the Gospel at all times", but it rarely inspires
and it almost never eventuates in concrete, practical action. It is vital
that ordained "leaders" of the Church correct this problem.

The State of the Church in the United States

Should there be any further reason for making evangelization our
uppermost priority, one need only point to the present condition of
the Catholic Church in the U.S. For those who claim that the Great
Commission is fulfilled by "everything else we are already doing",

we need to ask: where is all the fruit? What do we have to show for it? One would expect far greater fruitfulness than is evident today. At the very least, it would be reasonable to expect the Catholic Church would be holding its own in terms of numbers.

On the surface, it may appear as though we have. For many years, Catholics as a percent of the total U.S. population remained roughly even at between 21 and 25 percent depending on the method of enumeration that is used.[56] However, these aggregate numbers belied a huge attrition from the Church, an attrition that was offset by the disproportionate number of Catholic immigrants to the U.S.

> The ratio of departing Catholics to converts:
>
> *More than six-to-one*
>
> - Pew Research Center
> *America's Changing Religious*
> *Landscape,* May 2015

What's more, the most recent data from the Pew Research Center reveals that the longstanding Catholic share of the American population at about 23 percent has declined over the past decade. In fact, the entirety of Christianity in the United States has declined.

> In the Pew Research Center telephone surveys conducted in 2018 and 2019, 65% of American adults describe themselves as Christians when asked about their religion, down 12 percentage points over the past decade... Currently, 43% of U.S. adults identify with Protestantism, down from 51% in 2009. And one-in-five adults (20%) are Catholic, down from 23% in 2009.[57]

If we scratch the surface, the reality is that massive attrition has been taking place. Roughly 13 percent of all adult Americans are former Catholics.[58] In fact, it is a reality that ex-Catholics far out-number the second largest denomination in the U.S., Southern Baptists.[59] According to the Pew Research Center, "[a]mong U.S. adults, there are now more than six former Catholics (i.e., people who say they were raised Catholic but no longer identify as such) for every convert to Catholicism."[60] Moreover, one cannot help but wonder if the ratio is not even higher considering the fact that at least some Catholic "converts" lapse in the practice of the faith within a short time of being received into the Church.

What's more, most of those who are leaving the Church are not joining another Christian tradition. In fact, they are not joining any religious tradition at all. The ratio of American adults who have joined the ranks of the religiously unaffiliated vs. those who have joined *any* religion is approximately 4:1.[61]

Moreover, time is working against us. In 1965, fifty-five percent of Catholics participated in the Eucharist at least weekly. By 2014, weekly Eucharistic participation had dropped to 23 percent. In the space of two generations, Mass attendance had dropped by more than half. According to an analysis of published data from the Center for Applied Research in the Apostolate (CARA) at Georgetown University, in 2002, twenty-five percent of American Catholics reported attending Mass "rarely or never". By 2008, the "rarely or never" group had increased to 32 percent, a seven percent increase in only six years!

Adding to the bad news, according to annual data from the *Official Catholic Directory* certain other key sacramental participation rates have declined precipitously. Figures 1 through 4 depict historical data and average linear trend lines for the rates of U.S. sacramental marriages, infant baptisms, first communions, and adult conversions to the Catholic Church for the two decades between 1997 and 2016, respectively.[62]

Note that these graphs are normalized *per 1,000 Catholics.* In other words, the downward trends cannot be attributed to a decline in the overall Catholic population. Accordingly, the normalized data trends are important for revealing the whole story.

Figure 1

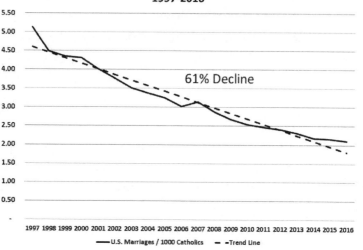

U.S. Sacramental Marriages per 1,000 Catholics: 1997-2016

61% Decline

Figure 2

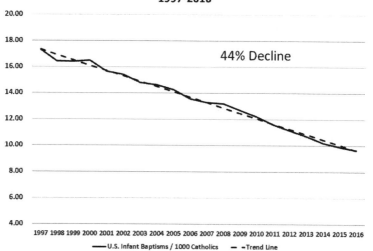

U.S. Infant Baptisms per 1,000 Catholics: 1997-2016

44% Decline

Figure 3

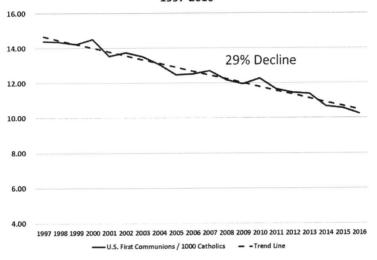

U.S. First Communions per 1,000 Catholics:
1997-2016

29% Decline

U.S. First Communions / 1000 Catholics — Trend Line

Figure 4

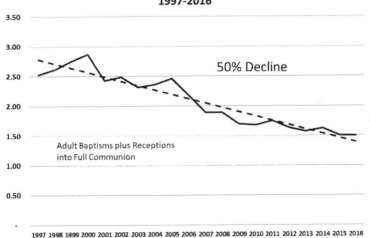

U.S. Adult Conversions per 1,000 Catholics:
1997-2016

50% Decline

Adult Baptisms plus Receptions
into Full Communion

U.S. Adult Conversion / 1000 Catholics — Trend Line

Sacramental marriages-per-1,000 Catholics have been in a virtual freefall, declining a shocking 61 percent in the decade between 1997 and 2016. No doubt related to the fall in marriages, infant baptisms-per-1,000 Catholics have plummeted 44% during the same period. Some have attributed this to a general decline in fertility rates. However, fertility rates actually increased in the period from 1997 to 2008, during which baptism rates steadily declined. [63] While first communions-per-1,000 Catholics have not dropped to the same extent as baptisms, there has still been a significant trend downward of 29% during the two decades from 1997-2016.

The falling trend in adult conversions to Catholicism has also been dramatic, if somewhat more erratic. Defined here as the sum of adult baptisms plus receptions into full communion in the Church, the linear trend line for adult conversions-per-1,000 Catholics between 1997 and 2016 fell by half in just twenty years!

Interestingly, the decline in the national confirmation rate during the same period (not shown here) has been fairly insignificant. Evidently, confirmation is viewed by many Catholic young people and their parents as a rite of passage into adulthood. Unfortunately, while these youth may pass into "adulthood", they pass right out of the Church shortly thereafter. The Dynamic Catholic Institute reports that during the past decade 85% of young Catholics leave the Church within seven years of their confirmation. [64] Notwithstanding this post-confirmation attrition, the fact that the national confirmation rate has not seen the same decline as the other sacraments of initiation suggests that there is an opportunity to evangelize and maturate our youth while we still have their attention. (See Chapter XII for further ideas on this subject.)

In any event, when one considers the full weight of these present-day realities, it is undeniable that something needs to change.

The Call of the Shepherds

At the opening of the Second Vatican Council, Pope St. John XXIII prayed to the Holy Spirit that He pour out a New Pentecost on the Church. Just as the original missionary thrust of the apostolic era began with the first Pentecost, the New Evangelization requires a whole new Pentecostal wave that will change our lives as surely as the first one changed the lives of the apostles. I frequently get the sense that the Holy Spirit has been saying "yes" to

> A compelling case can be made that the single most consistent theme of our recent popes has been the heartfelt plea for a new missionary wave of evangelism that involves the entire Church.

Pope St. John's prayer ever since he prayed it, but we are too frightened to accept the challenges that accompany the powerful gifts that God has already given us.

Twelve years after Pope St. John prayed for a New Pentecost, Pope St. Paul VI's issued the apostolic exhortation *Evangelii nuntiandi* defending the timelessness of the call to the missionary spirit of evangelization. Paul's call reverberated louder and more insistently throughout the pontificates of Pope St. John Paul II, Pope Emeritus Benedict XVI, and now Pope Francis I. In fact, a compelling case can be made that the single most consistent theme of our recent popes has been the heartfelt plea for a new missionary wave of evangelism that involves the entire Church – especially the lay faithful. If we include the documents of Vatican II – particularly *Lumen Gentium* –

the call for a new, widespread wave of evangelization in the Church has been going on now for a half-century.

This plea calls for a radical change in our self-understanding and in the ways we function on a day-to-day basis. If ever there was a papal vision of "normalizing" evangelization throughout the Church, Pope St. John Paul II expressed it:

> Above all, there is a new awareness that missionary activity is a matter for all Christians, for all dioceses and parishes, Church institutions and associations… I sense that the moment has come to commit all the Church's energies to a new evangelization and to the mission *ad gentes*. No believer in Christ, no institution of the Church can avoid this supreme duty: to proclaim Christ to all peoples.[65]

In 2011, when Pope Benedict XVI issued the guidelines for the General Synod on the New Evangelization for the Transmission of the Christian Faith, he stated rather bluntly:

> A new evangelization is synonymous with mission, requiring the capacity to set out anew, go beyond boundaries and broaden horizons. The new evangelization is the opposite of self-sufficiency, a withdrawal into oneself, a status quo mentality and an idea that pastoral programs are simply to proceed as they did in the past. Today, a "business as usual" attitude can no longer be the case.[66]

We cannot truly evangelize the world by limiting ourselves to "everything we are already doing". Even doing these same ministries better is not enough. Pope Francis said it this way:

> I dream of a "missionary option," that is, a missionary impulse capable of transforming everything, so that the Church's customs, ways of doing things, times and schedules, language and structures can be suitably channeled for evangelization of today's world rather than for her self-preservation.[67]

These excerpts from papal messages over the past few decades are but a fraction of all that has been said and written. Notwithstanding these multiple appeals from all our recent popes, an honest assessment of the U.S. Church in the early twenty-first century is that we have failed to respond in a focused way… so far.

* * *

Moving from the Past to the Future

This reticence to launch out into the "deep waters" of evangelization is certainly understandable in light of our history. From the early sixteenth century until the Second Vatican Council, we were taught to eschew anything outside the domain of the Holy Roman Catholic Church. Our fortress mentality basically left the world "out there", while we were safely ensconced inside. Moreover, here in the United States, wave after wave of immigrants in the eighteenth through early twentieth centuries brought about break-neck growth in the Catholic population. This growth strained the capacity of our bishops to keep up with the demand for new churches, schools, and hospitals. Moreover, the American *leitmotif* was anything but welcoming to Catholics. These elements all combined to make evangelization a low priority, at best.

> "I sense that the moment has come to commit all the Church's energies to a new evangelization and to the mission, *ad gentes*. No believer in Christ, no institution of the Church can avoid this supreme duty: to proclaim Christ to all peoples."
>
> ‐ *Pope St. John Paul II*
> *Redemptoris missio*

In any event, our history has left us in a position wherein we are not well prepared for evangelization. Father Raniero Cantalamessa, OFM Cap, the preacher to the papal household, has very gently summed up our situation *vis-à-vis* evangelization this way:

> We are more prepared by our past to be "shepherds" than to be "fishers" of men, that is, we are better prepared to nourish people

who come to the church than to bring new people into the church or to bring back those who have drifted away and live on the margins... There is a need, therefore, for the basic proclamation to be presented to us clearly and succinctly...[68]

In addition to all this, the pejorative caricature that we tend to carry around in our heads of an evangelist as "a street preacher on a soap box" probably also contributes to our disinclination to change.

> "Today, a 'business as usual' attitude can no longer be the case."
>
> - *Pope Benedict XVI*
> *Lineamenta, Synod XIII*

In reality, the new evangelizer will look very different. The full fruition of the New Evangelization will train and commission a teenage girl to put her Confirmation to work by sharing her excitement about Jesus with her friends on Facebook. It will help a soccer mom witness to her friend how she came to love the Lord, who gave her the strength and peace to forgive her ex-husband. It will train dads to lead their families in prayer. It will work through the lives of college students intelligently and respectfully defending the truths of natural law in a secular environment. It will have a huge presence in social media. It will find its way onto the street and into subsidized housing and onto commercial TV channels with 30-second "spots" and special programming.

> "We are more prepared by our past to be 'shepherds' than to be 'fishers' of men."
>
> - *Raniero Cantalamessa, OFM Cap,*
> *Preacher to the Papal Household*

It will necessitate line items in our budget with hitherto unthought-of amounts dedicated to evangelization. In short, it will require a wholesale change in our Catholic culture.

The *kērygma* will be proclaimed in many ways that will change our self-image as Catholics and change the "business" of the Church. More importantly, it will change the lives of many others, and with these changed lives, eternal destinies will be changed. We will also witness cultural changes in sexual mores, in the stability of marriages, in the health and well-being of children, in the incidence of poverty and drug addiction, and much more… if we only devote ourselves to the task.

XI. Purposeful Parishes

I pray… for those who will believe in me through their word, so that they may all be one, as you, Father, are in me and I in you that they may also be in us, that the world may know that you sent me.

John 17:20-21

On "Becoming a Catholic"

A challenge that Catholics have in evangelizing has to do with the fact that membership in a Catholic parish is not as simple as becoming a member in a Protestant congregation. To become a Catholic involves something of an identity change. You are joining a world-wide expression of the Christian faith, which has its own look and feel that is somewhat distinctive. As arrogant as it may sound to post-modern ears, the Church of God "fully subsists" in the Catholic Church (cf. *Lumen Gentium*, 8). Please understand that I say this in all humility. Whatever gifts God has given us we must receive with full acknowledgement that we "hold a treasure in clay vessels" (cf. 2 Cor 4:7). Simply being the recipient of the "fullness of the faith" does not *ipso facto* make us good Christians.

In any event, while *all* Christian communities strive to help new members grow in holiness, becoming a fully-engaged and mature Catholic embodies the expression: "God loves us just the way we are, which is enough not to leave us that way." Becoming a Catholic usually entails a long, drawn-out process called the Rite of Christian Initiation of Adults (RCIA) or its equivalent even when you are already a baptized Christian. Moreover, if an annulment is required (which is often the case), not only will attaining full-membership take time, it will also require a good deal of conviction and motivation on the part of the seeker. Even a returning Catholic who typically does not participate in RCIA should by all rights receive the personal care he may never have received in the first place; and, at a minimum, he should be expected to take on or resume a lifestyle of weekly Mass participation and routine confession.

An important reason why the *Proposal* places so much emphasis on *diocese-wide evangelization* has to do with "oneness" within and throughout the universal Catholic Church; it is a constitutive "mark" of our Catholicism. Unfortunately, at the present time, that unity is a long way from perfect. In an ideal world, any seeker should be able to walk into any Catholic parish and find equivalent degrees of commitment to accompanying her into full membership in the universal Church and beyond, to mature discipleship.

As a practical matter, this essential unity (not uniformity) is even more important today than it has been in earlier eras, because our society is so mobile and so diverse. As an evangelizer, the odds are extremely good that the friend to whom you have witnessed may not live anywhere near you. So, while you may agree to spend a year accompanying her through RCIA in what will become her parish across town, eventually you are going to want to return to your home parish. If there aren't people in *her parish* who are as committed as you are to involving her in the parish community and ministry, she may lose her new-found faith in short order. Moreover, if the folks in her future parish are more committed to the peculiarities of the *parish* than they are to Jesus and the *balanced theology of Catholicism* you may be leaving her in the hands of people who are not really up to the task.

If, because of the leadership of the bishop, evangelization becomes the priority in *all* parishes, a mechanism will at least eventually exist to help her truly become a *Catholic*, and not just a member of St. Gertrude's or St. John's or what have you. Of course, there is not a bishop on earth who can snap his fingers and instantly change every parish in his diocese into the ideal Christian community. And even if he could, there are many pastors who dread the thought – often with good reason – of another diocesan "program". From experience, they know that many diocesan initiatives have amounted to a lot of work for little or no long-term benefit. Consequently, implementing the *Proposal* at the diocesan level will necessarily take a long time and a steady hand. It will require a willingness to start small and "work with the willing" for as long as it takes, trusting that given enough time and enough visible fruit, all of the parishes will become willing. As Catholics, that needs to become our explicit, long-range goal. We are simply more than the sum of our parishes.

What Is Your "Particular Church"?

Ask a hundred Catholics what their "particular church" is and I would venture to say that all one hundred would answer with the name of their parish. That's not a bad answer. After all, it is in our parishes that we *experience* the Faith. Our experience of community happens within the parish. We baptize our children there. The Sacrament of the Holy Eucharist is offered there. We experience the forgiveness of our sins there. Memories of parish life are intimately tied up with our early education, the bonds of strong friendships, our weddings, the funerals of our parents. For many, our parishes serve as the center of our social lives. We volunteer there, we have fun there. We get involved in parish liturgical and service ministries. We pour our money into our parishes and get wrapped up in maintenance and financial decisions. Praise God! This is as it should be. In fact, when we evangelize, it is with the hope that the evangelized will come to love our parish (or at least another parish) with the same affection that we have; that they will experience greater love of God and fraternal love in just such a community.

Before going on, it is important to say that I too love parish life. In my years as a deacon, parish life has become increasingly more important to me rather than less important. That said, the parish – however good it may be – is not an entirely correct response to the question: "What is your particular church?"

The *Catechism* answers this question as follows:

> The phrase "particular church," which is the diocese (or eparchy), refers to a community of the Christian faithful in communion of faith and sacraments with their bishop ordained in apostolic succession. These particular Churches "are constituted after the model of the universal Church; it is in these and formed out of them that the one and unique Catholic Church exists (*Lumen Gentium* 23)." (833)

Okay, so what is a "parish"? Quoting the Code of Canon Law, the *Catechism* also gives us an answer for that question:

> A parish is a definite community of the Christian faithful established on a stable basis *within a particular church*; the pastoral care of the parish is entrusted to a pastor as its own shepherd under the authority of the diocesan bishop. (2179, *italics* added)

By now, you're probably asking, "So what? Why is any of this Catholic trivia important for the New Evangelization?" Here is the reason: While it is perfectly true that "[t]he Church of Christ is really present in all legitimately organized local groups of the faithful... in so far as they are united to their pastors..."(832), something is missing in the parish, taken by itself. One more quote from the Code of Canon Law may help to explain:

> A diocese is a portion of the people of God which is entrusted to a bishop for him to shepherd with the cooperation of the presbyterium, so that, adhering to its pastor and gathered by him in

the Holy Spirit through the gospel and the Eucharist, it constitutes a particular church in which the one, holy, catholic, and apostolic Church of Christ is truly present and operative. (CIC, can. 369)

In a special way, when the people of God along with the presbyterate (the priests) are "gathered by the bishop", a particular church is formed and it is in that particular church that the "four marks" of the Church (i.e., one, holy, catholic, and apostolic) are "truly present and operative." We have to a large degree lost sight of this teaching.

Catholicism that Ends in the Parish

What happens in most U.S. dioceses is that the people of God are rarely gathered by the bishop in any meaningful way. As a result, the individual parishes are left to determine their own identity and, to a large extent, their own destiny. Provided the sacraments are being administered in general accordance with established liturgical norms and the parish remains solvent, the expectation is that each parish independently decides what is important for how they are going to "be church".

This practical independence, or what might be called "congregational Catholicism", is among the more-subtle challenges to wide-scale evangelization. By "congregational Catholicism", I mean a Catholic identity that *emphasizes* membership in a specific parish over the Catholic Church or, in the worst of cases, even Christianity. In discussing the diocesan clergy, the Second Vatican Council taught:

In exercising the care of souls parish priests and their assistants should carry out their work of teaching, sanctifying, and governing in such a way that the faithful and the parish communities may feel that they are truly members both of the diocese and of the universal Church. They should therefore collaborate both with other parish priests and with those priests who are exercising a pastoral function in the district (such as vicars forane and deans) or who are engaged in works of an extra-parochial nature, so that the pastoral work of the diocese may be rendered more effective by a spirit of unity. Furthermore, the care of souls should always be inspired by a missionary spirit, so that it extends with due prudence to all those who live in the parish. And if the parish priest cannot make contact with certain groups of people he should call to his aid others, including laymen, to assist him in matters relating to the apostolate.[69]

This is a delicate subject to broach because we all love our parishes. Moreover, by comparison, we feel successively more distant from such "abstractions" as "deaneries", "dioceses", "provinces", or even Roman Catholicism at the national level. Fortunately, whatever alienation there may be tends to end at national borders and we come back full circle to a close identification with the universal Church. I would venture to say the "pope", the "Vatican", and "Rome" tend to evoke positive associations for most faithful Catholics. It is that intermediate level where personal identification breaks down. Many Catholics don't know the name of their bishop; if they know that much, they wouldn't recognize him walking down the street. Deans and vicars, mean virtually nothing at all.

Please do not read harsh judgment in this. Our best efforts to evangelize will require that parish life become stronger and more Christ-centered, not less. In fact, it is necessary. We need our parishes to be vibrant and growing communities that people want to be a part of. However, dangers can crop up when our attention is exclusively on our own parish life. There are also opposite and equally serious dangers associated with unrooted Catholicism that is not tied to a real-life local community. But, because the parish-or-nothing mentality poses a particular danger to widespread evangelization, for the moment let's deal with that problem.

Here are the dangers: First, without a solid identification with the larger Catholic Church (and the larger Mystical Body of Christ *in toto*), some parishes turn into a creature of their own making, emphasizing their own preferences over the core beliefs that make us truly Catholic in the first place. For example, we have the "arch-traditionalists", some of whom come very close to denying the validity of the *Novo Ordo* Mass and the Second Vatican Council. And then there are those who, "with itching ears" take their cues from secularism and pursue whatever is novel (which may be totally heterodox) or they may extract those parts of social justice teachings that align with their politics while ignoring the rest (cf. 2 Tim 4:3).

Second, insofar as we live in a *trans-parish* society, if we become too committed to our own particular ways of doing things, the larger movements of the Holy Spirit may pass us by. Our apparent self-sufficiency can isolate us. For example, widespread evangelization with the diocesan bishop leading the way may get missed altogether.

We need to work on seeing ourselves as belonging to something larger than our own parish. In fact, if we don't, we run the risk of ceasing to be fully Catholic. Regardless of what form it takes, "congregational Catholicism" is not unlike the Reformed Protestant model of Christianity that is entirely self-governing and for which there is no higher authority than the elders or church council. In the worst of cases, to the extent that a parish explains away those passages of Sacred Scripture that they don't like, it can become more "protestant" than our Christian brothers and sisters who take the Bible seriously. Any request (or, heaven forbid, correction) from the bishop is met with the anti-authoritarian, uppity response: "Who does this guy think he is?"

In these instances, the parish becomes my personal property. It is the fruit of *my* years on the finance committee or *my* involvement on the parish council or whatever.

In another version of "congregational Catholicism", the pastor makes *all* the decisions however miniscule and the parish simply becomes the "pastor's project". He is "the gatekeeper" and no one enters without his consent. Father has to "approve" everything down to the last detail. The greatest danger: It becomes all about the pastor and his parish and no longer about our risen Lord. When this happens, we lose sight of our purpose as the Church (with a capital "C") to heal, to serve, to evangelize; any of which takes more than just the pastor. Literally, "parochial" interests, in the pejorative sense of the term, replace the larger interests of God. Wittingly or otherwise, when a pastor assumes the perspective of the parish as his own personal project, he is functioning in direct contravention of canon law, which states:

> [A pastor] is to cooperate with his own bishop and the presbyterium of the diocese, also working so that the faithful have concern for parochial communion, consider themselves members of the diocese and of the universal Church, and participate in and sustain efforts to promote this same communion. (Can 529 §2)

In one parish where I served as a deacon (which I consider to be one of the best in our diocese), there are a total of 41 parish ministries listed in the stewardship brochure. Out of these, 27 (66 percent) are exclusively internal in focus (e.g., liturgical, financial, social, etc.). Nine groups, or 22 percent are service ministries for their own parishioners (e.g., shut-ins, grieving, bereavement meals, etc.). Only 5 (or 12 percent) are outreaches to the rest of the world (e.g., Habitat for Humanity, Haiti Mission, St. Vincent de Paul work, RCIA, etc.). The 88 percent are all good things; most of them important to the good workings of parish life. However, this culture of parish-centered ministry, if not balanced with an outward-oriented sense of mission encourages a kind of isolationism.

XI. Purposeful Parishes

To a great extent, the Church today in the United States is a collection of independent, largely self-serving parishes. This makes for a maintenance-oriented, self-satisfied attitude toward parish life. "Success" is measured in terms of social events that are as good as last year and continuing financial stability. In their excellent book, *Rebuilt: Awakening the Faithful, Reaching the Lost, Making Church Matter*, authors Father Michael White and Tom Corcoran coined the term *"churchworld"*. This is a parish environment where most "church people" – especially, professional church employees – live out their entire lives. Unfortunately, this all-too-typical inward-looking focus is of practically no interest to anyone outside the Church and does nothing to advance the cause of the Gospel of Christ. Moreover, to the rank-and-file Catholic who has little interest in *"churchworld"*, is it any wonder that the Church continues to hemorrhage her members? White and Corcoran's prescription for breaking out of *churchworld:* "… looking beyond the people in the pews to the people who are *not* there.[70]

Churchworld is a reality and it represents a serious cultural obstacle to the Church's efforts to evangelize. Jorgé Cardinal Bergoglio, the former archbishop of Buenos Aries, pointed out this problem to his brother cardinal-electors during the pre-conclave run-up to the last papal election. He spoke no longer than four minutes, but his words were so poignant many have speculated that they are the proximate reason he is now Pope Francis. Thanks to the action of Jaime Cardinal Lucas Ortega of Havana, permission was granted to release his words to the public. Here is what Cardinal Bergoglio – now Pope Francis I – said:

> 1. Evangelizing pre-supposes a desire in the Church to come out of herself. The Church is called to come out of herself and to go to the peripheries, not only geographically, but also the existential peripheries: the mystery of sin, of pain, of injustice, of ignorance and indifference to religion, of intellectual currents, and of all misery.

2. When the Church does not come out of herself to evangelize, she becomes self-referential and then gets sick. (cf. The deformed woman of the Gospel in Luke 13:10-17). The evils that, over time, happen in ecclesial institutions have their root in self-referentiality and a kind of theological narcissism.

3. In Revelation, Jesus says that he is at the door and knocks [Rev. 3:20]. Obviously, the text refers to his knocking from the outside in order to enter but I think about the times in which Jesus knocks from within so that we will let him come out. The self-referential Church keeps Jesus Christ within herself and does not let him out.

4. When the Church is self-referential, inadvertently, she believes she has her own light; she ceases to be the *mysterium lunae* [Latin, "mystery of the moon,"] i.e., reflecting the light of Christ the way the moon reflects the light of the sun] and gives way to that very serious evil, spiritual worldliness (which according to de Lubac, is the worst evil that can befall the Church). It lives to give glory only to one another.

5. Put simply, there are two images of the Church: Church which evangelizes and comes out of herself, the *Dei Verbum religiose audiens et fidente proclamans* [Latin, "Hearing the word of God with reverence and proclaiming it with faith"]; and the worldly Church, living within herself, of herself, for herself. This should shed light on the possible changes and reforms which must be done for the salvation of souls.

6. Thinking of the next pope: He must be a man who, from the contemplation and adoration of Jesus Christ, helps the Church to go out to the existential peripheries, that helps her to be the fruitful mother, who gains life from "the sweet and comforting joy of evangelizing.[71]

Venturing out of the Catholic 'Ghetto'

In order for evangelization to become a widespread dimension of our Catholic identity and culture, it is going to require the focused attention of our bishops and our pastors, both individually and collectively. Evangelization will have to be inculcated at *"all levels"* of Catholic life: the individual, the family, the school, within the parish and among parishes, throughout the diocese, and ideally, throughout the larger Church.

This fact begs the question: How can a bishop or a priest or a lay leader ever "draw new disciples to Christ" if he or she almost never interacts with a non-Christian or even a non-Catholic Christian? It is true that most lay people have opportunities at work to rub shoulders with non-believers. But the irony is that the most *active* Catholics – clerical *and lay* – become so engaged

> We live in Catholic 'ghettos' of our own making

in the Church that their interactions with people *outside* the Church are severely limited. Speaking for myself, as an active deacon, nearly all of our friends and all the people my wife and I routinely deal with are active, believing Catholics. While this is part of the joy of experiencing Christian community, it is this very joy that many of the disaffiliated so badly miss. If we never consciously reach out beyond the active Catholic community, something is terribly wrong.

All-too-often this reticence to mingle with "outsiders" even extends to ministries that are specifically aimed at them. My wife and I recently had the experience of trying to find a weekday Mass in a large U.S. city we were visiting. We found one at noon at an inner-city parish that clearly had a strong outreach to the poor. As we walked from the parking lot into church, we passed through a nicely-designed outdoor pavilion that was set up as a place for street people to gather and get a bite to eat. It wasn't until we were leaving after Mass with the priest's words to "go and announce the Gospel of the Lord" still ringing in our ears that it occurred to me that not a single one of the street people standing around had come in for Mass. I want to avoid jumping to conclusions. Perhaps, someone from the parish had invited them to come in for Mass on many occasions and they were rebuffed so many times that they finally gave up. Maybe it was just an "off day". But there is also the disturbing possibility that the parish had taken to heart the Lord's commandment to feed the poor and had divorced that from his commandment to go into the whole world and proclaim the Good News to the poor. It was a hot day. If for no other reason than to get in out of the heat, I would have thought that a few would wander in. It didn't happen. My suspicion is that they were simply not invited. There was a socioeconomic chasm that separated "them" from "us" and we didn't bridge it. At least that day, the poor did *not* have the Gospel preached to them (cf. Mt 11:5).

The Catholic Church in twenty-first century America is large enough to live within itself from birth to death. Outside of work, we may have very few interactions with secular types ("We don't really share their values") or with those who have left the Church ("Gee, whatever happened to Joe and Carol? We never see them anymore"). If we're not careful, we may even find that we have very few *Christian* friends who are not Catholic. In short, we live in a Catholic ghetto of our own making.

Parishes with a Purpose Bigger than Themselves

Have you ever been caught up in a project or ministry that "charged your batteries" and got you so excited you couldn't wait for the next day to come? One such memory for me occurred back in the late 1980s. Two west-side Protestant ministers and a Catholic priest – all mutual friends – began to sense that the Holy Spirit was calling them to reach out to the entire Christian community in Evansville, Indiana with the aim of conducting a regional evangelical crusade. The priest in that group was a friend of mine and he came over for dinner one evening and shared his excitement about what was being planned. Even though he knew this week-long event was not going to have much of a "Catholic flavor", he went to the bishop and asked for permission to be a part of it. Permission was immediately granted and Father Bill threw himself into it, over-and-above all his other parish duties.

At dinner when Father Bill shared his excitement about this grand event, something stirred in me. Unbeknown to Father Bill, for nearly a year I had been praying with a small group of Christian friends once a week for 2-3 hours at a time that God would unite his people and do something great in our community. I had even had a vision that this "something" would happen in our municipal stadium. So, when Father Bill told us what us afoot; that the stadium had already been rented and an evangelist already booked, I knew that while our little east-side group had been praying, our Lord had been independently working with a small group of west-siders – neither aware of the other – answering our prayers. From that moment, I was "all in". We organized, we made phone calls, we advertised, we prayed, we sang... together. The evangelist's organization was thrilled that the Catholic community was getting involved and they encouraged us to find a Catholic speaker to serve as the guest evangelist one night. By God's grace, we located a great Franciscan who came and proudly proclaimed Jesus to the crowd of thousands.

When the time came, congregations from all over the region, mostly Protestant, but several Catholic parishes as well – were represented with designated "counselors" to pray with individuals who responded to the call to come forward and give their hearts to Christ. In addition to praying one-on-one with the respondents, the counselors had all been trained and equipped with pencils and cards to take down their name and contact information. They were each invited to church the following Sunday and a multi-week Bible study had already been prepared and scheduled in the participating churches to help the respondents take the next step of joining a local Christian community.

Was this crusade perfect? Of course not. No single evangelistic outreach ever was or ever will be. Was it of value? *Absolutely.* I can no longer remember the number of commitments that were made that week, but I believe it was well over a thousand. Did it warm the heart of our Father? Without a doubt. Rarely have I ever felt such a strong sense of purpose in my entire life. I knew that by praying and throwing myself into that crusade, I was participating in something far larger than myself or even my family or my parish. People were coming to know Jesus as I knew him and what could be more wonderful than that?!

* * *

Church is meant to have a purpose bigger than ourselves. The church pastored by Father Michael White – Nativity Parish in Timonium, Maryland – serves as a sort of monument to the fact that it is possible to inculcate such a purpose in Catholic parishes. Nativity has experienced tremendous growth in both holiness and size. For Father White, it all starts, "… by looking beyond the people in the pews to the people who are *not* there." (*italics* in original)[72] Father White and his co-author Tom Corcoran make no bones that this requires a full-blown culture change and that such a change can make a lot of people unhappy. Unfortunately, many people think the purpose of their parish is to serve them; in other words, their concept of the parish's goal is to make *me* happy. In the United States parishes are perceived through the lens of a consumer mentality that equates parish life to a restaurant or hotel. If the pastor does not serve up just what *I* want, I'll complain and if that doesn't work, I'll leave in a huff and find a parish that does.

In describing the transformation of Nativity from a typical Baltimore suburban parish into the vibrant community it is now, the authors write:

We were doing a lot of things; we were just doing the wrong things for the wrong reasons and ignoring the one thing we should have been doing. Our parish had become a consumer exchange, and, as such, it had lost its *"transforming power"* in people's lives. We needed to repent and return to the purpose given us by the Lord. The purpose of Nativity is to reach lost people to help them become disciples, and then to help disciples become *growing* disciples.[73]

In 1995, an evangelical pastor by the name Rick Warren wrote a book entitled *The Purpose Driven Church*. At that time, Rev. Warren was leaving little doubt that he knew his subject matter, since he was in the process of building Saddleback Church in Orange County, California. Saddleback currently averages some 22,000 worshippers per week! (This is the same Rick Warren who seven years later wrote *The Purpose Driven Life*, which has since sold over 32,000,000 copies and been acclaimed by *Publishers Weekly* as the bestselling non-fiction hardback in history.)

In any event, Warren makes several fascinating points in *The Purpose Driven Church* that bear on the subject of purpose in parish life. He rightly claims that every church is driven by something... "It may be unspoken. It may be unknown to many. Most likely it's never been officially voted on." Then, he lists some of these driving forces: tradition, personality, finances, programs, buildings, events, seekers.[74] Without pronouncing judgment on nor endorsing any of these driving forces, he contends that it is important to identify what is driving your own church. He then asserts that through the lens of the New Testament, every church should have five purposes and they should all be balanced in a harmonious blend. These five purposes are:

- Purpose #1: Love the Lord with all your heart
- Purpose #2: Love your neighbor as yourself
- Purpose #3: Go and make disciples
- Purpose #4: Baptizing them

- Purpose #5: Teaching them to obey [75]

It comes as no surprise that Warren would list these five purposes of a church. Taken together, the first two are often called "The Great Commandment" (cf. Mt 22:37-39, Mk 12:29-31). The last three are the three constitutive aspects of "The Great Commission" (cf. Mt 28:19-29). I agree with Warren's list. Taken collectively, they are the two great, irreducible directives the Lord has given us.

Isn't it interesting that these five purposes are all *other-focused?* Yet, despite that fact, they ironically serve the needs of those who observe them. We all have a *basic human need for purpose* in life. We simply have to have something to live for. According to Mayo Clinic, a loss of interest in doing normal activities is one of the symptoms of depression. [76] Without a *raison d'être,* we are lost. If you want parishioners who are positively excited about their parish, give them a purpose that is greater than the annual summer social; a *great purpose,* one that is bigger than ourselves, that gives real meaning and direction to life.

Parishes that do not imbue meaning in the lives of their members are lukewarm, at best. Parishes with a clear sense of direction can be exciting places to be. But, if you want parishioners with enthusiasm that is "off the charts", give them a purpose that is bigger than their parish.

Viktor Frankl, the German psychiatrist who lived through the horrors of Nazi labor camp Kaufering, once wrote:

> For success, like happiness, cannot be pursued; it must ensue, and it only does so as the unintended side-effect of one's personal dedication to a cause greater than oneself or as the by-product of one's surrender to a person other than oneself.[77]

* * *

Let us pray that our leaders are inspired to rouse the sleeping giant called the Catholic Church. The world will never be perfect and the giant will never become completely alert until our Lord finally returns; but, in the meantime, great strides can be made in proclaiming the Gospel if we set our creative minds and hearts on escaping the prisons of our own making and running into the arms of our Savior.

Surely, we can do better.

Part III
On Achieving the Vision

XII. A Regional Strategy for Vision Achievement

Then the Lord answered me and said: Write down the vision clearly upon the tablets, so that one can read it readily. For the vision still has its time, presses onto fulfillment, and it will not disappoint. If it delays, wait for it, it will surely come, it will not be late.

Habakkuk 2:2-3

The definition of insanity is doing the same thing over and over again and expecting a different result.

attributed to
Albert Einstein

Taking Stock

In Part I of this book, a *Proposal* was offered for the Catholic Church in the United States to launch a large-scale, sustained evangelistic initiative; an initiative that would hopefully change the culture of the Church over the long haul. "Resolutions" were put forward for lay people, religious, and the various orders of the ordained. A defense of the *Proposal* was made based on evangelization being *the greatest single unmet need* in the Church today and in the world at large. The case for evangelization as the greatest unmet need was based on the discomfiting reality that proclaiming the Gospel is something ordinary Catholics hardly ever do in the developed world, despite the fact that it is a constitutive dimension of being a Christian. Can we really call ourselves "Christian" if we hardly ever think to do it?

199

PART III: ON ACHIEVING THE VISION

Part II was a series of reflections on a few of the *Challenges* that stand in the way of large-scale Catholic evangelization in the United States. It highlighted the cultural reluctance of Catholics to share our faith in Jesus, the widespread conviction that evangelization really isn't "Catholic", the tendency to insist on teaching *all* the truths of the Christian Faith before proclaiming the *central truths*, the clergy sex abuse crisis and the need for forgiving the leaders who have failed us, and the narcissistic inward-looking orientation of ordinary parish life that gives no attention to the myriads of people who are *not* in the pews.

In this new section of the book, the editorial tone of Parts I and II gives way to more practical matters. Specifically, it discusses two major questions: First, in this chapter, ***what*** might we do to implement long-range, sustained evangelization at a diocesan level? Specifically, the chapter proposes a missionary process for widespread evangelization within the context of a diocese. It is deliberately very practical in tone, attempting to fill the gap between high-sounding exhortations to evangelize and down-to-earth questions about how to go about it on a large scale. When appropriate, it tries to avoid vocabulary that tends to make us think only in "churchy" terms in favor of more earthy terms. For example, the adjective *regional* is usually used in lieu of *diocesan*. Accordingly, the process is referred to as *Regional Strategy for Vision Achievement* or simply *Regional Strategy,* for short.

Following a brief fictional interlude, Chapter XIV focuses on ***how*** to enhance the chances of actually implementing the *Regional Strategy* or another process like it. In the last chapter, the idea of a *National Strategy* is proposed in which questions of both *what* we might do and *how* to go about it are combined.

The scope of these questions is so daunting that it is bound to elicit: *"This is way too ambitious."* Or *"Oh, my goodness, he never* mentioned thus-and-so." Or: "We tried that and it didn't work." So, let me apologize in advance for the omissions, and perhaps, even downright mistakes. The fact is that no one really has a blue print of what a grand missionary process for the conversion of a region might look like, let alone a process for the conversion of a nation. We simply never talk in such ambitious terms. But I believe it is time we do.

What is offered here are only overarching processes with some suggested details added. In the real world and under the promptings of the Holy Spirit, nothing is as clear cut as it appears on the printed page. There may be several other fruitful ways to approach large-scale evangelization. I also apologize for my presumptuous temerity in taking on such an ambitious goal. My only defense is that we *need* to focus on this subject for the sake of a hurting and sinful world. Plus… our Lord asked us to do it. *Go and make disciples of all nations…* This includes our own.

Program, Project, Plan or Process?

Before describing the *Regional Vision Achievement Strategy*, it is important to understand what it is *not*. It is *not* a program. We Catholics are accustomed to "programs". While programs may become components of a regional evangelization process, they are not the process itself.

A program, no matter how fine it may be, is too often viewed as a magic wand. Once you have acquired the wand and waved it around a few times, the expectation is that "it" will automatically produce the desired fruit. Invariably, the result is disappointing, because whatever "it" is, its success (or lack thereof) is dependent far more on the spiritual earnestness of the people involved than on mechanically doing all the "right things". Any truly successful program starts on the knees of saints who are trying to discern what the Holy Spirit wants them to do and are willing to do it when he speaks. You can be sure that the original success of any evangelistic or catechetical program was the result of earnest people imploring God for grace and fruitfulness. When it comes to actual implementation, the merits of the program depend on the sincere thirst of its participants for souls. Fruitfulness is at least eighty percent passion born out of a deep love for God and neighbor and only twenty percent the specifics of the program.

Over the past forty years, I have worked on numerous teams putting on *Cursillo* retreat weekends in the Diocese of Evansville. These are always powerful evangelistic experiences that change people's lives. And yet, when I look around at the guys on the team, rarely are they exceptional men, except in one important way: their love for God and their sheer dependence on him. Each one considers it an honor to be called to help. Each one doubles down and begins fasting and praying for the men (aka, "candidates") who will be "making" the *Cursillo*. Starting six or eight weeks before the weekend, the team meets once a week for four hours at a time to celebrate the Eucharist, to pray, to confess our sins, to study and discuss Scripture, to do the detailed planning, and to share a meal. During this period of formation, the word goes out to the larger community to begin praying and offering acts of sacrifice for the candidates and this prayer/fasting surges during the "weekend" (actually, Thursday evening through Sunday). On the weekend itself, there is a crescendo of prayer and fasting by hundreds of people on behalf of the candidates and for the spiritual protection of the team members.

Is it any wonder that these are powerful events? I am convinced that if we all lost our talk notes and the music leader developed laryngitis, the Holy Spirit would still "show up" and the candidates (not to mention the team) would still go home changed men. In fact, by human standards the talks are rarely oratorical masterpieces. The liturgies are not always moving and the music is at best "a joyful noise offered to the Lord". Put another way, if all the speakers were professional preachers with the gifts of St. John Chrysostom, and every Mass was a liturgical masterpiece, and the song leader was Luciano Pavarotti, without the authentic, passionate concern of the team and without the committed support of the larger community, I doubt that we would see a single changed life. One need only look to numerous larger and better equipped areas of the country where the *Cursillo* movement has effectively died out to prove this point.

The point is this: to the extent that *Cursillo* or any other "program" or even movement is a success, it is first-and-foremost because *disciples* who are deeply and humbly in love with Jesus are begging him to change lives.

Unfortunately, when asked "what is your evangelization strategy?", I have heard more than one bishop reply with the name of a program; sometimes, several programs. We all want easy, pat answers – quick fixes. This faith in programs unwittingly borders on the idolatrous. The "program" becomes the substitute for the Holy Spirit. We don't have to pray. We don't have to struggle and put in the hard work to discern the Lord's promptings. All we need to do is follow the program.

So, I need to say categorically that the *Vision Achievement Strategy* offered in the following pages is *not a program*. It may, in fact, use multiple programs and these programs certainly have their value. But, in the final analysis, they are only tools. None of them by themselves are the solution to widespread neo-paganism and relativism. I would scrap every evangelization "program" in existence if it would ensure that people fall on their knees in the presence of the Blessed Sacrament and implore God for massive conversions, and commit themselves to the task. We need to struggle in prayer. Only then are we ready to think through what makes sense in our particular situations and design the course of action that our Lord reveals to us. And, in doing that, we will make it our own; not someone else's course of action that the Lord revealed to *them*.

* * *

In addition to the tendency to reduce evangelization to a program, there is also a tendency for evangelization to be viewed as a "project", as if the conversion and salvation of souls could be placed alongside replacing the roof of the church, or the summer social, or even the upcoming capital campaign. Evangelization is not one project among many. As Pope St. Paul VI put it, "[evangelizing] is in fact the grace and vocation proper to the Church, her deepest identity. She exists in order to evangelize..." (*Evangelii nuntiandi,* 14). To hear some speak of it, you would think it was the other way around: that we evangelize in order to exist; that it is a means to a very churchy, self-centered end, rather than an end in itself.

The *Strategy* is not conceived of as a project, one among several possible courses of action competing for limited resources. It would be better by far to refer to it as THE PROJECT. It is the essential purpose of the Church lived out within a locale. It is our very *raison d'être*.

* * *

So, if the *Strategy* is not a program or a project, what is it? It certainly has elements of a *plan,* but that's not quite it either. On the one hand, a vision without a plan is just a daydream. If we have not laid out a course of action for how to move us toward the vision of a thoroughly evangelized region, it is not likely that anything is going to happen. On the other hand, most people would rather face anything but another plan, and with good reason. Many plans have a way of becoming an end in themselves. After we have spent months in committee meetings compiling the plan, we are ready to be done with it and get back to all the other responsibilities we've been forced to ignore while we were planning. And, in the end, most plans just tend to be formalized lists of disconnected things we probably would have done even without the plan.

I would submit that the *Regional Strategy for Vision Achievement* must be conceived of as a ***long-range process***.

Why a Process?

Somethings have to happen before others can. Imagine the chief executive of a manufacturing company who has a vision to build the "World's Greatest Widget". He is consumed with this dream. He thinks and talks of nothing else. He knows his widget will be so superior to all other widgets that the marketplace will eventually demand the World's Greatest Widget; that it will accept nothing less. He just knows his company will grow and become the envy of all widget manufacturers throughout the world. Every widget wonk in the world will want to work in his company, because people will pay almost anything to get one of these widgets and the profit margin will be so overwhelming that every employee will become a millionaire. So, the CEO calls a meeting of all his employees and with rousing rhetoric, shares his dream and describes the functionality and beauty of his widget and the tremendous future they all have. He concludes his *tour de force* by urging them all to get out in the plant and start rolling the World Greatest Widgets off the assembly line.

> A vision is only a daydream without a plan and a plan is only a list without a process to execute it

A long, awkward silence follows. Finally, one bespectacled draftsman sitting in the back row raises his hand and respectfully ask what's on everyone's mind, "Sir, I love your vision and really want be a part of it. So, how soon can we see the plans for the new process?"

With a glance both patronizing and slightly befuddled, the CEO responds, "What do you need a process for? You know what to do. Just order more plastics and get to work."

Improbable as this sounds, it is not far from what all the talk about the New Evangelization has been like over the past 40-odd years. Rarely, do the clergy (including myself) move passed platitudes and pep talks. And yet, building a world filled with loving, passionate Christians requires a plan.

We need a recipe, not just a list of ingredients

Moreover, the plan needs to be more than a list of unconnected ingredients: a dash of Scripture, a splash of faith-sharing, a pinch of friendship, an ounce of charity. *We need a recipe, not just a list of ingredients.* We need a process. We have to be able to answer the question: Which ingredients come first and what do we do with them? And, once we've done that, what's next? If building widgets is a complex process, then surely building mature Christians cannot require any less understanding and dedication.

Back in the 1950s the U.S. Department of the Navy set out to build the first Polaris-class nuclear submarine. No one had ever built anything quite so complex. And not only did they have to build it, but it needed to be done on time and within budget. Out of this experience, the project management practice of "PERT charting" was born.[78] Through a series of lines and nodes, PERT charts literally "connect the dots." Interdependencies are identified. Work is *logically sequenced* such that a dependent action is not initiated until the completion of the antecedent action(s) on which it depends.

While it is absolutely true that the conversion and sanctification of souls cannot be reduced to a set of cold, sequenced steps, our standard approach to evangelization seems to be "so spiritual that it's of no earthly good". In fact, it is fair to say that most parishes and dioceses do not have any approach at all. The usual language of pastoral letters and homilies may be beautiful and inspiring, but if they are not accompanied with practical instructions laying out what we're going to do next and what's going to come after that, the inspirational message too often fades into a vague aspiration. Does it not make sense *first* to prepare parishes and individuals for evangelization *before* asking them to simply get out there and do it? And once a parish does begin wooing a few seekers, *what's next?* Is there a sequence of activities planned to move them forward to an actual decision for Christ? Have the RCIA teams been prepared for the task of doing what the Church asks of them? If so, what happens next? Does *Mystagogy* – as called for in the Rite itself – extend for a year after Easter Vigil? Does it go beyond a few hours of catechesis to include real, committed mentors who model what it means to be a twenty-first century Catholic who is in love with Christ; people who are well-prepared and willing to befriend and nurture and cultivate the fledgling faith of the neophytes? Is there a specific plan to engage them in the life of the Church and to use their gifts for service? How are the new Christians being formed into missionary disciples themselves, so that they can join in the Great Commission?

What about returning Catholics? Is the phenomenon of "reversion" such an informal, private matter that no one even notices they're back before they slip away again? Have we prepared ourselves to embrace them and celebrate their return and incorporate them into the work of the Church?

We need to recognize the need for a long-range, comprehensive regional evangelization plan carried out in love and unity. And, not just a plan that lists discrete, disconnected activities, but a *process* that recognizes interdependencies and sequences the activities in a logical order.

* * *

Businesses are organized with the end in mind: to sell a product or service. Like every business that has ever opened its doors, the Church must come to realize that she too is here to sell a product: *A relationship with the eternal Triune God.* Although we are not a business, there is much that the world of business can teach us. For example, businesses clearly understand the concept of *"processes"*. They eat and breathe it; live and die by it. They understand the process by which raw materials are purchased. The materials are then *processed* by an established *process* to create the end-product. They have *processes* for marketing and selling their products. And all of these *processes* require formal training for the workforce and accounting of all the costs involved. In her apostolic mission of evangelization, the Church must begin to develop the same process-oriented disciplines. We have to come to an understanding of the critical importance of *processes* that – when mingled with grace – help to cultivate a receptive spirit; *processes* that help to bring about explicit life-decisions to love and follow Jesus. And, once these conversions have begun, we must put in place clearly-understood processes of committed accompaniment to "stand behind" our product with a "lifetime warranty". And then we will have to learn to think even beyond accompaniment to a healthy spirit of self-evaluation and assessment, using all the modern methods available to us, and when appropriate, even including tools as foreign as quantitative metrics and data analytics.

* * *

Putting the Paradigm Shift into Practice

In Part I, a *Proposal* for the new Evangelization in the United States is described in terms of ten attributes which collectively represent a major "paradigm shift" from the *status quo.*

As the process for achieving the *Proposal,* the *Regional Vision Achievement Strategy* can be described in terms of seven key characteristics that are closely related to the attributes of the paradigm shift. It might be said that they add a more practical dimension to the ten attributes of the paradigm shift discussed in Chapter III.   We've already discussed one of these seven characteristics: its *focus on process.* The remaining six characteristics are just as crucial to the success of the *Strategy* or, for that matter, any other approach to regional evangelization. If even one of them is missing, the effort will falter. Accordingly, the *Strategy* must be:

- Comprehensive
- "Shepherded" in Unity
- Grounded in Prayer and Responsive to the Holy Spirit
- Fruitful and Growth-Oriented
- Accountable
- Perpetual

Comprehensive Much has been written in recent years about evangelization that is carried out by *missionary disciples* and *parishes.* It is not without good reason that the focus has been on these two groups, since most of the hard work of evangelization needs to be shouldered by impassioned individual Catholics and dynamic, caring parishes. That said, within the organizational structure of the Catholic Church, there remain other vitally important "players" that are often overlooked in the real world of evangelization. They, too, need to be pulled into the process. Hopefully, this will come as good news for all the lone evangelizers and rare parishes out there who are struggling on their own.

Typically left out of the literature is the role of the diocesan bishop and, by extension, "the Diocese". In fact, the central figure of the bishop in the apostolate of evangelization goes back to the words of Christ himself (cf. Matthew 28:1½-20). Moreover, the modern diocesan office that serves the bishop has come to play a vital role in *communications and coordination* that usually goes well beyond the canonically-required functions of the traditional chancery office. Accordingly, "the Diocese"- understood here as the bishop and his diocesan staff – can do a great deal proactively to encourage a sense of apostolic purpose, zeal, and unity among the faithful.

At this juncture, I suspect there are any number of diocesan evangelization staffers who are perplexed at the suggestion that they are not typically involved in evangelization. Surely some are thinking: "I don't know what he is talking about. I work on evangelization all day long." To this reaction, I would humbly suggest that there is a distinction between *working on* evangelization and actually evangelizing. The point is that over-and-above serving as a training and coordination resource to parishes (which is certainly a good thing), the bishop and his staff have their own evangelistic role to play. Moreover, the resources available to a diocese for evangelizing through the media as well as through large-scale evangelistic events can hardly ever be carried off by individual parishes, or even parish clusters, or deaneries. In this sense, the Bishop/Diocese has opportunities to evangelize in addition to just *working on* evangelization. There is far more that a diocese can do than is typically being done.

Given decisive episcopal leadership, with "the troops" fired up and pastors experiencing a new sense of unified direction, an entirely new dimension can be brought to the discussion of the New

Evangelization that ordinarily is left out of the conversation altogether.

Unfortunately, the subject of diocesan leadership often evokes a lot of eye-rolling at the parish level. Parish priests often resent the "Big D" due to the perception that all it does is heap unnecessary demands and policies on them that consume precious time and/or limit their freedom. Whether that perception is accurate or not, the diocese is often viewed as irrelevant. For many, if not most Catholics, it seems totally disconnected from their lives and their lived experience of the Church. This is problematic for reasons that are

Figure 5
EVANGELIZATION INVOLVING THE
ENTIRE CHURCH

"No believer in Christ, no institution of the Church, can avoid this supreme duty: to proclaim Christ to all peoples."
- St. John Paul II

both theological and practical. When one makes a commitment for Christ either as an existing Catholic or an inquirer, that person is aligning herself first and foremost with the most worldwide and ancient expression of Christianity that exists. In fact, for the first millennium, the terms "Christian" and "Catholic" were typically used interchangeably. So, first-and-foremost, when a person becomes a *Catholic* Christian (or reaffirms her Christian commitment

211

inside the Catholic Church), she is joining a *large community* with visible expressions at the local, regional, national, and world-wide levels. As important as the parish is, it should leave only one of several imprints on her *identity* as a Catholic Christian.

Moreover, from a practical standpoint, evangelization plays out in a *trans-parochial* context. In the lived arena of evangelization, the relationship between evangelizer and seeker typically involves more than one parish. The evangelizer lives in one part of town, the seeker in another. Very often, different cities and even dioceses are involved. So, we have to get used to the idea of thinking and acting regionally and even across dioceses, at least when it comes to the great work of evangelization and the institutional mechanisms that support it. Eventually, we probably will need to move to *trans-diocesan* thinking that takes place at a national level. But, regardless of that, the point is this: no one parish, deanery, or even diocese is always going to encompass the relationships between the evangelizer and the evangelized.

This, of course, is not to suggest that there is no role for evangelizing parishes. Quite the opposite. It is only to suggest that there is an important role for the diocese and the Church at-large when it comes to evangelization, a role that is commonly overlooked today.

As suggested in Figure 5, there are other players that have a role to play as well. For example, Catholic schools are often treated as autonomous entities with little relationship to the very parishes in which they usually function. Similarly, Catholic Charities, the Knights of Columbus, Catholic hospitals, Catholic medical associations, and even old-name Catholic universities all need to be coopted into the process (difficult as that may be). Moreover, the multiplicity of ecclesial movements all have a vital role to play in the evangelical work of the Church. In this sense, the *entire* Church needs to understand and exercise its place in the process of regional evangelization. In a few words, the *Regional Vision Achievement Strategy* is best conducted as a *process* that is carried out *comprehensively*.

* * *

There is yet another sense in which regional evangelization must be comprehensive. Often in Catholic circles, one hears: "The only kind of evangelization that works is based on one-on-one relationships." Or, "The only kind of evangelization that works comes from personal example. Words just get in the way." Or, "Such-and-such a strategy [fill in the blank] is worthless. Only Fundamentalists do that." All one must do to falsify any of these claims is listen to more than one conversion story. Every story is different and as unique as the individual doing the telling. Reductionists who simplify the process of conversion to only "one way" neglect to recognize the uniqueness of the individual, not to mention the myriad means used by the Holy Spirit to effect a work of grace. Given the unique experiences, personality, intelligence, and background of any individual, the initial spark that sets a person on the road to conversion may…

> … be as "spiritual" as walking into the quiet of a Eucharistic chapel by accident and recognizing the presence of God.

> … be as "human" as a friend telling his story, which triggers the recognition of something authentic and beautiful.

> … be born in a soup kitchen where a poor woman is treated as someone special.

> … have started by participating in a *Habitat* project sponsored by the Knights of Columbus.

... have been the invitation heard on a *Catholics Come Home* TV spot.

... be founded on the gradual respect earned over many years by the life of a Catholic spouse.

... be attributable to the witness of a teacher or a caregiver.

... have come about by reading one of the "Church Fathers" or a contemporary apologist.

From these *real* examples, it should be obvious that no one method of evangelizing can begin to suffice to reach the soul of everyone. This doesn't mean that a bishop struggling to formulate a regional evangelization process won't have some hard choices to make. But it does mean that the process should be as **comprehensive** as possible, allowing the Holy Spirit many avenues through which to work the miracle of faith.

Shepherded in Unity The evangelization of an entire region will not happen by itself. If left to the efforts of the relatively small number of the faithful who are currently concerned about spreading the Gospel, the New Evangelization will continue in the future as it has in the past: as relatively isolated and dramatically different apostolates. Someone must call us *together* into this great mission and the bishop is the only person with the authority to do that. The bishop sets the tone and establishes the direction for his diocese – no one else. If he doesn't do it, it won't happen. That's why his leadership is so important.

Moreover, it is not sufficient for the bishop to say: "Okay, everybody. Now listen up. Let's all get out there and evangelize." This is equivalent to a shepherd merely unlocking the sheep gate and nudging his sheep out to graze. Without him staying with the flock and guiding them to the best pasture, they scatter, "each going his own way" (cf. Is 53:6). They disperse and are eventually lost.

To use a different metaphor, the existing state of affairs in which evangelization is *not* "shepherded in unity" can be compared to the "warm-up" of an orchestra prior to the beginning of a concert. Among the many talented musicians practicing their upcoming difficult musical phrases, only a trained ear can discern the underlying beauty of what they are playing. To the untrained ear, it is simply noise, a cacophony of chaotic virtuosity. But, let the maestro approach the podium and call all those individually-talented musicians to order, and what was just noise a few moments before turns into an experience of incomparable beauty.

The local Church that is not working together will, at best, be a warm-up for the real thing. Only the bishop – read maestro or conductor – can call us all into order and bring about the needed unity to do something great for the Lord. Note that it is not the maestro who is playing the music. That said, he will not have the respect of the members of the orchestra if he himself is not an accomplished musician. In the same way, a diocesan bishop must lead both by word and by example in order to bring about the harmonious work of the entire local Church.

Continuing the orchestra metaphor a little further, each of the musicians gathered around the maestro must be willing to sacrifice his own virtuosity for the good of the orchestral effort. In any given piece, the genius of any given musician may not be put on full display. But, in due time the strengths of the different sections and even the individual players will all be highlighted.

The bishop needs to call us all to one great united purpose. When this unifying episcopal direction is lacking, a noticeable "silo mentality" develops. People have a natural proclivity to view problems and needs through the lens of their own particular interests and talents. In a complex culture, we become a great mass of specialists. For all the strengths of specialized perspectives/

responsibilities, the perspective of the specialist has the drawback of blinding us to common problems and opportunities that we can all share when it comes to the transmission of the Faith.

This silo mentality is not only an organizational dysfunction, but it is also an expression of the extreme individualism of secular society that has infiltrated the Church. Consequently, it has subtle spiritual implications. We profess that the first "mark" of the Church is her "oneness", in modern parlance "unity". Unity should be an observable characteristic by which the fractured world is able to recognize something truly unique and desirable in the Church; something that goes beyond theological agreement to a clearly visible lived reality. For example, Catholic parishes and Catholic schools should be easily recognizable as part of the *same institution* sharing the same passion for Christ.

Another manifestation of the silo mentality is the phenomenon of disparate parishes that evolve merely into collective expressions of the personality and ecclesiology of their pastor. Of course, to the extent that different parishes serve different people groups, a degree of diversity is appropriate. But, to the extent that different parishes reflect widely divergent values and priorities, we lose our oneness and our catholicity. At best, this impairs our Christian witness. At worst, it destroys it.

This state-of-affairs has implications for how we plan and how we implement those plans (or not). For example, our contemporary approach to the implementation of a diocesan pastoral plan can be described as the "smorgasbord approach" that allows pastors to pick-and-choose what suits them and to implement it or not. Moreover, diocesan pastoral plans are often developed by asking specialized staffs and people with particular interests to define their own goals and objectives, and then pursue their respective solutions in relative isolation from one another.

Unfortunately, the Church today faces a huge secular behemoth that encourages sin and threatens the very salvation of souls and the long-term communication of the Gospel itself. Insofar as each decision-making entity (e.g., vicariate, department, pastor, etc.) has a role to play in the great evangelistic enterprise, they all must recognize their interconnectedness and work as a unified team in a coordinated way on the execution of *one grand missionary process for the conversion of the region,* a process that involves the participation of everyone. For example, the Vocations Department may need to take explicit responsibility for the cultivation of a deep personal relationship with Jesus in the lives of each young man currently discerning a vocation to the priesthood; in the long haul, this pays off in priests who are passionate about sharing their love for Jesus and credible witnesses of the Gospel. Similarly, the Vicar for Clergy may need to take responsibility for the training and formation of parish priests in the pastoral art of infusing a passion for Christ into their homilies and into marriage preparation and baptismal prep for parents. None of this is meant to obviate the need for departmental plans, but it does require that all the various perspectives seek a unified "high-level perspective" that asks the question: What can I/we (our parish, our department, etc.) bring to our common problem? Where do I/we fit into the grand evangelistic enterprise that will help us execute it better? In the final analysis, it belongs to the bishop – no one else – to facilitate this conversation.

* * *

One might ask: Is the *Strategy* a creature of "top-down" management? The answer is "yes" and "no". "Yes", insofar as we, the Church, are constituted hierarchically. As a human organization, no system is perfect and I am confident our Lord was well aware of all the plusses-and-minuses of a hierarchical system when he founded his Church on Peter and the apostles. Yet, despite the negatives of established ecclesial authority, our Savior chose it (cf. Mt 16:18-19, Mt 18:18, Jn 20:23). Moreover, with centuries of clericalism and its corollary – lay passivity – to expect a broad-based, unified movement in the Church to simply materialize without the leadership of the bishop and the cooperation of the presbyterate is simply unrealistic.

Having said that, inasmuch as the regional evangelization process starts at the grass roots of the most-committed individuals and parishes, it is not top-down. From the most-committed it works its way out in successively wider circles with the leadership and support of the bishop. So, rather than top-down, a more apt description of the strategy is "from the center moving outward".

Grounded in Prayer and Responsive to the Holy Spirit One of the mysteries of salvation is its admixture of faith and works; providential grace and free will; ultimate reliance on God's mercy while struggling to execute his will. There is a risk that the *Regional Strategy* may be understood in such a way that its strongest advocates lose sight of this mysterious reality. If entered into in the wrong way, mounting a widespread movement to win souls for Christ in a systematic way has the potential to morph into modern-day Pelagianism. If we place too much importance on what we do and forget that apart from God we can do nothing, we will be guilty of just that (cf. Jn 15:5).

Here's the problem: Suppose the *Regional Strategy* was pursued with little or no reference to the role of the Holy Spirit in bringing about the conversions we hope for. The almost inevitable result would be to begin to view ourselves as the prime movers, taking matters into our own hands and working so hard that we're saving ourselves and others to boot. As much as this mindset may appeal to our American, can-do sensibilities, it is an idolatrous heresy in which we place ourselves on the throne of God.

The cornerstone of the *Regional Strategy* is prayer – intercessory, discerning, adoring, persistent – and an absolute openness to being directed by our Lord in ways that we cannot anticipate today.

Fruitful and Growth-Oriented Having warned about the danger of Pelagianism, there is an opposite danger that is equally concerning. This is the blasé attitude which denudes us of all passion and concern for conversions by putting the entire responsibility in the hands of the Holy Spirit. It is the mindset that allows us to treat evangelization as a box to be checked without caring about the results. As suggested earlier, this attitude is a form of presumption that exonerates us of real responsibility. If placing all responsibility for results on ourselves is a form of Pelagianism, then just as assuredly placing all responsibility for results on God is a form of Calvinistic predestination.

If we are serious about evangelization, we should aim toward not only reversing the massive exodus away from the faith, but toward real growth; toward *making disciples of all nations,* including our own. In her landmark book *Forming Intentional Disciples,* Sherry Weddell includes a chapter entitled "Expect Conversions".[79] In it, she relates the story of a priest-friend who found it utterly amazing that a life-changing conversion came about through the witness of a less-than-qualified layman. She reminds us of our Lord's words to his disciples: *Do you not say, 'There are yet four months, then comes the harvest'? I tell you, lift up your eyes, and see how the fields are already white for harvest* (Jn 4:35). We have set our sights so low, that we hardly know how to handle success.

There is impressive evidence from the parables that Jesus is deeply concerned about the fruitfulness of his followers. *He expects us to produce.* Consider the Parable of the Talents (cf. Mt 25:14-30). When it came time to give an account of the treasure the master had entrusted to his servants, he commended the servant who risked the most and yielded the highest return. Conversely, to the one who buried his portion of the treasure and returned it with no profit, the master had him thrown into the darkness *where there will be wailing and grinding of teeth* (v.30).

The Parable of the Tenants makes a similar point (cf. Mt 21:33-46). The land owner invested heavily in his vineyard, entrusted it to his tenants, then went away expecting them to produce a rich harvest for him. When they tried to keep the harvest for themselves instead, the landowner made it clear what was to happen to them: *[T]he kingdom of God will be taken away from you and given to a people that will produce its fruit* (v.43).

In Luke 16:1-8, Jesus describes the situation of the dishonest steward who squandered his master's property. Even though the master fired him, he commended the scoundrel for "acting shrewdly" by dishonestly recovering at least cents-on-the-dollar. The telling insight into this teaching comes when Jesus says: *For the people of this world are more shrewd in dealing with their own kind than are the people of light* (v.8b, NIV). Apparently, not everything that originates in the secular world is bad, simply because the focus is not spiritual. If we can borrow the business world's concern about profits, learn from it, and apply it discriminately to the work of evangelization, that's a good thing; not bad.

Christ's concern about the Church's fruitfulness shows up over and over again in the Gospels. He cursed the unfruitful fig tree (cf. Mt 21:18-22) and He was willing to pay unreasonably high wages to workers who didn't enter the vineyard until late in the day (cf. Mt 20:1-16).

* * *

The great evangelical pastor, Rick Warren, refers to the following statement as a myth: "All God expects of us is faithfulness." To place this assertion in the proper context, it appears in his book *The Purpose Driven Church* in a chapter entitled "Myths About Growing Churches". So, in making this statement, Pastor Warren's intent is not to deny that there are times and situations in which faithfulness really is all our God expects from us; when it is all we *can* give. His point is this: when it is within our power to do a great work for the kingdom and we know it is our Lord's will for us to do it, he expects us to do it. And his point applies equally to individual Christians as it does to churches. In fact, our Lord himself said so:

> That servant who knew his master's will but did not make preparations nor act in accord with his will shall be beaten severely; and the servant who was ignorant of his master's will but acted in a way deserving of a severe beating shall be beaten only lightly. Much will be required of the person entrusted with much, and still more will be demanded of the person entrusted with more. (Lk 12:47-48)

Two aspects of the *Regional Strategy* need to be held in delicate balance simultaneously: We must approach our task grounded in prayer and responsive to the Holy Spirit *and* at the same time be fruitful and growth-oriented. Warren put it this way:

> All our plans, programs, and procedures are worthless without God's anointing. Psalm 127:1 says. "Unless the Lord build the house, its builders labor in vain." A church cannot be built by human effort alone. We must never forget whose church it is. Jesus said, "*I* will build *my* church". (Mt 16:18, *italics* added)
>
> On the other hand, we must avoid the error that there is nothing we can do to help a church grow. This misconception is just as prevalent today. Some pastors and theologians believe that any planning, organizing, advertising, or effort is presumptuous, unspiritual, or even sinful, and that our only role is to sit back and watch God do his thing... This way of thinking produces passive believers and often uses spiritual sounding excuses to justify a church's failure to grow.[80]

Perhaps the best way to end this discussion on the balance between dependence on God and our own fruitfulness is to return to our Lord's words:

> Remain in me, as I remain in you. Just as a branch cannot bear fruit on its own unless it remains on the vine, so neither can you unless you remain in me. I am the vine, you are the branches. Whoever remains in me and I in him will bear much fruit, because without me you can do nothing... If you remain in me and my words remain in you, ask whatever you want and it will be done for you. (Jn 15:4-5,7)

Accountable It is more-than-a-little interesting that in all of the parables about fruitfulness (see above) there is an accounting. The servants who were entrusted with varying talents had to give an accounting of what they had done with those talents. The tenants were expected to produce an abundant yield for the landowner and there was eventually "hell to pay" when they continued to willfully betray his trust after multiple chances to redeem themselves. The dishonest steward was called to give an account for squandering his master's property. In the Parable of the Sower, our Lord spoke of the yields produced by the seed that fell on good soil in the accounting language of profits: *thirtyfold, and sixtyfold, and a hundredfold*.

In a Church that sets annual monetary goals for parishes' responses to the bishops' annual appeal, why is it that there are no expectations about the fruitfulness of our evangelization efforts? I suspect because we don't really believe we can be fruitful. How has it happened that we have divested ourselves of any accountability for helping to bring people into personal relationships with Christ? Perhaps, because we're afraid the accounting won't be very positive. And yet, our Lord told his disciples that there was no reason to wait; that *the fields are already ripe for the harvest*. It is our Lord who creates the harvest, but we are expected to help sow the seeds, water the sprouts, and when the time comes, bring in the sheaves.

The *Regional Strategy* is not envisioned as optional. If evangelization is to become a bishop's top priority, then the cause of unity demands everyone to participate – every parish, every Catholic. While we cannot flip a magic switch to make that happen overnight, we can establish the expectation and require the discipline of reporting on the efforts made and the apparent results. Not every parish can be expected to maintain the same pace and to achieve the same levels of fruitfulness, but every parish can be required to do *something* and to work toward the eventual achievement of fully-alive individuals and communities reaching out proactively to people on the peripheries of the Christian Faith.

All of this will require the establishment of research, milestones, and long-range schedules, not just vague promises. The *Regional Strategy* calls for clearly-defined measures of progress, scheduled self-evaluations, and parish assessments. When we don't achieve those deadlines and milestones, the question should be: Why not and how can I/we do it better the next go-round?

If the Church in America is going to make an impact in the lives of individuals and the culture as a whole – which we have the potential to do – the *laissez-faire* culture of diocesan and parish life will have to give way to a more responsible, disciplined outreach. Moreover, accountability is for *all* levels of regional ecclesial life – the individual missionary disciple, evangelizing communities and teams, parishes and pastors, diocesan staff, and the bishop himself. (More on these subjects later.)

Perpetual – In Chapter III, we saw that the *Proposal for the New Evangelization* is long-range in expectations and permanent in commitment. Any practical process for achieving the vision of an evangelizing Church must reflect this commitment.

I also quoted earlier the words of the long-standing preacher to the papal household, Father Raniero Cantalamessa, OFM Cap when he wrote: "We are more prepared by our past to be 'shepherds' rather than to be 'fishers' of men, that is, we are better prepared to nourish people who come to the church than to bring new people into the church or to bring back those who have drifted away and live on the margins..."[81] Any honest self-assessment must recognize the truth of this statement and come to grips with the fact that it is likely to take a very long time to change our largely pastoral culture to a *pastoral and evangelical* culture. The Christianization of the Mediterranean world and Europe did not take place over night, although the conversion of Constantine and the ensuing Edict of Milan in 313 A.D. was the "tipping point" that clearly accelerated the process. The spread of the Christian faith in the Americas occurred much faster, but this was due to colonization by at least nominally Christian Europeans and, in no small part, to the apparitions of Our Lady of Guadalupe, which led to the baptism of 9 million Aztecs in Central America and the complete cessation of infant sacrifices in about in six years.[82] Perhaps, the Lord will send us an intervention such as the conversion of a great leader or a widely-recognized miracle that will be a "game changer". But, even if this happens, we have to be prepared to be "in this" for the long haul. After all it took some 300 years from the Resurrection to the conversion of the Roman emperor and it has taken some 300 years since the inception of the Enlightenment to morph a largely Christian society into the hyper-secularized society we live in today.

The last thing we need is for the New Evangelization to go the route of an ecclesiastical fad. Despite our modern expectation that great success at anything can be achieved quickly and with minimal effort, we must consciously brace ourselves for a long, gritty struggle until that time in the future when *evangelization* becomes a permanent feature in the culture of the Church.

Imagine saying: "We are going to invest our efforts into Catholic Charites for the next three years until we have eradicated poverty. Then, we can move onto something else." Of course, that's a laughable proposition. Despite our best efforts, we will never be able to eliminate poverty altogether. Moreover, as faithful Catholics, no one would even think of such a thing. Care for the poor and the down-trodden is in our bones. It is part of our ecclesiastical DNA, just as it should be. We know that to be an authentic Christian entails tireless, frustrating, committed care for the poor. And that, despite our Lord's words: *The poor you will always have with you* (Mt 26:11).

Jesus prophesied something very analogous with respect to unbelief when he said: *But when the Son of Man comes, will he find faith on earth* (Lk 18:8b)? Until he comes again, there will always be distractions, skepticism, cynicism, sin, and all the other human problems that hold people back from the embrace of our loving Father. Unless the *eschaton* is right around the corner, I do believe that we will see at least a season of re-Christianization, a "new springtime of hope" that St. John Paul II foresaw as an aspect of the twenty-first century. But whether I am right or wrong has nothing to do with the attribute of permanence in the *Regional Vision Achievement Strategy*. What does is the will of our God who no more desires humanity's detachment from God than he does needless poverty and suffering. This is why evangelization can never merely be a program or a project, but must become a passion, a holy obsession that consumes our lives. This is why all the other attributes of the *Strategy* – prayer, unifying episcopal leadership, comprehensiveness, fruitfulness, and accountability – must become permanent features in the landscape of the Church.

Reasoning from the End to the Means

Now, let's construct the *Regional Strategy*. In his blockbuster book *The 7 Habits of Highly Effective People*, Stephen Covey lists as "Habit 2" the following adage: *"Start with the End in Mind"*.[83] This makes perfect sense, of course, since without "the end in mind" we can't begin to lay out how to get there, whether the "end" is being a better leader or creating a literary masterpiece or any other goal. The strategy that follows starts at the end point by asking: "What would a fully-evangelized region look like?

Let me invite you to enter this reverie with me. Let's envision a fully-evangelized diocese (aka, region) as the "end" we have in mind and start working backwards to the beginning.

Let's imagine a place fifty years or more from now where every inhabitant – rich, poor, educated, illiterate – has heard a very compelling

> "If you don't know where you're going, you might wind up somewhere else."
>
> - *Yogi Berra, Late New York Yankees All-Star Catcher*

presentation of the most fundamental truths of our Faith. By some amazing process, they have all heard convincing presentations that everything really did come into existence in an instant (aka, *The Big Bang*), suggesting the reality of God; that the mathematical probabilities of the universe being supportive of any life – let alone human life – can be demonstrated to be infinitesimally small, and yet here we are, also pointing to God;[84] that God must have willed the advent of human beings into the physical universe out of sheer love; that if God loves us, he would surely reveal himself, which he has done in Sacred Scripture; that in their freedom, our earliest forbears rejected God's love and that we have all tended to follow suit ever since; that God didn't give up on us, but rather proved his unconditional love by becoming one of us; that as a human, he actually died for us so that we might be liberated from our willful rejection of him; that he returned to human life (albeit, in a new kind of glorious life) to give us a chance at sharing that same life with him forever, and; that to this very day God has provided a trail of inexplicable phenomena over the past two millennia that continue to point to him; that God deeply hopes we will accept him and love him in return for his love and take him up on his offer of eternal life.

Having heard this message laid out in various loving and compelling ways, many people (though definitely not all) have accepted the message who otherwise would not have; these people have entered into personal relationships with our Lord, come into the Church, are reforming their lives, and even spreading the Good News themselves.

Moving backwards from this "end state", it is actually possible to **_reason to_** the means by which the end was achieved. We need to ask ourselves some questions systematically, starting with: How in the world did the Church get the Christian message out there in such a thoroughgoing and compelling way that many people accepted it? This almost certainly could not have happened by one-on-one word-of-mouth alone. It must have also involved a large-scale, coordinated communications effort making use of the Internet, broadcast radio and TV, cable TV, maybe even satellite media, billboards, and the like. For the sake of giving this great evangelistic outburst a moniker, let' call it the **Regional Catholics Initiative**.

Okay, so let's think about the cost of all this media involvement. How did we possibly afford such a thing? Step backward one more step away from the endpoint toward the beginning point. In order to have raised all this money and in order for all these conversions to have taken place, two prior things must to have occurred: By some means other than massive media involvement, the Church must have previously grown. Where else would the money have come from?

Moreover, if the media was really effective, this grown Church must have previously grown not only in number, but also in zeal. How else could the Church have accommodated all the people who responded to the media without the help of not only a larger Church, but a Church filled with disciples who were thrilled to befriend and teach and accompany and correct and support? How else but through Catholics willing to take substantial amounts of time out of their own pursuits to help others? The answer is simple: Other, earlier Christians had to have been there to befriend and help them. There must have been a virtual army of missionary disciples witnessing through their words and lives the truth of our salvation *before* the *Regional Catholics Initiative*. Let's refer to these prior phenomena as the **Missionary Disciples Initiative.**

Now, we have to step backward toward the beginning yet another step. Where did all these on-fire missionary disciples come from? Well, way back in the day (in about 2020) some parishes must have been transformed at their very roots into communities filled with serious believers willing to commit their lives to introducing others to Christ and nurturing them into committed Christians. Let's call this the **Purposeful Parishes Initiative.**

Fine, so how on earth did that happen? Those pastors didn't all wake up one morning and say: "Gee, I think it's time to convert the pew-warmers and overhaul parish life." Well, we have to step back toward the beginning one more time. Through great prayer and faith, a visionary bishop way back when must have called his pastors together and begged, cajoled, and pleaded with them to share their own love for Jesus with their people; to inspire them to an exciting vision of parish life that is willing to reach out beyond themselves to friends and strangers alike, to the hurting and broken. And that same bishop, almost single-handedly at first must have undertaken the formation of priests and lay ecclesial ministers into missionary

228

disciples. His infectious love for people and passion for Jesus quickly won a larger circle of missionary disciples and within a few years, discernable progress could be seen. Let's call the work of this bishop-saint the **Episcopal Initiative.**

There you have it. Starting with the end in mind and working backward to the present moment, we can trace the broad outline of the interdependencies and chronological order of a prototype *Vision Achievement Strategy for Regional Evangelization.*

The Regional Strategy: A High-Level Look

This section provides a broad-brush description of a prototype *Vision Achievement Strategy for Regional Evangelization.* It is not a magic bullet that will solve all the problems we struggle with as evangelizers. Rather, it is offered in humility and with hope that dioceses will use it as a starting point for scaling up the New Evangelization to a regional movement by bringing a modicum of organization to the process.

The Four Initiatives Now let's turn around and move from the beginning to the end. As proposed and depicted in Figure 6, the *Strategy* is comprised of four staged, but continuing initiatives: (1) the Episcopal Initiative, (2) Purposeful Parishes Initiative, (3) the Missionary Disciples Initiative, and (4) the Regional Catholics Initiative.

It is important to understand that these initiatives proceed in a logical and chronological sequence and that *they all begin with the bishop.* This *Episcopal Initiative* is all the more important today given the present ecclesiastical state-of-affairs. Today, many rank-and-file Catholics are so disenchanted by the institutional Church that the bishops *must* do something to make a clean break from the scandals of the recent past and promise a humble, repentant new beginning.

Figure 6
THE 'FOUR INITIATIVES'

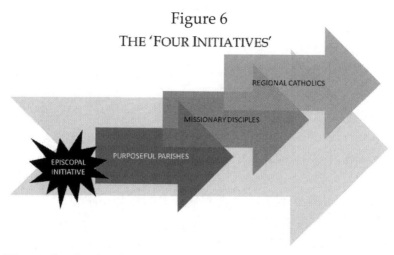

We might think of this new beginning as spiritually "rebooting the system". We have all had the experience of our computers becoming so fouled in Internet cookies and multiple applications running simultaneously that we have to shut it down and start over. More will be said later on the sustaining aspects of the *Episcopal Initiative*. Suffice to say that this initiative will require humble transformational leadership from the diocesan bishop that conveys a new direction for the local Church. It will entail radical dedication to holiness and service lived out in the public arena, diocese-wide intercession, discernment of the Holy Spirit's promptings, top priority given to evangelization, clarity in communications, and more.

If there is a silver lining to the troubles of the Church, it is that they provide a clear opportunity for change and make for a startling contrast against a backdrop of ecclesiastical irrelevance, *status quo*-thinking, and, in some cases, even sin. But, scandals aside, as suggested earlier, it is unlikely that anything as ambitious as the thoroughgoing evangelization of an entire region will ever happen without the bishop enthusiastically leading the way and establishing a new, higher level of expectation.

Once the *Episcopal Initiative* has excited enough pastors and parish leaders, the *Purposeful Parishes Initiative* is kicked off. Through this initiative, parishes working in concert with the diocese will gradually begin to bear fruit by: working to stem the outbound tide of their youth; encouraging all their members to enter into or deepen their own personal relationships with Jesus, and; becoming Christian communities capable of inviting and welcoming new members. As the new evangelical purpose of the parishes begins to solidify in their self-identity, a growing number of parishioners will mature in their capacity for nurturing the faith of new members.

... the bishops must do something to make a clean break from the scandals of the recent past and promise a humble, repentant new beginning... We might think of this new beginning as spiritually "rebooting the system".

As this happens, the *Vision Achievement Strategy* will begin to shift its focus from the *Purposeful Parishes Initiative* to the *Missionary Disciples Initiative*. Increasingly conscious of their own longing to lead others to our Savior, a growing number of motivated Catholics will receive training and formation in the sacred task of sharing their faith in sensitive and compelling ways; sharing carried out both individually and in communities of fellow missionary disciples; sharing that takes place with their children, and grandchildren, siblings, among their circles of friends, with their co-workers, and on and on. At first, their harvest may appear small. After all, we can't expect the Holy Spirit to march to our brand-new drumbeat. But, in time there will be growth. These modest successes will circle back and help to stimulate the development of new purposeful parishes. At the same time, some parishes and missionary disciples will find themselves reaping what they themselves did not sow, becoming the beneficiaries of the witness of Catholics from other parishes and even other cities. With the continuing encouragement of the bishop and a growing number of pastors, the long-term fruits of the missionary disciples will begin to yield a larger harvest and more missionary disciples will join their number. Will there come a "tipping point" when the number of converted lives becomes impossible to overlook? Will the growing trickle turn into a stream and then a river? Only God knows.

That said, at some point, the Church will desire to make an even bigger impact for Christ. After having prepared both parishes and individuals for the missionary apostolate, the goal is that there will be a veritable army of well-formed, mature missionary disciples capable and desirous of accompanying a huge surge in the number of prospective seekers; a surge responding to large-scale, well-organized evangelistic efforts undertaken as part of the fourth initiative: the *Regional Catholics Initiative*.

To summarize the four initiatives, the bishop kicks-off, motivates, and continuously sustains the *Regional Vision Achievement Strategy*.

The *Purposeful Parishes Initiative* focuses on developing their own members – including their youth and young adults – into deeply-committed Christians and transforming their communities into parishes capable of reaching out, welcoming, and sustaining new members.

The purpose of the third initiative is to form and equip average Catholics as *missionary disciples* who work both individually and collectively for the evangelization of all their environments: family, work, and social. This initiative also involves the formation of permanent communities of mature missionary disciples to support one another and evangelize through natural gatherings of friends and families.

Finally, the *Regional Catholics Initiative* engages in far-reaching activities designed to penetrate larger society and bring in a large harvest. This initiative might include a well-funded *Catholics Come Home* media campaign (www.catholicscomehome.org) combined with region-wide protocols to embrace and accompany those who respond. It might also include organized outreaches to troubled neighborhoods; multi-parish "come-and-see" events; large, regional repentance/conversion events, etc.

By its nature, the *Vision Achievement Process* is growth-oriented with each successive initiative building on the fruitfulness of the antecedent initiative(s). The *Purposeful Parishes Initiative* evangelizes parishes, moving them into working Christian communities that are stemming the exodus of people from the Church and transforming ordinary Catholics into deeply-converted Catholics. The ultimate milestone of the *Purposeful Parishes Initiative* is *net growth* in the number of registered Catholic who are actually showing up and demonstrating signs of personal conversion. These deeply-converted Catholics are transformed into evangelizers in the *Missionary Disciples Initiative* and these new missionary disciples begin intentionally sharing their faith in Jesus with those around them. The fruit of the missionary disciples are new Christian converts who are cultivated in RCIA (or an analogous process for the previously-baptized). In turn, these converts begin to multiply themselves as their children, grandchildren, friends, and others cultivate deep relationships with their Lord. Finally, when the number and maturity of missionary disciples has grown to the point of being capable of accompanying a large surge of growth, the *Regional Catholics Initiative* brings together the apparatus of the diocese and all the parishes into a unified effort to bring every person in the region into a personal, fruitful relationship with their Savior in the Church.

An important thing to understand about these four initiatives is that – once begun – they *never really end.* Each initiative has its own definable beginning that happens once the antecedent step(s) on which it depends has become well-established. Then, each initiative must continue on as a *permanent feature* in the life of the local Church. *In this sense, the initiatives are* <u>not</u> *discrete phases.* Even *after* the bishop has kicked-off and sustained a great evangelical movement, and *after all* the parishes in the diocese reform themselves into purposeful, dynamic communities of faith, and *after all* the missionary disciples are winning converts for Christ, and *after* the entire Church works together to convert the entire region, the continuing work of the Enemy will not cease. Moreover, human inertia, triumphalism, and all the ordinary distractions of life can force a reversion back to old ways without a firm commitment to sustain the Great Commission *in perpetuity.*

The Four-Step Cycle With the exception of the Episcopal Initiative, a 4-step cycle is imbedded within each of the remaining three initiatives. This cycle is depicted in Figure 7. Within each of these last three initiatives, the same four steps are cycled through multiple times on the way to a thoroughly evangelized region.

STEP 1 – PREPARE – has to do with the assessing, planning, and personal formation needed to evangelize fruitfully. Any endeavor worth doing requires planning and preparation and the work of the apostolate is usually no different. Since nothing happens in an historical vacuum, the assessing (or evaluating) aspect of Step 1 looks at what has already taken place, learns from it, and then plans. At the level of the individual, the "preparation" translates into "formation"; not just theological or ministerial formation, but also a deepening of one's own personal conversion. This personal formation in missionary spirituality and faith-sharing skills takes place regardless of who you are, although it has a somewhat different spin depending

Figure 7

THE 'FOUR-STEP CYCLE'

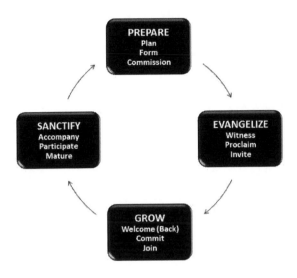

on your role in the Church – pastor, catechist, pastoral associate, engaged lay person, diocesan staff, etc. The content also changes depending on which *Initiative* you are in – *Purposeful Parishes, Missionary Disciple,* or *Regional Catholics.* At the completion of each formation period, the bishop formally *commissions* the "graduates" to establish that they have been truly "sent" by the Church into the work of evangelization (cf. Rom 10:15).

The actual work of evangelization begins in STEP 2, following naturally from the preparation step. The specifics of the *Witness-Proclaim-Invite* activities in the EVANGELIZE step will vary depending on which initiative one is participating in at the time. Obviously, the specific methods of witnessing, proclaiming, and inviting look very different depending on whether they happen in a letter from a pastor to an estranged parishioner – typical of the *Purposeful Parishes Initiative* – or between two close friends over coffee or on a street corner between two strangers – a work of *Missionary Disciples* – or in the ether of the airwaves watching a TV ad in the comfort of your family room – typical of the *Regional Catholics Initiative*.

In any case, STEP 2 leads into STEP 3: GROW. Responding to the work of evangelization in Step 2, *Welcome* may consist of the Sacrament of Reconciliation for one who is coming home to the Church after years away (in which case, it is really "Welcome Back"). But whether returning or quietly "trying out church" for the first time, it will involve a "welcome" attuned to the circumstances.

The entire *Vision Achievement Strategy* is ordered to a moment of decision on the part of the evangelized: a conscious decision to *COMMIT* one's life to our risen Lord, ideally in the Church. Once again, the *way* in which that commitment is elicited and the *way* the seeker makes the commitment depends on the circumstances of the strategic initiative and the individuals involved. That said, this commitment is a particularly important step, because outside of the *public* liturgical rites of the Church, we Catholics have a tendency not to ask for a *personal* decision to love Christ and put him first in our lives. While the RCIA's public moments of decision such as the Rite of Acceptance and Baptismal Promises can be extremely powerful, they can also be perfunctory and pressured. The same can be said for the Rite of Confirmation for catechized Catholic youth. The ultimate decision *should be* a big deal in our lives, one that stems from a personal recognition of the truth of God's amazing love and an uncoerced choice to love Him in return with all our heart, soul, mind, and strength (cf. Mt 22:37, Lk 10:27). This should happen in a

> This commitment is a particularly important step, because we Catholics have a tendency not to ask for a personal decision to love Christ and put him first in our lives

memorable personal setting sometime *before* public promises are given. This is particularly important in a culture that tends to delay or even avoid important commitments altogether.

Critical to STEP 3 is the seeker's entry or re-entry into the Church. (On the subject of "re-entry", see section entitled *Welcoming Catholics Home* later in this chapter.) The name for Step 3 – GROW – is appropriate for two reasons. First, the newcomer begins to *grow* in Christ. Second, all things being equal, the Church grows in number. While each person's decision to commit to Jesus is a personal moment, the Lord never leaves us isolated. The conversion of St. Paul illustrates the point. After our Lord dramatically revealed himself to Saul, he was led to Damascus where Ananias found him, ministered to his needs, and baptized him (cf. Acts 9:10-19). Luke recounts how Saul "stayed some days with the disciples in Damascus" (v 19b). Here is the precursor of the Rite of Christian Initiation of Adults (RCIA). No one can *join* the Mystical Body of Christ in isolation from others. There is always some kind of welcoming, orienting, and educating which culminates in formal recognition as part of the group.

Of course, this marks the *beginning* of life as a conscious Christian and hopefully not the beginning of the end, which all too often happens at the present time. Hence, STEP 4 – SANCTIFY – is what follows *after* joining. During the period in which a commitment to Christ is being considered and for a significant period of time thereafter the evangelizer or another trusted missionary disciple commits to *accompany* the newcomer in order to solidify her decision and help her grow in her fledgling relationship with our Savior as a member of the Church. For an extended time, thus big sister or brother must "be there" to accompany the convert/revert to the sacramental life, to be a friend through life's stresses and joys, to provide mature Christian guidance, and to fully incorporate one's friend into the daily life of the Church. (See *Creating the Ministry of Mentor* later in this chapter.)

There's more. The aim of SANCTIFY goes beyond the one-on-one relationship between the newcomer (i.e., neophyte, newly-received, or revert) and mentor. The end game is to solidify the newcomer's life in the Church through real *participation* in both the sacramental life of the Church, in service within the Church, and in outreach to those who may not be members of the Church. Ultimately, we are interested in the person's maturity as a Christian; in his becoming a saint.

While this marks the end of one four-step cycle, it is also the beginning of a new cycle. Once again, the Church *prepares* for this new cycle through planning. In this context, the term *Plan* should be understood as a serious evaluation of the cycle-just-ended. (See *Research: Getting It Better the Next Time* below.)

Splicing It All Together When the four initiatives and the four-step cycles are spliced together in a single graphic, a "high-altitude" view of the *Vision Achievement Strategy for Regional Evangelization* emerges, as shown in Figure 8.

Note that the three initiatives that follow from the *Episcopal Initiative* can be understood in terms of "target groups". The *Purposeful Parishes Initiative* is aimed at ordinary "Sunday Catholics" as well as marginal Catholics who are (or have been) loosely associated with the parish and/or school.

As this target group is solidified through the initiatives of the parishes, the growing number of formed missionary disciples take aim at the large number of individuals whom we might refer to as the "Distracted and Uncommitted". These may be our children, neighbors, and friends who have no particular animus against the message of Jesus, but who are so preoccupied with life's demands

Figure 8

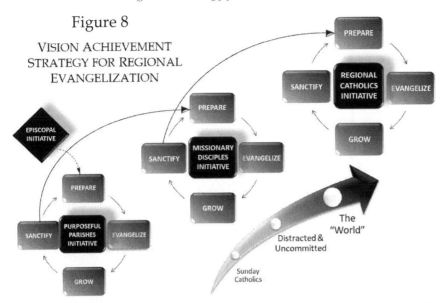

VISION ACHIEVEMENT
STRATEGY FOR REGIONAL
EVANGELIZATION

and distractions that commitment to Christ is not a high priority. The Distracted and Uncommitted may be Christmas-and-Easter-Catholics or they may be loosely associated with some other expression of Christianity, but are not seriously committed to Christ. They may also be 'nones' for no particular reason other than the fact that Christians have not yet loved them enough to lead them to Jesus.

Finally, the *Regional Catholics Initiative* is aimed at "the World". As used in this context, "the World" is understood in two senses: First, in the sense that our Lord used the term when he said, "In the *world* you will have trouble, but take courage, I have overcome the *world*" (Jn 16:33), and second, as the world that is outside the sphere of influence of most parishes and missionary disciples. In the first sense, the world is the domain of the secular culture where power often resides. It is antagonistic toward the Gospel, either because God and his Church represent a way of life that calls people away from sin or because of widespread misunderstandings about the teachings of the Church. In the second sense, the world is those masses of

239

people who for any number of reasons are living outside the ordinary influence of either the institutional Church or most missionary disciples in the United States. Examples of such populations might include certain low-income neighborhoods that may have been thriving Catholic communities a few generations ago, but have been largely left behind in recent times, now infested with gangs and drugs. Isolated, rural areas of the country might be another. This is the world that will need the benefit of creative media interventions or other highly visible apostolates.

The *Vision Achievement Strategy* envisions a succession of initiatives that begins small, working only within and through parishes...

In any event, the *Vision Achievement Strategy* envisions a succession of initiatives that begins small, working only within and through parishes. Over time, as the ecclesial culture changes and a growing number of Catholics begin to understand that being "Catholic" entails a conscious effort to spread the Good News in their personal lives, then the target group grows substantially to include everyone who can be reached in the ordinary lives of ordinary Catholics missionary disciples. Finally, as both human and financial resources grow, the target group expands to *everyone* residing or working in the region, some of whom live on the peripheries of society. Hopefully, as proposed in the first part of the book, the Church will ultimately undertake a systematic, united apostolate to evangelize at the national level.

... Next, the target group grows substantially to include everyone who can be reached in the ordinary lives of Catholic missionary disciples...

Staged Processes within a Larger Process The *Regional Strategy* presupposes that in many – if not all – cases the diocesan bishop will have to deal with circumstances that prevent moving all the parishes in the diocese along in perfect unison at the same time. Hopefully, this will not *always* be the case. However, in most episcopal sees, not every pastor will be willing or, for that matter, able to embrace the vision of regional evangelization. Others will be constrained by health and age. Diocesan financial constraints may be a

> ... Finally, as both human and financial resources grow, the target group expands to everyone residing or working in the region, some of whom live on the peripheries of society.

factor as well. Rather than force the matter on pastors who would only resent the *Strategy*, it is better to stagger the participation of the parishes, working first "with the willing" and gradually moving out to the others over time.

The Diffusion of Innovation Theory developed by E.M. Rogers in 1962 observed that only about 2.5 percent of a target population are willing to adopt an innovation immediately (which in many instances may be a good thing). These "innovators" are followed by "early adopters", who are opinion leaders that recognize the need for change and are willing to take a risk. According to Rogers, these early adopters represent about 13.5 percent of the population. In a series of cascading events, the "early adopters" are followed by the "early majority" (34 percent), the "late majority" (34 percent), and the "laggards" (16 percent). All of this follows the normal bell-shaped distribution.[85]

Recognizing this reality, in most dioceses the implementation of the *Vision Achievement Strategy* should be planned as multiple, staged processes moving forward within the context of the overarching meta-process. Each of these processes begins with a group of parishes moving through the *Purposeful Parishes Initiative*. Hopefully, key parishioners who are involved in these parish reforms are so energized that they will then move on to the *Missionary Disciples*

241

Initiative. At first, the number of participating parishes and missionary disciples may be small with only a few innovators and early adopters clearing the path for those to follow. Meanwhile, the *Purposeful Parishes Initiative* will continue to cycle through the "four steps" for the "early majority" and "late majority" parishes while the "innovators" and "early adopters" are sowing seeds and beginning to collect the harvest of their labors as missionary disciples. In time, enough parishes will be generating enough missionary disciples and mentors to accommodate the work and the fruits of the *Regional Catholics Initiative.*

The point is this: under the leadership of a bishop or succession of bishops who are not easily distracted by lesser matters, an evangelizing diocese will take time to establish. Notwithstanding, with prayer, leadership, and perseverance the number of the willing will grow and the bishop(s) can establish the expectation that within a reasonable number of years *all* the parishes will learn to evangelize and thousands of people will commit themselves to being missionary disciples.

As the Lord spoke through the prophet Zechariah: "… even those who were scornful on that day of small beginnings shall rejoice…" (Zech 4:10a). In any event, just as the Great Commission will never be finished until our Lord's Second Coming, the *Regional Vision Achievement Strategy* does not envision a time in the future when it will ever come to an end. The initiatives are iterated over time with successively growing numbers of parishes and individuals participating and with a growing number of people professing and living the Catholic Faith. In time, due to normal human inertia and changes in pastoral leadership, some of the early adopters will need a "retread" with the process beginning over.

Relation to a Diocesan Pastoral Plan The *Vision Achievement Strategy* is an example of a "*process plan*". A process plan "determines the sequence of operations or processes needed to produce a part or an assembly" [86] . Process planning is well understood in the manufacturing, design, and construction industries, but I have found that it is rarely understood in the Church.

By its nature, a *process plan* is different from the more-common diocesan pastoral plan. Pastoral plans normally have several goals and pastoral planning usually is consensus-driven. There are frequently many evenings devoted to town hall meetings and soliciting the opinions of all comers. The pastoral planning model of multiple open meetings makes sense given the fact that pastoral planning usually involves perceived needs that are *internal to the Church*; is implemented during a defined period of time, and; is updated every so many years.

The big difference between *process* planning and *pastoral* planning is that the former is much more constrained and, once it is established it typically does not change except in the details. As a *process*, the *Vision Achievement Strategy* should become a permanent feature in the life of the diocese. The only question should be: *Is the process achieving the desired goal?* Not: *What should our goals* (plural) *be for the next x years?* That said, the process is constantly being evaluated with lots of thought going on as to how it might be modified in its details to achieve the goal *better*.

The meeting of a group of contractors working together on a large construction project is an example of process planning. There is no question as to what they are building; just, how best to get it done on time and in budget. By contrast, pastoral planning tends to be more analogous to an architectural designer's charette, where the question is: *What shall we build?* In the context of regional evangelization planning, the goal is clear: Bring as many people as possible into a living, permanent relationship with Christ in the Church.

With this thought in mind, it is recommended that the *Regional Vision Achievement Strategy* be seen as distinct from the normal diocesan pastoral plan, which may only be updated once every so many years. Both may exist side-by-side and run parallel to one another.

Formation: Bootcamps for the Faithful

 We have to begin to multiply the small number of troops that are currently in place. Formation is the key to that multiplication process.

In Defense of Formal Formation In *Evangelii Gaudium* Pope Francis wrote: "… it would be insufficient to envisage a plan of evangelization to be carried out by professionals while the rest of the faithful would simply be passive recipients." [87] I understand his concern. Proclaiming the Gospel is the birthright, privilege, and responsibility we all received in our baptism. It really is the work of every Catholic. Pope Francis is right to have a concern about creating a cadre of "professional" evangelists, lest the rest of us use that as an excuse to let ourselves off the hook. In the very next paragraph, he also recognized the importance of training: "Of course, all of us are called to mature in our work as evangelizers. We want to have better training, a deeper love and a clearer witness to the Gospel."[88]

But, is there a place for formal preparation? Should we be concerned about knowing when and what to say during an evangelical moment? On the one hand Jesus said, "When they persecute you, do not worry about what to say, because the Holy Spirit will give you the words." (cf. Mt 10:19) True enough, but he had persecution in mind when he said that. Moreover, this fact remains: If Jesus was not convinced of the necessity of preparation for proclaiming the Gospel, it's difficult to explain why he spent so much time with his disciples apparently doing just that.

I suspect the disciples weren't much different from us in terms of their need for preparation and a degree of proficiency. The problem is that few of us ever think about sharing our faith, and if we do, we feel inadequate to the task. Perhaps, if we had grown up in an era of sound religious formation and apologetics, the feelings of inadequacy would not be so overwhelming. Regardless of that, it is difficult to imagine changing the entire culture of the Church first to accept evangelization as the responsibility of us all, and second, to become effective evangelizers without the Church making a huge investment in forming ordinary Catholics as evangelizers.

The fact is: It works. Those apostolates that have seriously invested in training evangelizers are now reaping the good harvest they have sown. The Fellowship of Catholic University Students (FOCUS) invests in months of training and spiritual formation for their campus missionaries before sending them out and the response has been stunning. Considering the fact that FOCUS has only been in existence since 1997, it is nothing short of amazing that their biennial SEEK gatherings today attract nearly 20,000 college students from all over the country. Many of these ordinary university students came to the Lord through the loving and *prepared* apostolate of the FOCUS missionaries and now they, in turn, are making converts of their friends.

Granted, the typical diocese would find it difficult to replicate what FOCUS does either in the time commitment or financial resources that FOCUS requires. Moreover, they probably shouldn't try, since college campuses are not typical American workplaces or social settings where the great majority of the population lives out their lives. Nonetheless, FOCUS has much to offer the larger Church. In addition, ministries such as St. Paul Street Evangelization (streetevangelization.com), Mission of the Redeemer Ministries missionoftheredeemer.com), the Catherine of Siena Institute

245

(siena.org), and a few others are great evangelist formation resources aimed at adults who are longing to learn how to share the Faith and accompany others into Christian maturity.

The Common Elements of Formation The *Vision Achievement Strategy* envisions three formation processes, one for each of the initiatives.

- Formation to create *Purposeful Parishes*.
- Formation to build up the army of *Missionary Disciples*.
- Formation for leadership roles in the *Regional Catholics Initiative*

Each of the three formation processes should contain content that is unique to that particular initiative. At the same time, there are elements that are common to all three initiatives. These common elements include:

† **Advancement in our own personal conversion** to Christ through the Eucharist, Eucharistic adoration, daily personal prayer and Scripture, and periodic fasting

† **Liberation and healing** from habitual sins and the deep wounds that often accompany these sins through the routine reception of the sacraments of Penance and, when needed, Healing of the Sick. Prayers of Deliverance may also be a part of this.

† **Cultivation of a missionary spirituality** through readings and lectures

† **Fellowship** experienced in both small groups and larger community contexts

† **Commissioning** by the bishop at the completion of the formation

The Rationale for Commissioning The formal commissioning by the bishop serves at least two purposes. Firstly, Catholic laity as a rule do not feel *authorized* to share their faith. One of the negative aspects of clericalism that permeates Catholic culture is the sense that anything of a specifically religious nature is the sole purview of the clergy and religious; trained lay ecclesial ministers may be considered acceptable. Typically, the laity's self-perception is that they are not duly authorized to share the Gospel or otherwise represent the Church outside of tightly scripted liturgical ministries. Although the ecclesiology of the Second Vatican Council stressed the "priesthood of the laity" arising out of our baptism, this ontological reality has not deeply pierced lay consciousness or identity. However, following a period of formation, public commissioning of the participants can help to bring about that consciousness. Furthermore, it has the psychological effect of officially authorizing and, thereby, obligating the participant to a life of evangelization.

Secondly, Catholics generally do not feel *qualified* to share their faith. We live in a world of specialists and accreditation. If you do not have the creds, you don't have a right to provide the service. The fact that we have certain qualifications by virtue of baptism and confirmation *ex opere operato* is not widely appreciated. Once again, commissioning has the effect of conferring credentials or bringing out those creds people may not even know they have.

We do nothing significant in the Church on our own authority. The Church has always had a concern about itinerant preachers "out there" doing things on their own. One of the earliest inklings of this concern can be found in St. Paul's Letter to the Romans when he wrote:

> ... how can they call on him in whom they have never believed? And how can they believe in him of whom they have never heard? And how can they hear without someone to preach? And how can people preach unless they are sent? (v14-15a)

When all is said and done, the episcopal commissioning should be thought of as a formal "sending" of well-prepared missionaries into the world.

That said, a reasonable argument *against* commissioning well-formed evangelizers is that it can have the effect of elevating the status of the *commissioned,* thus providing a convenient excuse to others for demurring from their baptismal obligation to share the faith. It could be viewed as creating a new quasi-clerical caste, which is exactly what the formation is attempting to obviate. In my opinion, commissioning has more advantages than disadvantages when one considers that the excuse-makers are usually so marginal in their faith life that they would not even consider evangelizing anyway. In the end, it will be up to the diocesan bishop to weigh these arguments and make the call.

Planning Implementation of the *Strategy*

Having said that the *Vision Achievement Strategy for Regional Evangelization* is not a *program,* it *is* 'programmatic'; it is an orderly, long-range, systematic process comprised of common-sense, progressive steps designed to lead to a fully-evangelized particular Church and regional population. However, within the broad parameters of the *Strategy* there may be great variation from one diocese to the next.

You may think of the *Strategy* as a freshly-cut fir tree waiting for Christmas ornaments to be hung. Any fir tree has a trunk, it has branches, it has a recognizable shape; but there are thousands of ornaments and a variety of lighting schemes that can be hung on the tree. Once fully decorated, each tree is beautiful and unique, but they all are recognizable as Christmas trees. Insofar as there is a wide array of Christmas ornaments and decorating schemes, many families decorate their tree *as a family.* In the same way, the diocesan bishop needs to collaborate with others committed lay and clerical disciples on planning the details of the *Strategy*. The only thing that is *not* up for discussion is the "kind of tree to be decorated". We are talking here about planning for the evangelization and conversion of an entire region, *not* some other worthy goal. Clarity on this point is crucial.

As to the specifics of the planning, numerous decisions will have to be made, to cite just a few:

- For the *Purposeful Parishes Initiative,* how many and which parishes should be in the first cohort?

- How long should the formation period for the *Purposeful Parishes Initiative* run?

- How many people should be in the first formation 'class' and how should they be recruited/selected?

- What should the *specific* content include and how should the formation meetings be divided between personal spiritual formation and ministerial formation?

- Who will be the primary formators (aside from the bishop)?

- What specific actions should be included in the first year of the *EVANGELIZE* step?

- What performance standards and possibly even quantifiable metrics might be used for evaluating each initiative and each of the four steps that comprise an initiative?

- What should we use as performance milestones before moving the *Strategy* to the next initiative?

Research: Getting It Better the Next Time Regardless of how these and other questions are answered, the planning should always be as much about *pre-* and *post-facto* analysis and critical evaluation of the steps that have already been taken as they are about what should happen next. In fact, planning for the next cycle should not be finalized until evaluation of the last steps has taken place. The Church is in this for the long haul and needs to learn from what we have done "wrong" in order to adjust the process and do it better the next time. I can't help but think of the adage often proffered by a Scripture professor I once had during my deacon formation: *God's people deserve only the best.*

For this reason, a commitment to serious, long-range, empirical research is important. For example, research is the only way to get a handle on what has been effective during missionary disciple formation in strengthening the participants' ability to share their faith? Research will also be needed to learn what aspects of our youth programs and Confirmation preparation helped to keep young adults in the Church ten years after they were confirmed? Accordingly, for some purposes, observing Mass attendance numbers before and after a particular outreach may be very helpful in evaluating its fruitfulness. In other cases, *pre-* and *post-action* surveys may be needed.[89]

The Short-Range Tactical Plan As stated earlier, the *Vision Achievement Strategy* has a very long-range horizon. Within this long-range perspective, a four-step cycle can take from 1 to 7-or-8 years, depending on the initiative, the size of the diocese, and the resources that are available. Moreover, different formation processes can be going on simultaneously. For example, there may be 4 or 5 parishes in the *Purposeful Parishes Initiative* while parishes that got started earlier have their people moving through the *Missionary Disciples* formation process. As one would expect in an undertaking as ambitious as the thoroughgoing evangelization of an entire region, let it suffice to say, there are a lot of moving parts.

Consequently, a short-range *Tactical Plan* is needed to manage the implementation of all the details. The *Tactical Plan* breaks down all of these activities into bite-sized, *manageable pieces that can be achieved in one year.* Tactical planning meetings should be held about once a quarter between the bishop and key evangelization staff to: (1) keep track of and report on the progress of all the "moving parts"; (2) identify delays and other obstacles, and; (3) to decide on remedial steps to get things back on track or, if necessary, revise expectations. Without this tactical perspective, communications will break down and the needed remedies never provided.

Subjects of Concern in All the Initiatives

 Before focusing in a little more depth on each of the four initiatives, two subjects of concern that are common to all the initiatives are highlighted in this section to call attention to them as special needs. They are deserving of particular attention because of the outsized effect they have on the subject of regional evangelization.

Welcoming Catholics Home If we were to liken Catholic evangelization to the task of fishermen "hauling in the catch", the job is complicated by fact that the "fish" have to be sorted by "species". The various species may include 'nones', members of other world religions, non-Catholic Christians, Catholics who were never fully initiated (e.g., baptized and perhaps childhood receivers of the Eucharist, but non-Confirmed), fully-initiated Catholics who have been away from the Church for many years, and former Catholics who are desirous of returning. Added to all these "species", there is the additional question of whether or not the individual has been divorced and civilly re-married.

About the only thing that they all have in common is that they are in some stage of opening themselves up to a deeper relationship with Christ. In the U.S., there are literally millions of inactive or lapsed Catholics who have never ceased thinking of themselves as "Catholic". Among these, many who return prefer not to be openly

251

identified as having lapsed in the practice of their faith and want to come home with as little fanfare as possible. Others recognize that they are at the brink of the most important decision of their lives and they are thirsting for an entirely new identity in the community.

For this last group, it seems to me that we would do well to adapt an individual approach to their return and avoid the "we've-always-done-it-this-way" mentality. After all, when a person returns to Church after many years away, they are taking a big step. From a strictly juridical standpoint, they are just putting things back in order; a sincere Confession and return to Sunday Mass will do. From the perspective of their heart and will, this is their *conversion*. Often, it is the *first* time they have made an intentional, adult step toward God. In these cases, to call them a *revert* is a bit of a misnomer. They are not really reverting back to anything. They are embarking on something entirely new and our objective should be to facilitate and celebrate it to the fullest extent that we can. If the individual wants to publicly solemnize his "reversion" in some way, there should be a way for that to happen.

In any event, isolation is not the answer. Sometimes the way back is so private that only one person other than the revert herself knows it: her confessor. Not being a priest, I have no way of knowing how often this happens. But when it does, if the process begins and ends in the confessional, there is no open acknowledgement of it. In the grace of the sacrament, the penitent is indeed reconciled with the Church. By her participation in the Holy Eucharist, her re-unification with the Body of Christ becomes visible. However, as essential as these graces are, the revert is left up to her own resources and resolve as to whether or not she will take further steps toward serious participation and maturation in the Faith.

All of the above-mentioned "species" of converts have at least the potential for pursuing a public conversion process that involves the larger community: the Rite of Christian Initiation for Adults (RCIA), either as an "inquirer-catechumen" or an "inquirer-candidate". (I hope the reader will overlook my loose phraseology.) For the revert whose re-entry into the Church is exclusively through Confession and the Holy Eucharist, there is no formally-sanctioned path to a public declaration of faith aside from reciting the Creed along with everyone else.

While this may be all anyone needs to meet the minimum standards of membership in good standing, if we want to actively pursue the return of inactive Catholics, anything that we can do to publicly solemnize that return could only serve to reinforce it and enhance the chance that the "revert" is returning home "to stay".

Unfortunately, the *General Instruction of the Roman Missal* seems to prohibit any ritual deviations during Mass (cf. GIRM, 24). Accordingly, a public liturgical rite similar to the Rite of Acceptance during Mass is not a possibility without the Conference of Bishops receiving permission from the Holy See for *recognitio* of a new rite. To make the matter more problematic, a priest-friend recently reminded me that in this age of questioning the seal of confession, it would be particularly awkward for a pastor who may have heard the penitent's confession to preside at a public rite that acknowledges his return.

One possibility worth considering is the bishop under his own authority offering a blessing outside of Mass for all returning Catholics on a designated date who have received Confession or perhaps are even considering such a step. In any event, serious regional evangelization warrants some thinking outside the box.

Confessors faced with the quandary of how to provide outside support and encouragement for the returning penitent might encourage him (during Confession) to contact a priest or pastoral associate who can help him take appropriate next steps in his faith formation and service in the Church.

Creating the Ministry of "Mentor" One of the most serious needs
 in the RCIA as it is lived out in the United States is
for godparents and sponsors to be mature
disciples who can really serve as a role model for
the newcomer. Unfortunately, in my experience,
godparents and sponsors who are also mature disciples are the
exception rather than the rule.

Before the Church can effectively evangelize in the most fruitful
way possible, pastoral leadership should go to great lengths to
identify, recruit, and train spiritually mature and balanced
missionary disciples in the parish for the ministry of *accompanying* the
newcomer for as long as it takes to solidify her conversion. I would
recommend further that these individuals be *commissioned to a new,
special ministry of "mentor"* and then *"matched"* in a one-on-one
pairing with each of the catechumens/candidates. These mentors
must invest themselves in cultivating sincere friendships with their
catechumen/candidate/neophyte and, over an indefinite period of
time, cultivate a sense of responsibility for their growth into mature
disciples who may eventually be able to mentor others. They should
concern themselves with *all* aspects of discipleship: friendship,
spiritual growth, catechetical knowledge, and a commitment to
Christian service.

Serious, mature discipleship – which is too often ignored in the
catechumenate – is the ultimate measure of evangelical success, since
it requires a serious commitment to the good of others. As our Lord
put it: "Not all those who say 'Lord, Lord' will enter the kingdom of
heaven, but only the one who does the will of my Father." (Mt 7:21)

In the current state of the Church, this mentor – who will "stay"
with the neophyte long after Easter Vigil – should typically be
someone other than the godparent or sponsor. Often, the "official"
sponsor or even the "evangelizer" who led the convert into the

catechumenate has different gifts than are needed for the ministry of mentoring or that person may simply lack the personal maturity to help a person grow as a Catholic over a sustained period of time.

I have experienced that failure in myself. A number of years ago, I sponsored a young woman (a baptized Christian) in the RCIA. She went through the RCIA process, made her profession of Faith, was confirmed, received the Eucharist, and underwent a *very brief* period of Mystagogy. Unfortunately, I lapsed in my commitment to her as a spiritual mentor and in less than a year, she was coaxed back out of the Church.

In any event, Sherry Weddell, author of *Making Intentional Disciples*, one of the most influential contemporary books on Catholic evangelization, points out the same need. Referring to the important role of Ananias in the conversion of St. Paul (cf. Acts 9:10-19), she asks:

> How can we call forth and form "Ananiases," that is spiritual companions to walk with and mentor new and renewed disciples? Because we have learned that in the absence of discipleship-centered Christian community, even the most independent and committed Catholics cannot flourish, and they begin to wither – and even leave.[90]

Fortunately, since she wrote these words, Weddell has created a formation process for "Ananiases" through the Catherine of Siena Institute. Bishops who are deeply concerned about evangelization would do well to look into this or a similar ministry. In the Church of the future, it should be a goal of the formation processes imbedded in the *Vision Achievement Strategy* to produce enough mature missionary disciples that no seeker will have difficulty finding a mentor who will walk with them through the stages of conversion and into committed discipleship themselves.

* * *

Drilling into the *Episcopal Initiative*

The Announcement The *Regional Strategy for Vision Achievement* begins with the bishop making an announcement. Among the "resolutions" for diocesan bishops offered in Chapter II is his announcement that evangelization is to become his "highest personal priority" and "the highest priority of the entire local Church". The stark clarity of the announcement cannot be overemphasized. It is a demarcation between past and future. It kicks off the beginning of a new era. It serves as a policy "reboot" of the ecclesial system if you will. The *public nature* of the announcement is critical, because as the highest priority, the bishop

Episcopal Initiative

Aim:

To stimulate and sustain widespread regional evangelization through the impetus of the diocesan bishop and his leadership team

is effectively announcing that every decision from that moment forward must use the spread of the Gospel as the #1 criterion for adjudicating whatever the issue *du jour* happens to be. Other considerations may enter in, but "the mission of the Church" is #1 (cf. *Evangelii nuntiandi*, 14). The announcement simplifies the *modus operandi* of the Church. Given any particular decision that needs to be made, the question should be: *Might "it" have an impact on the proclamation of the Gospel?* If so, then the next question should be: *How can we do "it" so that "it" enhances the proclamation of the Gospel?*

This *announcement of highest-priority* is also fraught with symbolic significance. Unless contradicted by the bishop himself, it signals the bishop as the leader of evangelization within his diocese. The great evangelical movements at work in the Church today can all point to a specific individual as their founder and leader. Examples that leap to mind include Curtis Martin, leader of the *Fellowship of Catholic University Students* (FOCUS), Ralph Martin, leader of *Renewal Ministries*, Dave Nodar, leader of *ChristLife*, Steve Dawson, leader of *St. Paul Street Evangelization*. Still, the *bishop's* announcement is different from the genesis of all these wonderful movements insofar as he is the leader of the entire Church in a particular region and, by virtue of that position, he is *announcing the normalization of evangelization throughout* the Church, not merely announcing a movement *within* the Church for those who may feel specially-called to share the Gospel.

The *Episcopal Initiative,* however, goes well beyond a one-time announcement, a kind-of cornerstone once laid and then forgotten. The announcement portends a fresh start; a public process of regret, repentance, and conversion; but also, a dividing line between fatalism and hope, a beginning filled with anticipation and expectation that the Holy Spirit can and will change us.

Episcopal leadership is imbedded throughout the *Vision Achievement Strategy,* leading it and supporting it for the duration. As Figure 9 highlights, there are at least three ways in which the diocesan bishop infuses the entire process of regional evangelization.

- First-and-foremost, he leads in prayer by establishing a diocese-wide prayer movement in support of the conversion of the region
- Second, he leads by inspirational personal example
- Finally, he unambiguously pursues evangelization as his own highest priority

Diocesan Prayer Movement Over three decades ago when the number of men entering the seminary in America practically dried up, our local bishop requested people to commit themselves to pray for priestly and religious vocations. There was a gratifying response to this request. Holy hours started being scheduled in many parishes,

Figure 9
THE EPISCOPAL INITIATIVE

votive masses were celebrated, and much more. Some of those prayer times remain in existence today. While our diocese could still use more priests and religious, the situation is dramatically better now than it was then. In fact, four young men were ordained priests for our diocese just this year (an unheard-of event in recent times). I am convinced that much of the credit for the increase in vocations can be traced back to the humble people who began interceding in response to the bishop's appeal.

Suppose in your own particular Church, a new prayer initiative was launched at this point in history for the evangelization and conversion of people who are lost in sin and living without reference to God? I have no doubt that in time we could expect a fresh move of the Holy Spirit and many changed lives. Moreover, in my view, the purpose of the prayer movement should be expanded to include discernment of the Lord's will for regional evangelization in all of its specifics, as well as reparation for the many sins of the Church and the world at large.

Perhaps, a general intercession could be added to the Prayers of the Faithful at every weekend Mass "for the conversion and salvation of souls" throughout the region. It is an indictment of the Church that our general intercessions include prayers for every kind of human suffering, but rarely, if ever, for the conversion and salvation of those who perpetrate serious personal

> It is an indictment of the Church that our general intercessions include prayers for every kind of human suffering, but rarely, if ever, for the conversion and salvation of those who perpetrate serious personal sins.

sins and often contribute to all the other human suffering. The bottom line is this: Some people – we can never say who – are almost certainly in the process of consigning themselves to Hell. We are not doing much to show the Lord that we really care. As the Mystical Body of Christ, we know that our prayer and fasting have a powerful impact on the lives of people, in the opposite way that our sins do (cf. Gen 18:16-33, Ex 17:12-14). We need people seriously committed to praying.

In addition to individual prayer warriors, religious communities and existing lay prayer groups should be contacted and expressly invited to dedicate themselves on a daily basis to the bishop's prayer movement. Examples of such groups may include the Legion of Mary, Third Order Carmelites, perpetual adoration groups, *Cursillo* reunion groups, charismatic prayer communities, etc. Shut-ins, the sick and/or elderly would be invited to offer their pain, loneliness, and sense of uselessness in this great movement of redemptive suffering and reparation for the heinous sins committed every day even within our own communities (cf. Col 1:24).

Transformational Episcopal Leadership Since this is a key focus of the next chapter, little will be said about it here. Let it suffice to say at this point that a key aspect of the *Episcopal Initiative* requires a no-holds-barred self-evaluation of how effectively the diocesan bishop is leading. *Spoiler Alert:* According to perhaps the most rigorous study of transformational leadership, I would say that most bishops possess several – though not all – the qualities needed to lead their dioceses into great evangelical fruitfulness. It will take work. To a great extent, the success of that work will depend on whether or not bishops *give themselves permission to be heroically holy leaders,* rather than the stereotype they believe is expected of them. It will be up to the rest of us to encourage and support them in that effort.

Highest-Priority Commitment to Evangelization As observed earlier, evangelization is not yet mainstreamed as a normal activity in the Church – either at the personal level or corporately. It will only be considered "normal" when sharing the Faith becomes a commonly-understood aspect of what it means to be a good Catholic; just as participation in the sacraments, personal prayer, service, and financial support of one's parish are all considered "ordinary" aspects of being a serious Catholic. Infusing a high priority into what most Catholics consider the esoteric concern of a few specialists will require a high-priority commitment on the part of the bishop.

Making evangelization one's highest personal priority is one thing. Making it the highest priority of the local Church is another. By itself, the announcement may be viewed as only one more unwelcome mandate, and by itself, prayer can become an excuse for inaction. A true highest-priority commitment to evangelization will entail several episcopal actions, such as the following:

- To recognize and legitimize the longings of "the willing"
- To create a permanent Bishop's Evangelization Advisory Group,
- To prioritize through normalizing,

- To create a culture of accountability, and
- To permanently fund evangelization

Recognize and legitimize the longings of "the willing" In Christ's time, there was a strong messianic current within Judaism. From the time of the Babylonian Captivity, the people of God had been subjected to one foreign power after the next and they were longing for the advent of their savior. Many were *expecting* the arrival of the messiah. They

> There are those who *are willing* to do far more for the Gospel than is being asked of them. Identify who they are. Legitimize their longing. Ask for their help.

had read the apocalyptic words of Daniel 7 which were interpreted by some as pointing to that general period of history in which the Christ would make his appearance. But, regardless of whether or not they believed the time was near at hand, they had a strong yearning for it.

We live in a similar time today. Christianity has been rejected, is maligned and increasingly oppressed by secular powers. The Catholic Church's convictions about sexual morality, social justice, and plain old civility have been replaced by personal libertarianism, extreme individualism, growing violence, societal polarization, and derision towards those who hold countervailing views. Some even seem to be intent on open, hateful rebellion against the very Person of Christ and his Mother. At the same time, we remember very well the impassioned appeals of all our recent popes for a "new evangelization" and what seemed to be the expectation of St. Pope John Paul II for a "springtime of hope" in the twenty-first century.

Many priests and lay faithful have a deep longing for that new springtime. They are doing what they can within their own areas of influence, but feel stymied by what they perceive as ambivalence or confusion from ecclesiastical leaders.

Perhaps the most immediately fruitful thing a bishop can do at this point in history is to recognize who these people are, bring them together, and legitimate the longing of their hearts. There are those who *are willing* to do far more for the Gospel than is being asked of them. *Identify who they are. Legitimize their longing. Ask for their help. Then, bring them together into a formation process for missionary disciples and, in some cases, into a working unit.*

Create a Regional Evangelization Leadership Team To ensure that evangelization is sustained over time as Priority #1, it needs to become a part of the formal institutional framework of the Diocese. One of the most important steps a bishop can take is to create of a high-level working *Regional Evangelization Leadership Team* that is made a permanent part of the diocesan organization chart.

Although not a creature of canon law like the diocesan Finance Council that provides an independent source of accountability for financial matters (Can 492) or a diocesan Pastoral Council for consultation on pastoral matters (Can 511-514), the *Regional Evangelization Leadership Team* can serve an equally vital role. From an organizational standpoint, it would make sense if membership in the *Team* partially overlaps with the bishop's College of Consultors (Can 502) and the diocesan Pastoral Council.

The recommended functions of the *Team* include:

- Assessing the diocese's progress toward established regional evangelization performance criteria and metrics
- Creative brainstorming and new idea development
- A low-keyed form of accountability for ensuring the bishop maintains ongoing focus on regional evangelization
- Friendship and support for the bishop during the tough times

- Research into best practices and periodic analysis of related data
- Evaluation of the strengths and weaknesses of a just-completed cycle
- Planning improvements for an upcoming cycle

The members of the *Team* should be so highly-respected that they genuinely serve as leaders in the diocese. Meetings need to be disciplined and run on time. They should report on the progress of parishes, formators, schools, youth and campus ministries as well as the bishop's progress on his own roles in the *Vision Achievement Strategy*.

The Regional Evangelization Leadership Team (or simply, *the Team*) is to become the bishop's primary group of evangelical Catholic advisors and leaders, at least by example and influence, if not by formal authority.

The *Team* should be the most mature and talented lay and clerical disciples of Jesus in the regional Church. Its priest-members must be among the most-enthusiastic pastors in the presbyterate; men whom the bishop respects and considers friends. Their presence is absolutely essential, even if they have to drop other commitments in order to become a member.

Barring unusually preclusive circumstances, the pastors on the *Team* should be prepared to be the first to shepherd their own parishes through the *Purposeful Parishes Initiative*. Subsequently, they will become the cheer leaders and informal coaches for future pastors who get involved in the *Initiative*.

Lay involvement should comprise a significant portion of the *Team*. The initial group of lay members should include individuals who are likely to be included in the first cohort of *commissioned missionary disciples*. At least some of them should be on the team responsible for helping to form other missionary disciples in the future. (See the discussion on missionary disciples later in this chapter.)

Each of the members – lay and clergy – should be very goal-oriented and in possession of wide experience in the grass roots of at least one of the following areas: pastoral ministry, family life, and/or business. In other words, they need to bring something significant to the table from the various milieu in which most personal evangelization takes place. They need to be creative, "can-do" people who believe in the singular importance of evangelization in all its aspects; who are willing to embrace the *Vision Achievement Strategy* and participate in its implementation, plan its details, and humbly evaluate its outcomes.

Together, the *Team* will form a small community supporting each other as brothers and sisters, with the bishop not only as a spiritual father, but in another sense, as a brother as well. In return for their commitment, they will receive the best formation available at the expense of the diocese; for priests and deacons, formation aimed at best practices in parish renewal and ministry; for laity, missionary disciple formation as evangelizers.

Prioritizing through Normalizing In a *maintenance-driven culture*, there are no priorities. Since the working assumption in a maintenance-driven culture is that everything is as it should be, the very act of prioritizing one value or aspect of work over another is a threat to the *status quo*. In a *vision-driven culture*, the goal is to normalize policies and practices that support the desired vision.

What this means in the case of prioritizing evangelization is that all other important policies, values, and work must become subservient to the missing feature of the culture that needs to become normalized. This does not necessarily mean that all the other commitments of the diocese need to become *un*important, although a few of them may need to. It is more a matter of incorporating evangelization-related objectives into all of those other commitments. Finding the right questions to ask is critical. For example,

- Liturgists might ask: How can we do liturgy and what music can we select that helps to remind the assembly of Jesus' sacrificial offering for them?

- Pastors and pastoral councils should consider asking: Who has the potential to lead evangelization in the parish and who have the gifts to help these leaders?

- Priests should ask: How can I preach so as to elicit a firm commitment to love and follow Jesus in response to what he has done for me on the cross and the altar?

- Comptrollers and diocesan finance councils need to find ways to carve evangelization budgets out of existing operating funds (a painful process) and pursue grants for new funds.

- Catechists and religious education teachers need to decide: How can we convey the Incarnation and *kērygma* as the very heart of all Christian truths?

- Event planners need to ask how to convey the message of God's personal love for all who will attend any of their events.

- Foundation boards need to ask how to encourage long-term giving to permanently endow the work of evangelization.

- The bishop and evangelization staff need to ask: What criteria can we use as benchmarks for evangelical progress in our own work? In the parishes? How can we form thousands of passionate missionary disciples throughout the rank-and-file Catholic population of the region?

Over time, a focus on these and similar questions will help to normalize evangelization in the culture of the local Church.

Create a Culture of Accountability: Faithful → Bishop In my experience, the idea of parish-level accountability to the bishop for anything other than the annual diocesan appeal and canonically-required sacramental statistics is usually not well-received, especially by pastors and pastoral councils who have been overly influenced by a congregational decision-making model and overly "Americanized" by the anti-authority ethos of our culture. As a result, it seems that the only way many bishops hear about what is going on in their parishes is from the continuous stream of complaint letters they are forced to read. At this point in history, a greater degree of parish reporting to the bishop about their evangelistic activities is both warranted and reasonable. This could be implemented in any number of ways, three of which are mentioned below:

- requesting parishes or parish clusters to respond to relevant "normalizing evangelization" questions;
- establishing clear parish objectives for conforming to the *Vision Achievement Strategy*, and;
- following up at appointed times to review the responses and progress *vis-à-vis* the objectives.

For example, suppose the bishop requests the responses to the above parish-related questions in accordance with certain guidelines for the first year of the *Purposeful Parishes Initiative*. Accordingly, in response to the bishop's request St. Athanasius – a 2,000-member parish – assembles a music/liturgy team, a priests/deacons' preaching team, and a catechesis team to respond to the "normalization questions". Furthermore, they establish the clear objectives of: training and scheduling a 2-person welcoming team at every weekend Mass; recruiting ten parish leaders for in-depth missionary disciple formation/training (to be provided by the diocese); and organizing a couple-to-couple faith-sharing ministry with two mature mentor-couples who meet regularly with engaged or newlywed couples. Finally, the pastor commits to meeting personally with each newly-registered member (typically, about 30-per-year) and inviting them to the next *Christ Renews His Parish Weekend*. All reasonably achievable and consistent with a first-year *PREPARE* step in the *Purposeful Parishes Initiative*. Not every parish will respond as faithfully as St. Ath, but over time the discipline of knowing that an accounting is required and being expected to communicate with the bishop's office will gradually move the recalcitrant parishes in the right direction (and/or to early retirements).

Create a Culture of Accountability: Bishop → Faithful

Historically, it has been difficult to broach the subject of episcopal accountability, since bishops function without a board of directors and are canonically answerable only to the pope. As recent events have brought to light, accountability really needs to be a two-edged sword. While parishes and other institutional subsets of the Church owe accountability to the bishop, there is also the matter of the bishop's accountability to the Church. It is relatively easy for a bishop to commit privately to God that he will make evangelization his highest personal priority. It is more difficult to make a public announcement to that effect. With the announcement, he is at least on-record. It is even more difficult to repeat the pledge over-and-over again and to institutionalize a mechanism to ensure a bishop will remain accountable for his repeated pledges.

While most U.S. bishops seem to have made some kind of provision for evangelization in their diocesan organization charts, it is often unclear what these "departments" or "offices" do. Unlike the catechetical function of a diocese with a well-known constituency among parish-level directors of education and Catholic schools, evangelization does not have an analogous constituency at the parish level. Rarely are there evangelization staffs or even passionate champions in all but a handful of parishes. I am not necessarily advocating for the catechetical model as the solution to this problem, although that would be an improvement over the current situation.

The current deficiency of episcopal accountability for evangelization seems to be due to a combination of cultural laxity and uncertainty about how to evangelize at the diocesan level and support local evangelization efforts. No doubt, part of the problem derives from uncertainty about how to be accountable for activities that do not often produce a known outcome. A diocesan trainer, for instance, can advertise for a training session that only three people show up for. That said, those three people may go out and turn the world upside down, whereas twenty lukewarm people may not accomplish anything.

The U.S. Bishops recognized the problem of a lack of diocesan support as early as 1992, when they wrote *Go and Make Disciples: A National Plan and Strategy for Evangelization in the United States*. Since that time, many bishops have, in fact, provided some kind of institutional status to the work of evangelization within their organizations. In a random sample of 45 American (Latin Rite) diocesan websites, 31 (or sixty-nine percent) demonstrated at least some organizational commitment to evangelization on their websites (sometimes without using the word "evangelization"). That's the good news. The bad news is that 14 (or 31 percent) demonstrated absolutely no commitment to evangelization, even though almost three decades have elapsed since the USCCB published the above statement.[91] Moreover, where evangelization staffs do exist, it is not uncommon for them to be used as jacks-of-all-trades for handling the bishop's special projects or other business that does not fall clearly under the charge of another department.

The Regional Evangelization Leadership Team is one way the bishop can exercise greater accountability to the local Church for his own evangelical leadership. Reporting his activities in the diocesan paper and/or e-news is another. Ultimately, the episcopal and diocesan staff evangelization work should be evaluated as part-and-parcel of the *PREPARE* step of the *Four-Step Cycle* and Tactical Planning Meetings.

Permanently Fund Evangelization Any culture – ecclesiastical or secular – has many facets and one of these facets is financial. Endowments are a good indicator of the financial aspect of our Catholic culture; they are a measure of what we value. While I am not an expert on the range of endowments one can find in a typical diocesan Catholic Foundation, my impression is that endowments expressly established for unambiguously evangelistic work are exceedingly rare.

Some Catholic philanthropic foundations have modified their goals in recent years to consider grant applications for evangelistic projects, which is a step in the right direction. However, in order for evangelization to become mainstreamed in our Catholic culture, a diocesan bishop should give serious thought to putting out a "call" to the well-heeled laity in his diocese to solicit funds for a substantial endowment to support the evangelistic activities of the diocese. Such calls are made periodically for seminary education funds, priest retirement funds, special building projects, and the like. This is not to suggest that annual operating budgets should not include a strong evangelization component. Clearly, they should. However, as bishops come and go, priorities may change, and along with them budgets and organization charts. Endowments with clearly-stated donor intent statements remain.

Outside of foreign mission fields and some impoverished domestic dioceses, proclaiming the Gospel to the non-Christians in our midst ceased to be a lived priority at some point in the history of the Church in the United States. Diocesan evangelization endowments can help to ensure that such a thing never happens again.

* * *

Drilling into the *Purposeful Parishes Initiative*

 Once it has "sunk in" that the bishop is serious about evangelizing his region of the country, the *Purposeful Parishes Initiative* will become the lynchpin for the ultimate success of that goal. Just as there is no way for evangelization to be taken seriously by the Church without the impetus of the bishop, there is no way for it to become normalized in the life of the Church without the enthusiastic participation of

> The quickest route to growth in the Church is to halt the attrition

the parishes. Without the parishes, the "army" of missionary disciples needed to carry the message into the world will never grow beyond a platoon.

As mentioned earlier, there are over six persons leaving the Catholic Church in America for every Catholic convert. At this rate, by far the quickest route to reversing this ratio is to halt the attrition, especially among our young people. Accordingly, a conscious, concerted effort must be made at the parish-level to repair the leaks in the ship. If former Catholics had "found" our Lord in the Church, it is a safe bet that most of them would never have left. Unfortunately, they often didn't. Accordingly, the first priority of the *Purposeful Parishes Initiative* is to remake parishes into communities of faith where people are intentionally introduced to Christ, where they are

270

given opportunities to accept him as their Lord at a personal level, where they can get to know him and fall in love with him. Much of this effort must be directed toward youth, who research has shown are leaving at surprisingly young ages. If we can do this, the reasons for ever leaving in the future will be greatly diminished.

The second aim of this initiative is to raise awareness among believing Catholics that – as Christians – they have an *urgent obligation* to our Lord to introduce him to others. In other words, parishes can no longer be content to be cozy clubs organized and

Purposeful Parishes Initiative
Aims:

To bring unevangelized parishioners into a conscious personal relationship with Jesus

To imbue a missionary spirit into parishioners' self-understanding

To transform parishes into welcoming communities

To engage in acts of parish evangelization, accompaniment, and outreach

sustained just for their members. They have a *purpose* beyond their own wants and desires (however spiritual those may be) and that purpose is to bring others to Christ, ideally in the Church where the fullness of sacramental life can be found.

With this awareness, the third and fourth goals of the *Purposeful Parishes Initiative* are to do just that: to remake our parishes into communities that people *want* to joint and to take steps *as a parish* to evangelize. This parish evangelization can involve any number actions, such as re-establishing contact with those we know have

271

drifted away and inviting new, uncommitted friends to "come and see" (cf. Jn 1:46).

The *Purposeful Parishes Initiative* is a long-term, diocese-wide renewal effort to reform all the parishes into truly Catholic evangelical communities. Committed clergy, staff, and parishioners alike will reform the business-as-usual operation of their parishes from the *status quo* into communities that actively draw people to Christ.

The Pastor's Announcement Insofar as the aims of the *Purposeful Parishes Initiative* represent a sea change for most parishes in the U.S., a clear prophetic announcement is needed to kick it off, in the same way that the *Episcopal Announcement* starts with an announcement from the bishop. In this case, the announcement must come from the pastor in a visionary and compelling way. He is not announcing a Men's Club Steak Dinner or a quilting bee, but the advent of a new chapter in the history of the parish; a substantial remake of its underlying culture and *modus vivendi.* The announcement conveys the fact that the parish is about to undergo some radical changes, most notably a change in decision-making criteria that places evangelization at the top of the list.

The announcement will only be effective if a pastor is seriously willing to lead. For this reason, for the first few years of a diocese implementing the *Purposeful Parishes Initiative,* only the most motivated and dynamic pastors should be chosen to participate and the bishop should invest heavily in getting them the support they will need to succeed. They *must not fail,* because what they accomplish will establish the expectations for those who follow.

As Father White pointed out in *Rebuilt,* there is a price to be paid in a few unhappy parishioners. Some members will leave over the announcement, finding in it an unintended criticism of their past leadership. But, just as our Lord explained to those who were reluctant to follow him after he had extended a clear invitation, *No one who sets his hand to a plow and looks back to what was left behind is fit for the kingdom of God* (Lk 9:62). Once a pastor has tied himself to the vision of the bishop, there can be no turning back.

Many pastors will find it intimidating to have to respond to an accusation such as: "You've been here five years. If what we've been doing is so wrong, why didn't you start this sooner?" There will be some hurts and misunderstandings, but the response must be one of unabashed humility and a vulnerable longing to serve the Lord better.

Having said this, the announcement for most members will elicit excitement about a future with a purpose. In any event, once the proverbial bomb has been dropped and the smoke cleared, the following kinds of parish reform can ensue.

Purposeful Reforms The envisioned parish reforms can be summarized under three headings:

- Proactive Parish Reforms
- Pastoral Parish Reforms
- Missionary Parish Reforms

"Proactive" parish reforms should be understood as actions taken to prevent bad things from happening *before* they occur. "Pastoral" reforms are steps taken to undo bad things that have already happened, plus actions to evangelize and imbue evangelical purpose into *existing* parishioners. Some pastoral reforms may also have collateral benefits for non-parishioners who interface closely with the parish and/or school staff. After taking conscientious steps to get our own house in order, "Missionary" reforms are aimed outward to people who are not (yet) parishioners.

"Proactive" Parish Reforms The biggest "bad thing" that has already happened in our parishes was the fact that we fell asleep while literally millions slipped away unnoticed. We were so caught up in internecine battles and thoughtless routines that we missed the fact that we were hemorrhaging vulnerable souls.

Examples of proactive reforms designed to head off more attrition include, but are not limited, to:

- Decision-oriented youth ministry
- Modeling mature Christian adulthood
- Appeals to those on the periphery of parish life

Decision-oriented youth ministry One of our highest parish priorities should be to protect children and young people from the many distractions that can entice them away from God and to assist them in making a ***conscious, explicit commitment*** to Christ in the Church. This commitment should be so strong that it carries them on throughout the rest of their lives. Moreover, our commitment to them should be so strong that we use every conceivable to stay in touch with them even after they move away for college or career.

At a time when many young people are delaying adult responsibilities and the world is saying they are incapable of making serious decisions, the Church needs to be countercultural and help them grow up. Our history abounds with childhood and teenage saints who prove that youthful holiness is really possible: the Little Flower, St. Dominic Savio, St. Maria Goretti, St. Agatha, St. Lucy, Bl. Chiara "Luce" Badano, and many more. Many of our older priests living even today entered the seminary out of grade school and have never wavered. In Chapter VI, I recounted my own story which involved hearing the *kērygma* preached in my parish church when I was about 12 years-old and undergoing an incredible experience of Jesus' personal love for me right there on the spot. The Gospel needs to be proclaimed clearly and children need an opportunity to make a decision. The point is: It is possible!

The *Purposeful Parishes Initiative envisions dioceses in which parishes truly evangelize their children*; places where it is a real priority for the pastor to take time to sweetly communicate the message of Jesus' love to first communicants and *ask* the little ones to love him back; schools where children are given time to spend with their Lord in quiet Eucharistic adoration chapels, and teachers and coaches who will pray from their hearts.

By the time the children are in high school, purposeful parishes will ask their young people to step up to *an affirmation of their baptism by solemnly promising very explicit things*: never to leave our Lord or the community of the faith; to receive the sacrament of Reconciliation frequently, and; to receive the Lord at Sunday Eucharist minimally every week, regardless of their feelings or other time commitments; to strive to remain virginal until marriage and chaste throughout their lives; to use their gifts in service to others. As daunting as these promises are, they will not be made in a group setting or class environment where peer pressure can influence behavior, but rather between a student and her mentor or between a father and his son, always free of pressure and respecting the freedom of the individual.

Assuming the diocese customarily confers Confirmation during the teen years, when young people are ready and have made these mature promises to God in the presence of an intentional disciple, Confirmation can be received at the first available opportunity and truly celebrated as the reception of God's holy gifts to young men and women who are ready to use them.

When the time comes for the young adults to move away, purposeful parishes working in coordination with the diocese will already have in place committed mentors who are willing to "accompany" from afar each graduate by cell phone and take them out when they come home on break. These young people will mean enough to the local Church that the diocese will treat each one as their own special child, forwarding their new address and contact information to the parish or Neumann Center nearest them.

Our Lord asked Peter, "Do you love me?" The *Purposeful Parishes Initiative* will repeat the Lord's question to our young people and pray for a mutual response. If we don't ask the question, we will never get an answer and we run the risk of losing them permanently.

Modeling mature Christian adulthood In *The Art of Forming Young Disciples,* Everett Fritz makes a compelling case for "why youth ministries aren't working and what to do about it".[92] As a seasoned youth minister who has watched the Church hemorrhage young people for years, Fritz zeros in on the primary reason: *We have allowed young people to become isolated from mature adult Christians.* They are saturated in a youth culture – even inside the Church – and then we wonder why they cannot make grown-up decisions. In the *purposeful parishes* of the future, youth ministry will look very different. With a new emphasis on family life, committed Catholic families will regularly come together as a *community* for friendship, meals, fun, praise and worship. More will be said under the *Missionary Disciples Initiative* about these "communities of families", but let it suffice to say here that they will strive to unify people across age groups. As a boy, I recall being influenced not only by my own dad, but by an uncle and other friends of my dad. By and large, these were positive influences that happened simply by casual exposure. Imagine the blessings that could come from being *purposeful* about it! Imagine the gradual realization that there are *other* adults out there aside from your parents who love the Lord and are committed to the Catholic Church; that your own mom and dad are not isolated weirdos.

In addition to communities of families, *purposeful parishes* will work with Catholic men's and women's ministries and associations to bring boys together with men and girls together with women. The Knights of Columbus, parish Men's Clubs, men's *Cursillo* groups, women's groups such as *Walking With Purpose* will intentionally include activities together with their children.

There are yet other avenues the *Purposeful Parishes Initiative* will explore to expose our young people to mature adult Christian disciples. I have found it not-a-little disturbing how insurance regulations and organizational policies have unintentionally limited the exposure of youth to Christian ministry. A case in point: Habitat for Humanity actively builds homes for poor families using church volunteers... as long as the volunteers are 18 or older. This is not an unusual policy.

Another interesting case: A couple years ago, I was distributing Holy Communion one Saturday to patients in a local Catholic hospital. I brought along with me our then 10-year old grandson. It was a new and meaningful experience for Gavin as we went room-to-room chatting and praying with people, and bringing our Lord to them. Gavin comported himself in every way that I hoped he would. To a person, each patient seemed thrilled to get an unexpected visit from a genuinely friendly child. Gavin and I both thought the experience was fantastic and as we left, he asked if we could do it again. Well, even though he comported himself perfectly and he conscientiously used the dry soap dispensers before entering every room, and even though there were no age restrictions for visitors, and even though he did not have a runny nose, and the entire experience was amazing, I received a somewhat apologetic phone call the next day from the chaplain's office. A nurse had noticed my grandson with me and informed the hospital administration that I had broken the age rule so, "please do not bring him along again".

Policies such as these that obstruct the exposure of young people to adult ministry are often driven by insurance underwriters or myopic institutional concerns. The bishop can help to point out these issues and bring influence to bear on changing them.

Appeals to those on the peripheries Of course, youth are not the only people who have walked away from the Church. Many adults have left for a host of reasons and there are others who may still be coming to Mass, but are just going through the motions. Any provocation could induce them to fade away and never look back. The *Purposeful Parishes Initiative* will proactively seek to identify these souls and provide the attention, involvement, and the answers they may need. A pastor I used to work with instituted a weekly practice which came to be called "Tea with Father Tom." Every week Father Tom would simply make himself available to have a cup of tea and talk to anyone who showed up about any topic or question the person(s) might want to raise. This and similar practices to reach out to those on the periphery of parish life can be very helpful.

"Pastoral" Parish Reforms Of course, in many cases, the damage has already been done or is still in the process of being done. This damage can be both the result of missed opportunities that – had they been noticed – could have had a tremendous evangelical effect or it can be outright pastoral gaffs that had the effect of running people off. The reality of parish life in twenty-first century America is that many people in our pews come under the heading of "baptized but unevangelized" (to borrow an expression used by our current and last pope). Pastoral parish reforms focus on those things that parish clergy and staff can do to facilitate a deep personal conversion for the uncommitted who are still in the pews or have recently left.

Examples of pastoral reforms intended to redress past problems and institute best practices for the future include:

- Outreach to those who have left
- A reformed weekend experience
- Homilies that evangelize
- Sacramental prep that evangelizes
- Support staff reforms
- Getting the initiatory 'rites' right

Outreach to those who have left Jesus addressed a parable to those who prided themselves on being an example for others – the Pharisees and scribes. In this parable, he spoke of a shepherd who would go in search of a single lost sheep that had wandered off from a flock of one hundred (cf. Lk 15:3-7).

The problem in these situations is first, noticing a sheep is missing and second, finding him. Pastors are not omniscient and omnipresent. But, *purposeful pastors* will enlist the help of others to identify who has left and to track them down. The parish bookkeeper might conduct a spreadsheet "sort" of the membership database to identify registered members who stopped tithing within the last few years. Senior parish staff may be able to identify the names of some former members who walked away in a huff. An appeal could be put out from the pulpit to parishioners to feedback information on those they know who have left and to communicate the circumstances.

Once a list of possibly estranged members has been compiled, purposeful pastors will make systematic efforts to reach out to these people in the most personal way possible. In some cases, a telephone call from the pastor followed by a home visit might make sense (as time consuming and uncomfortable as that may be). If applicable, a sincere apology may be needed along with a request to "start over." In some cases, a letter might be appropriate.

Sometimes, just knowing that a person "is missed" can be enough to bring back a "lost sheep". In any event, there is greater potential for these lost sheep who have wandered off to be wooed back to the flock than unknown sheep who were never part of the flock in the first place.

Of course, there are numerous other outreaches to lapsed Catholics that a *purposeful parish* might pursue. Father Dwight Longenecker, an evangelical convert to Catholicism, has mused about one possibility:

> In this age when so many Catholics are drifting away from the church and there are so many others who are genuinely interested in the Catholic faith, I wish we had some form of non-Eucharistic worship where we could evangelize and catechize effectively. This would also provide a way for Catholics who, for whatever reason, cannot receive communion to belong to the church and worship God while they are working out how they can be full members of the church. These forms of worship would also get around the clericalism in the church because they could be conducted by laypeople–both men and women.
>
> It would be pretty radical, but what if once a month we actually put in place a simple, dignified act of worship which was not a Mass?[93]

Without endorsing a particular method, Archbishop Allen Vigneron of Detroit has challenged his parishes to sponsor non-sacramental gatherings as a way of providing a "shallow end" for those on the periphery of the Church; for people who want to know more, but are not yet ready or able to jump into (or back into) the "deep end".[94]

Reformed Weekend Experience The authors of *Rebuilt* speak of the importance of creating vibrant Christ-centered parishes, lest we invite lapsed or former Catholics back to the same places they left. They ask a very good question: "Why should people come to church or come *back* to church if their experience week after week is unhelpful, or maybe even offensive?" Who could blame them for finding other things to do?"[95] The place to start is the creation of a *different weekend experience.* As a deacon who has spent a number of years in parish ministry, I can attest that the experience of the weekend Eucharistic celebration – the most important thing we do all week – is often the thing we work on the least. Others have made the same point: Quoting White and Corcoran again: "Even after we had come to understand our mission... we continued to treat the weekend as an afterthought... We were too busy Monday through Friday to worry about Sunday."[96]

Since Mass is often considered as a passive spectator sport, White and Corcoran coined the motto: "Every member a minister." If you want to be a member of this parish, a basic requirement is that you minister to the community on a regular, scheduled basis. This policy unleashes a wealth of human resources that make for an outstanding weekend Mass experience.

When most people think of "volunteering at church", what usually comes to mind are all the traditional liturgical support roles (e.g., music ministers, sacristans, ushers, lectors, extraordinary ministers of the Eucharist, etc.). These are all wonderful forms of ministry, but with a little creativity, many other non-liturgical ministry teams can be exercised, for example, a...

- Host Team
- Transportation Team
- Driving Team
- Parking Team
- Operations Team (audio-video)
- Young Children's Team
- Refreshment Team
- Ministry Recruitment Team

This is what Father White has put in place at Nativity Parish in Timonium, Maryland. Properly-trained and entered into enthusiastically, these ministries can completely change the experience of a typical weekend Mass, not only for parishioners, but for the guests as well. Who would have thought that it is possible to evangelize by parking cars for church-goers on a rainy day?

Beyond the improved experience for those non-members who visit, the reformed weekend experience also will move ordinary parishioners into the first steps of becoming missionary disciples as they learn to "invest and invite" friends and neighbors to Mass on Sundays.

Homilies that evangelize As part of the *Purposeful Parishes Initiative,* parish priests will receive the formation needed to become *kērygmatic* preachers. Preaching the *kērygma* is so important, and yet many preachers rarely mention it. There is good reason that they should preach the most central mysteries of our salvation on a regular basis at weekend masses. The reality is that our churches are filled with people who cover the gamut from committed saints to nominal Catholics to visiting agnostics with absolutely no commitment to God. Even in the case of those who are baptized, Archbishop Michael Byrnes of Guam reminds us: "… the preacher must be aware that many in his congregation may not have met the grace of their baptism with a conscious faith (cf. Heb. 4:2) so as to enter into a committed, personal relationship with Jesus and the authentic conversion of life that characterizes a disciple."[97]

There is one message that applies equally to all present and, speaking as a long-time believer, I still can't get enough of it. It is simply this: *God really does love us.* More than that, He loves *me.* In fact, God loves us so much that He – the God of the Big Bang and of all times and places – willed to become one of us. And, if that wasn't enough, God *died* for us to bridge a chasm that only the God-Man could.

A purposeful pastor will deliver homilies that are special. His homilies will be well-prepared and check a lot of boxes. They will be laced with low-keyed humor. He will speak with only rare reference to a text and will allow people a glimpse of his own vulnerability. He will know his congregation and offer messages that are grounded in lived experiences. His exegesis will be flawless and his theology fully orthodox. But what it really boils down to is that he will speak of the love of Jesus *with personal conviction*, not forgetting the central reason we are all there in the first place.

The *coups de grâce* that is virtually never heard in a Catholic Church will become part of the common reformed weekend experience. The homilist *will invite* anyone who might want to consider surrendering their life to Christ to meet him after Mass. That can be the start of a whole new beginning.

Pastoral ministry that evangelizes St. Paul's self-description of becoming "all things to all people in order to save some" (1 Cor 9:22b) will effectively become the motto for all pastoral ministers – clergy or lay – serving in future purposeful parishes. Those of us who represent the Church in a "professional" capacity have the responsibility to recognize that the least little thing we say and do is scrutinized under a closer lens than the average person in the pew.

With this added responsibility, however, comes a multitude of opportunities to influence everyone who walks through the doors of the parish office to take a step closer to Christ. As part of the *Purposeful Parishes Initiative*, pastoral ministers will be "re-formed" to view all of the ordinary aspects of everyday ministry as having a potential evangelistic impact. Conversely, the formation will illuminate the obstacles they create through self-absorption and insensitivity.

Something as simple as the way a priest or pastoral associate engages a person who has a question has the potential either to attract or repel the questioner. In a 2012 article in *America* entitled "Why They Left", one former Catholic made the observation: "Ask a question of any priest and you get a rule; you

> Filling the young parents' heads with a lot of theology that presupposes personal belief serves very little purpose... We will learn to evangelize first; then catechize.

don't get a 'let's sit down and talk about it' response."[98] In a world filled with people who want to understand the *"why"* of an issue, a brusque, hurried answer does little to elucidate the truth and can do more damage than good. The reforms of the *Purposeful Parishes Initiative* will address these common pastoral mistakes.

Nowhere is this more needed that in the ministry of sacramental prep. This ordinary task is a *huge evangelistic opportunity* that has traditionally gone unrecognized. The operating assumption of most parish ministers seems to be that everyone who wants to marry in the Church understands marriage as a reflection of Christ's love for his Bride (cf. Eph 5:32) and that couples who present their children for baptism are longing for their little ones to be adopted by God the Father and to become a tabernacle of the Holy Spirit (cf. Gal 4:6, Acts 2:38-39).

Of course, this is pure phantasy. Nearly everyone who comes to the parish for these two sacraments does so for a "good reason", but rarely for the *right* one. For example, many couples who approach the Church for marriage preparation today are simply jumping through an ecclesiastical hoop. They have made little or no commitment of their lives to Jesus. As often as not, they are there to appease a parent or because of some vague sense of obligation that often accompanies the "sacramentalized, but not evangelized". There will never be a better opportunity to share our faith with a young couple than their marriage prep sessions. Insofar as the center of any truly successful marriage is a personal and joint encounter with Christ as a couple, our marriage prep should first and foremost be focused on bringing that couple into a deeper conscious relationship with their Savior.

Baptismal preparation offers exactly the same opportunity. If we miss the truly essential by focusing these "classes" on checking off the box, we have missed a potentially graced moment to evangelize. Filling the young parents' heads with a lot of theology that *presupposes* personal belief serves very little purpose if belief is not there in the first place. A *purposeful parishes minister* will learn to evangelize first by witnessing to his own relationship with Christ. Then, he can check the boxes: sacramental catechesis and planning the rite.

Support Staff Reforms On a day-in-day-out basis, the "face" of the parish is the person sitting at the front desk. She or he can be either the front line of pastoral service or the dreaded "gatekeeper". Purposeful parish reforms will include an investment in the formation and training of those who staff the front desk. It will also include training directed to welcome committees and teams.

In many of the monasteries of an earlier era, one monk or nun was assigned the role of "porter". In fact, for a long time, porters were one of the "minor orders" leading up to ordination. The porter had the often-lonely job of waiting near the entrance of the monastery to welcome any one who came to the door seeking material or spiritual help. In effect, he or she was the liaison between the monastic community and the outside world. St. André Bessette and Bl. Solanus Casey are recently recognized examples of porters who changed the lives of the "seekers" who came to them – often with outright miracles.

Whether the person at the front desk of a parish office is a volunteer or employee, he or she is the "porter" of the Church in modern times. Like the porters of earlier times, theirs is a privileged, *unique ministry*, not just a job. They are the ones who welcome Christ himself in the disguise of a "stranger" (cf. Mt 25:35).

Many who fall into the category of "marginal Catholics" have been hurt at some point in their lives by a perception (real or imagined) that the Church does not care about them. We can all think of priests, pastoral associates, receptionists, catechists, St. Vincent de Paul members, and others who "represent" the Church, but do so without much obvious personal care and concern; or, at least, they have not learned how to show it. St. Paul said it well when he wrote: "If I have all faith so as to move mountains, but do not have love, I am nothing" (1 Cor 13:2). The staffs and volunteers at *purposeful parishes* will be taught to understand their privileged role of *welcoming* people who call or walk through the door. They will learn to recognize that the way they handle everyday human situations can make the difference between a person who "comes home" to stay or one who only "visits" because he has to.

Parish staff members often work with a specialist's "silo" mentality that is crafted to accomplish a narrow purpose that overlooks the larger opportunity to bring people to Christ. In a reformed *purposeful parish,* the silos will be torn down. People who work in service to the poor will come to an understanding that hidden under the immediate need may be a person with a deep need and longing for Christ; not just money to pay the utility bill. A deacon praying with a hospital patient will learn how to discern when there is a deeper need for spiritual healing. A catechist will learn how to recognize manifold opportunities to witness her faith at a personal level, in addition to teach the day's lesson.

Getting the initiatory 'rites' right I recall Archbishop Charles Thompson of Indianapolis telling a story about one of his experiences as a young priest. He confessed that as a newly-ordained priest he felt particularly insecure about the Rite of Christian Initiation of Adults (RCIA), because it was one of those elective classes his seminary schedule just didn't allow him time to take. As divine providence would have it, in his first priestly assignment, he was asked to work on the parish RCIA team. It didn't take long before he came to a deep appreciation of the critically important role of RCIA in the lives of the participants and the parish as a whole.

One of the truly great reforms arising out of the Second Vatican Council was the restoration of the ancient catechumenate, a prolonged period of prayer, discernment, and progressive conversion leading up to and including baptism, confirmation and Eucharist at the Easter Vigil Mass. The 'Rite' itself, is an absolutely inspired compilation of instructions for leading the RCIA and for the rubrics that guide its preparatory 'rites'.

Unfortunately, there exists a serious problem in the way RCIA is typically practiced in the United States: We Americans aren't been very good at following directions. When we follow the actual Rite the way the Church has given it to us, I have personally experienced how powerful it can be. Father Jim Sauer, a recently-retired pastor in the Diocese of Evansville said it best: "RCIA is not a program. It is a way of life." Moreover, it is intended as a way of life not just for the catechumen/candidate, but *for the whole parish*.

In my experience, many pastors have not had the blessing of experiencing what Archbishop Thompson did. The RCIA is often handed off to a pastoral associate or director of religious education who in turn hands it off to a catechist who may or may not have any training or ever read the Rite. The result is something far less than it could be with most parishioners hardly even aware that RCIA is going on and, to the extent that they are aware, assuming it is just one more "program" among many.

PART III: ON ACHIEVING THE VISION

Having said this, despite its less than perfect implementation, the RCIA usually "delivers the goods". Due to ignorance and I suspect the deceptions of the enemy, there is a pervasive myth that upwards of 50 percent of people who come into the Church via RCIA leave the Church shortly thereafter.[99] In a recent article, Mark Giszczak, Ph.D. of the Augustine Institute pointed out that Georgetown University's Center for Applied Research in the Apostolate (CARA) investigated this widely-repeated claim in 2016 and concluded that conservatively, 84 percent of RCIA converts remain "in the pews" more-or-less permanently. [100] Would that cradle Catholics could boast of such a number! The point is: Parishes need to own the RCIA and fully participate in it.

As part of the formation for the *Purposeful Parishes Initiative*, pastors will be expected to sit down and take the time to study the actual Rite as given to us by the Church... and then implement it. Pastors, who typically delegate everything except the liturgical aspects of the Rite, will come to appreciate its evangelical and formative importance and make use of it. The catechumenate will be pulled from the periphery to the center of parish life – which is where it is *supposed* to be. The participants will be introduced and then re-introduced on Sunday mornings and at every other parish community event. They will be made to feel special and truly welcomed as they come to know the members of the parish on a personal basis. Gradually, they will be co-opted into some form of service in the parish. In some way, every member of the parish will welcome them and make them feel that they are joining a real family rather than an assortment of isolated individuals.

The Rite of Enrollment, the Rite of Sending, and Easter Vigil will become *gigantic* events for the entire parish community, such that the convert comes to the full realization that she is on the brink of joining both a universal and a local communion of people that will literally *change her identity*.

The same will hold true for the bishop as he presides over the Rite of Election in the cathedral. It would be unheard of for a diocese not to have a jammed cathedral for the ordination of a priest or for a religious community not to gather for the profession of solemn vows. The bishop's "election" of his

> The convert should come to the realization that she is joining both a universal and a local communion of people that will literally change her identity

catechumens into the final phase of preparation will be celebrated with the same solemnity and excitement.

As recommended by the outstanding evangelistic ministry known as TeamRCIA (www.teamrcia.org), the ritual steps in the RCIA process need to be "done well". By that they mean that such celebrations as the Rites of Acceptance and Sending, not to mention the Easter Vigil itself, need to come across as more than tightly prescribed liturgical steps. For example, TeamRCIA points out that there is no reason why the Rite of Acceptance cannot be done on more than one occasion throughout the year. The common practice of holding only one Rite of Acceptance per year can strip the convert of the personal nature of his/her journey and/or force the parish to accept a person into the catechumenate before he/she is ready. Again, TeamRCIA makes the point that the official Rite of Acceptance *permits unscripted* (albeit affirmative) responses by the convert to the celebrant's questions: "Are you prepared to begin this journey today...?" "Are you ready with the help of God to live this life?" "Are you ready to accept these teachings of the Gospel?" A legitimate and personal response to any of these questions could be: "With the help of God, I am trying" or "Although I am a little afraid, I want to. Please pray for me," rather than the usual "I am".

The *Purposeful Parishes Initiative* will improve both the quality of the experience of the catechumenate as well as the prospects for a *lifelong conversion* by making the ministry of RCIA a priority in their evangelization planning.

"Missionary" Parish Reforms If we think of a parish as a community of committed Catholics disciples who have been conscientiously prepared as a missionary band of disciples with a longing to serve, bring, and keep their neighbors in a loving relationship with God, then you have a mature *Purposeful Parish*. Let's consider what such a parish might look like....

Eucharistic missionary outreach Imagine a (fictional) mid-sized, historical urban parish called Ascension. Ascension's pastor – let's call him Father Luke –recognizes that the clear majority of people attending the funerals at his parish are unchurched and seem almost completely unmoored from the message of salvation. Most of these good people are there because they are experiencing the loss of a grandparent or work associate, and many of them seem disoriented during Mass; it's clear they're not used to being in church. Realizing that this is a common occurrence in his parish, let's imagine Father Luke carefully crafting a tender funeral homily about how even Jesus wept at the death of his friend, Lazarus, and he goes on to connect Jesus' final meal with the sacrifice of his own body and blood on the Cross a few hours later and the incomprehensible shock of his return to life some forty hours later; an event that changed the world from that day till the present.

Now, imagine further that the parish has a standing group of well-formed missionary disciples who have organized for just such a situation. This group, who call themselves the "Mary and Martha Team" are mainly retired folks who serve the funeral masses as readers, sacristans, ushers and the like and who also serve a bereavement meal for the mourners after the internment. At the meal, Father Luke notices two mourners he had seen at the mortuary the night before and at Mass this morning; two mourners who seemed to be particularly affected by the passing of the deceased and were especially attentive during the homily. He discreetly points them out to two members of the Mary and Martha Team. They know exactly what to do. They grab some food and a drink, go over and sit down near the two mourners who are seated at different tables, and they unobtrusively introduce themselves.

Two months later, one of these two team members shows up at Mass with her new friend. She introduces her to friends in the gathering space adjoining the old church and later Father Luke shakes hands. The two become close friends and start coming together to Mass frequently. Two years later, the former mourner is joyfully baptized at Easter Vigil with her friend at her side... But, even before that, she became a member of the Mary and Martha Team herself. Multiply this story by hundreds of similar stories and you begin to get a picture of a *purposeful parish*.

Purveyors of beauty Now, imagine a different team – this one comprised mainly of young singles. They're involved in a different kind of missionary outreach and have proudly named themselves after St. Bridget of Sweden. They mainly run the after-hours Tenebrae and Taizé services that are widely advertised at the local coffee shops. These eclectic, non-Eucharistic gatherings have a decidedly contemplative feel to them; deep, yet lyrical and undeniably Christ-centered. Following one of the services, three of the gals join up with Father Luke who didn't arrive until after the last Taizé chant was over. The coffee drinkers have a decaf latté together and the subject that night turns to the unlikely subject of natural family planning. As it turns out, it was not so unlikely after all, because several of the guests were attracted to the "natural, non-chemical" element of NFP and expressed a sadness and dissatisfaction with the "hook-up" culture they had all experienced first-hand. They really never knew anything else. The following year, two of the guests that night moved to a state university a hundred miles away, where they were connected with the campus FOCUS team thanks to the introduction of one of the St. Bridget guys. In time, both of them were baptized, confirmed, 'eucharisted' at the Newman Center and a few of the 'St. Bridget old-timers' drove up to celebrate the occasion with them.

Community Outreach Missionaries A few years ago, three of the guys went through the dioceses' Missionary Disciples Formation and were commissioned by the bishop. Shortly before their commissioning, they had a "strategic brainstorming session" with the bishop and some of his Regional Evangelization Team to figure out how they might work together to witness their love for Jesus and Mary. They came out with an idea that nobody was thinking about on the way in – to work with boys as Christian mentors. Ironically, the population at Ascension was mainly people their age and older with grown kids or they were young Millennials without kids. Since the guys had a love for kids who simply didn't exist at Ascension, they decided to serve kids in the larger community. The little group of three has now grown to fourteen third- and fourth-degree Knights of Columbus who call themselves St. Joseph's Helpers. Once a month, the Helpers – who have all cleared their background checks – go out in pairs to pick up pre-teen and teenage boys from neighboring parishes and a few other churches. They start the day with the boys the way they do every other Saturday – with Mass and rosary. Then, it's off to the local pastry shop and whatever has been planned after that; sometimes, just fun stuff like basketball or a chess match; sometimes cleaning out gutters and doing repairs or yard work where needed. Who knows where it will all go?

And then there are the St. Thomas Talkers, men and women who do love to talk, but also do a lot of listening. They are passionately concerned with bringing the Truth to unlikely places such as weekend community wine festivals or any public place where there is a lot of people. Affiliated with St. Paul Street Evangelization (SPSE), they set up outdoor booths with loads of Miraculous Medals and rosaries and scapulars as free gifts and they listen-talk-pray as people stop by. The St. Thomas Talkers can also be found teaching *Why We Believe* classes and leading *Alpha* programs for young people in the former convent next door to the junior college. They have re-structured Ascension's RCIA into the year-round apostolate it is supposed to be, providing a clear next step for *Alpha* "graduates".

If you could sit down and talk to Father Luke, he'd tell you about all the *other* ministries going on at his parish, like the…

- Companion and mentoring ministries to poor families
- Transportation ministry working with the American Cancer Society to get sick patients back and forth to their chemo sessions
- *Forty Days for Life* intercessors who gather outside Planned Parenthood to pray for the young mothers intent on aborting their babies
- Camillus ministers bringing Jesus to the homebound, infirm, and aged in area hospitals, and nursing homes
- Advocate-companions befriending the homeless

And then, he'd tell you his wish list.

Formation for the *Purposeful Parishes Initiative* In the section entitled *Formation: Bootcamps for the Faithful,* common elements for each of the (post-episcopal) initiatives in the *Vision Achievement Strategy* were listed. In addition to these common elements, each initiative will have specific content relevant to the aims of the initiative. Currently, no standard curriculum exists. Accordingly, at least for the time being, each diocese will need to create their own content taking into consideration the resources they have available and sharing what they learn with each other.

That said, the aims of the *Purposeful Parishes Initiative* dictate content that addresses the following subjects:

† **Discernment and cultivation of individual gifts** – human, spiritual, and ministerial. Personal inventories such as Gallup's "StrengthsFinders" and the Siena Institute's "Called and Gifted" can be useful at helping the participant get an idea of how he/she can best "fit" into the various parish ministry teams. They can also guide the participant and formators alike in identifying areas of concentration that will be useful in the *Missionary Disciples* and *Regional Catholics* initiatives. Each participant's gifts need to be connected to the ministries required for building purposeful parishes, such as: Sunday welcomers, long-term companions and mentors, teachers, and RCIA leaders.

In addition to these well-known roles, many dioceses make use of procurator-advocates who assist people going through the annulment process to prepare their case for judgment by the diocesan tribunal. This is a highly-valued service, since the annulment process can be daunting, even to the point of discouraging petitioners from completing the process. Often, RCIA catechumens and candidates are in an irregular marriage that requires an annulment before they can receive the sacraments of initiation. While it is doubtful that the *purposeful parishes* formation process itself would incorporate the degree of training needed to serve as a procurator-advocate, the formation's discernment aspect could help to identified prospective lay people with the gifts to be a good procurator-advocate. These people could then look to the diocese for specialized training.

Other content specific to the *Purposeful Parishes Initiative* must include specialized tracks for:

† **Priests** – Necessary elements include the art and science of inspirational pastoral leadership, building a healthy parish leadership team, recognizing evangelical moments in day-to-day ministry, reaching people who are not currently in the pews, planning for growth, setting meaningful and measurable goals, and transitioning from "consumer-oriented" to "mission-oriented" decision-making criteria.

† **Homilists – priests and deacons** – How to proclaim the *kērygma* effectively during weekend masses, and inviting personal commitments to the Lord

† **Pastoral associates** – Bringing the invitation of Jesus into daily ministry, and evangelical prep for the sacraments of marriage and child baptism

† **School principals and teachers** – Demonstrated and articulated love for Jesus in all aspects of school life

† **Catechists** – Developing the art of evangelizing first and catechizing second

† **Parish support staff (volunteer or paid)** – Moving from a job to a ministry mindset; the reception of strangers who so often interrupt their "work"; cooperating as a ministry team vs. a specialist mentality

† **Ministers of charity (volunteer or paid)** – Integrating the spiritual works of mercy with the corporal works of mercy and leading "clients" into a relationship with Christ

Now, imagine several other parishes like Ascension scattered throughout the region... Together they represent a great start, but in reality, Ascension and her sister *purposeful parishes* would only constitute a tiny "beachhead" on the shores of the enemy; a muscular, secular society, but also a largely ambivalent one that is vulnerable to infiltration by love.

Even working together, these reformed parishes can only reach as far as a few organized parish ministries can reach. There are still many more, mainly small parishes out there without strong leadership that are struggling just to survive. Praise God for our allies, those other Christians with the same hopes and serving the same Lord. But they too are overwhelmed; waiting off-shore, as it were.

The picture isn't complete yet. Missing is a massive "army of missionary disciples" capable of moving equipment and provisions into enemy-held territory, all the while preserving the infrastructure and liberating the civilian population. They are the spearhead of a new civilization founded on fighting the enemy with the most powerful weapon available: sincere love. Imbedded in that vast array are "special forces" who can get out the message and follow behind the retreating enemy, filling in the void with a new order; an order that respects the dignity of life and the beauty of God's creation. For the moment, we are forced to ask the question: "Where is that army of missionary disciples?" The answer is it doesn't exist yet. But, it can through the particular Church that makes a systematic, sustained effort over many years. This effort will entail taking "typical" Catholics as they are today to the next level of their own personal conversion where they experience God's love and healing first hand; where they receive training, and; from which they are sent out into the world.

* * *

296

Drilling into the *Missionary Disciples Initiative*

If the intent of the *Purposeful Parishes Initiative* is to reform parishes into holy communities with an outward-looking missionary perspective, the intent of the *Missionary Disciples Initiative* is to form and commission individuals from these parishes to proclaim the Good News of Jesus

Missionary Disciples Initiative

Aims:

To inculcate in Catholics a missionary passion and equip them with the sensitivities and skills to evangelize fruitfully

To engage these missionary disciples both individually and in community in the apostolate of faith-sharing and witness of life

in every facet of their lives. In effect, the *Missionary Disciples Initiative* equips those who have been affected by the *Purposeful Parishes Initiative* and are committed to being formed into missionary disciples capable of sharing their faith. The long-term goal is to raise up an "army of missionary disciples" who are fruitfully converting and raising up more disciples.

While parishes can engender conversions through their communal ministries, most serious conversions come about as the result of an individual disciple sharing her faith and inviting another individual to take the next step of faith in his/her life. In the Catholic Church, we see this most often between spouses and engaged couples, but also between parents and children and between close friends.

Small Christian communities of disciples such as *Alpha* or *Cursillo* teams or street evangelizers also work together to proclaim the Gospel. Sometimes, these teams originate in parishes, but more often they cross parish lines.

The *Missionary Disciples Initiative* is an infusion of (ideally, commissioned) well-formed disciples into all the "worlds" in which they live: domestic, work, personal/social, volunteer. Accordingly, the missionary disciples are parents, grandparents, siblings, teachers, co-workers, supervisors, colleagues, competitors, coaches, pastors, mature students, friends, neighbors, even strangers witnessing in all sorts of ways and situations; most commonly, as individual disciples, but also in intentional communities.

Outside of the immediate family, today we live within communities of interest where we communicate with each other via the text messages or Internet rather than across the back fence. Our best friends may just as easily live a thousand miles away as in the same city. As vital as it is, parish life is only one of the social mechanisms that bind us together and, of course, most of our lives are spent in a different environment than the parish campus. Accordingly, if we are to imbue a new evangelical spirit into Catholic culture, it must happen in the lives of individual Catholics, not just in the context of parish communities.

On the Need to "Equip the Holy Ones" The problem is that many *good* Catholics feel unequipped to evangelize. This was born out very clearly in a 2013 survey of registered parishioners in the Diocese of Evansville, Indiana.[101]

In that survey, two open-ended questions were asked about evangelization in the diocese. One question asked: *What is the single most important thing your parish or diocese could do to reach out to people who don't go to church at all?* The second question asked: *What is the single most important thing your parish or diocese could do to reach out to people who still consider themselves Catholic, but only rarely come to church?* The first question pertains to the disaffiliated (or *'nones'*), while the second pertains to inactive Catholics. The open-ended

Figure 10

Top Four Proposed Evangelization Activities: 2013 Evansville Diocese Survey of Catholic Parishioners

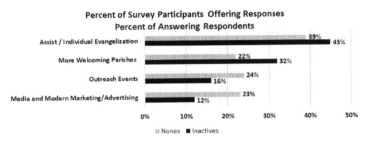

Percent of Survey Participants Offering Responses
Percent of Answering Respondents

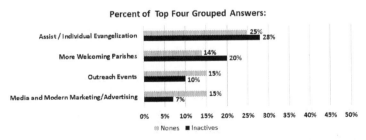

Percent of Top Four Grouped Answers:

Nones: What is the single most important thing your parish or diocese could do to reach out to people who don't go to church at all?
Inactives: What is the single most important thing your parish or diocese could do to reach out to people who still consider themselves Catholic, but only rarely come to church?

nature of the questions was deemed important to prevent inadvertently suggesting any particular answer. Respondents were invited to give as many responses as they would like in 30 words or less.

Out of the 608 respondents, 82 percent offered response(s) to the 'inactives' question and 72 percent to the 'nones' question. About 1.6

answers were offered to both questions. All responses were eventually grouped into 13 categories. As can be seen in Figure 10, the top four categories (or "grouped answers") were the same in regard to both 'inactives' and 'nones', although the ordering of the third and fourth grouped answers were reversed. By far *the largest response for both 'nones' and 'inactives' related to evangelization by individuals or assisting individual Catholics to evangelize,* abbreviated as *"Assist/Individual Evangelization".* With respect to 'inactives', 45 percent of the survey participants who responded to the question gave a response that fell into this category of individual evangelization or assistance in becoming an evangelizer; for 'nones', 39 percent of the survey participants offered the same general response. The next highest grouped answer among respondents was 32 percent for 'inactives' and 22 percent for 'nones'. One can see from Figure 10 that not only was "Assist/Individual Evangelization" the largest response among participating respondents, but it exceeded the next highest group answer – *Welcoming Parishes* – by substantial margins for both 'inactives' and 'nones'.

When counting the grouped answers themselves (instead of the respondents), the same marked priority of the "Assist/Individual Evangelization" shows up *vis-à-vis* other responses.

Figure 11 provides a breakdown of the major sub-categories subsumed in the "Assist/Individual Evangelization" group answer. Probing the responses at this level of specificity, two significant take-aways become evident. First, the importance of individual evangelization (aka, *missionary disciples*) comes through loud-and-clear. Out of a total of 225 responses to the 'inactives' question, fully 169 of them (or 75 percent) emphasize the importance of individual, one-on-one contact; moreover, if you count "a priest/pastoral associate" as an individual right along with other individuals in the evangelization of 'inactives', the importance of the individual jumps to 188 responses (or 84 percent). Regarding 'nones', 113 out of 169 responses (67 percent) emphasize the importance of the individual.

The second takeaway is the theme of *forming Catholics* in the work of evangelization. With respect to evangelizing 'inactives', 27 responses out of 225 (or 12 percent) expressed how important it is to "inspire/convert/teach how/teach duty". This need for formation is

Figure 11
Histogram of Sub-Categories for the 'Assist/Individual Evangelization' Grouped Response: 'Nones' and 'Inactives'

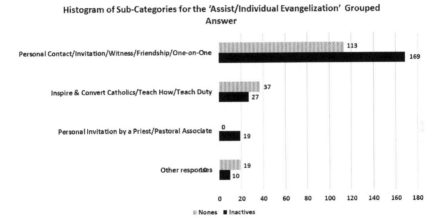

viewed as even more important when dealing with 'nones'; 37 out of 169 (or 22 percent) explicitly articulate this need. In fact, when considering the wording of the questions – *"What is the single most important thing your parish or diocese could do to reach out to..."* 'inactives' or 'nones' – it is not much of a stretch to interpret the entire category summarized under the heading "Assist/Individual Evangelization" as an appeal to "equip the holy ones" for the apostolate of evangelization (cf. Eph 4:12).

If the results of this survey are suggestive of a true *sensus fidei*, it may well be that the most important of the four initiatives in the

301

Vision Achievement Strategy in terms of producing conversions to Christ is the *Missionary Disciples Initiative*.

On Forming Missionary Disciples As a practical matter, the chief 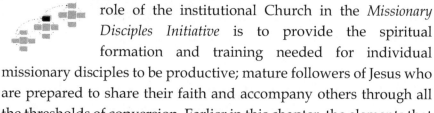 role of the institutional Church in the *Missionary Disciples Initiative* is to provide the spiritual formation and training needed for individual missionary disciples to be productive; mature followers of Jesus who are prepared to share their faith and accompany others through all the thresholds of conversion. Earlier in this chapter, the elements that are *common* to formation in each of the post-episcopal initiatives are discussed, including the spiritual elements. Below are the proposed subjects *specific* to the *Missionary Disciples Initiative*:

- The biblical and magisterial authority to evangelize
- Learning to trust the Holy Spirit
- The importance of intentionally forming friendships outside of the "Catholic ghetto" to reach 'inactives' and 'nones'.
- Planning for and participating in apostolic Christian communities (see following section)
- Recognizing the "moments" of evangelization
   o Learning the art of listening
   o Sowing – Fertilizing – Harvesting – Sustaining
- Weddell's Thresholds of Conversion[102]
   o Trust – Curiosity – Openness – Seeking – Intentional Discipleship
- Identifying, articulating, and practicing your "witnesses"
- Sharing God in different settings
   o At home – at work – with friends – with strangers
- Pre-evangelization and apologetics for different people

    o   'Post-moderns' Millennials and Generation Z –
        scientific skeptics – distracted and busy –
        Fundamentalist-leaning Protestants, etc.

- Articulating the *kērygma* effectively
- Praying with and for your friend
- Accompanying and mentoring for the long haul

The specifics of the curriculum, the candidate recruitment process, the length of formation, the intervals between formation sessions, etc. all need to be worked out as part of the implementation planning process for the *Regional Vision Achievement Strategy*. That said, priority for recruitment should be given to people who, by virtue of who they are or the positions they hold, have an outsized influence on others. Catholic school principals, teachers, and coaches come to mind. In any event, a formal assessment should take place at the end of a cycle to avoid past mistakes and do better the next time.

In today's "virtual" world, the bishop and his planners might consider including the flexibility and unique resources that online distance learning can provide working in tandem with scheduled face-to-face gatherings for the sacraments and spiritual growth, discussions, and practicing personal witness stories.

The number of resources for training Catholic evangelizers is growing quickly. Two such resources are the *St. Paul School of Evangelization* sponsored by St. Paul Street Evangelization featuring Mary Healy, Ph.D. from Sacred Heart Major Seminary in Detroit and "reLit" training by Michael Dopp, STL of the *Mission of the Redeemer Ministries* out of Quebec.

The *Missionary Disciples Formation* process should be seen primarily as a responsibility of the diocese as opposed to the parish in order to promote consistency and unity throughout the particular Church. Moreover, an aspect of the formation is learning to work together across parish boundaries and developing apostolic communities that may draw from a wide area. That said, the parishes should take an active part in recruiting and nominating candidates for the *Missionary Disciples Formation* and should continue to involve them in parish ministries.

Two Essential Ingredients for Recruitment There are two absolutely essential ingredients of the *Missionary Disciples Formation* without which the formation will turn into an academic exercise that bears little fruit or will not take place at all. As mentioned previously, Catholic laity are reluctant to do anything without the assurance of knowing they are *authorized* to do it. This ultra-cautious aspect of our Church culture demands that candidates in *Missionary Disciples Formation* come to a deep understanding that they are not only *authorized* to evangelize, but they have been *commanded* to do so. With this thought in mind, the *recruitment* of candidates must emphasize this point. Without it, all the usual reasons for not making the commitment (e.g., "too busy", "what is this thing?", etc.) will be added to our Catholic reticence with the effect being to inhibit many prospective candidates from stepping up.

The second *sine qua non* for a successful *Missionary Disciples Formation* is an absolute commitment to developing friendships *outside of* Catholic circles. Sadly, there is a tendency for even serious Catholics to understand all formation "programs" in a very ego-centric way; they exist for my own "growth" as a Catholic. Candidates must understand that *Missionary Disciples Formation* represents a paradigmatic shift in our understanding of religious education: It is given for us to share, not hoard. Without an unambiguous willingness to make friends outside the boundaries of our 'Catholic ghettos', candidates should not be admitted.

Communities of Missionary Disciples Isolation is not the answer to anything except the spread of contagion. Obviously, our aim as evangelizers is the exact opposite of containment. An aphorism in the *Cursillo* movement is: "An isolated Christian is a paralyzed Christian." Especially in our highly individualistic, over-worked culture, isolation has become one of the foremost tactics of the enemy. How often it happens that an individual or a family will get so busy that they gradually isolate themselves from parish life; then, they start skipping Mass, and before you know it, they cease coming altogether. After enough time in this situation, even basic human values can change. With these thoughts in mind, the experience of Christian community is an essential part of the formation and ongoing ministry of missionary disciples.

In the context of the *Missionary Disciples Initiative* the Christian community is a place where we inspire one another by our mutual presence, prayer, fun, meals, praise, and service. As Psalm 133 reminds us: *How good it is, how pleasant, where the people dwell as one!* (v1). The very fact of being part of a Christian community is its own reward.

Hospitality as Evangelization At first blush, the last statement may sound like a contradiction of the previous dictum to make friends outside the Catholic ghetto. In fact, it is not. In addition to being a powerful means of sustaining and growing our own faith, Christian communities are a critical component of *regional evangelization*. Sometimes, we can accomplish together what we cannot accomplish on our own. So, the previous point still stands. We must make friends with those who have never (or only rarely) heard the *kērygma*. That said, those very friends can be invited into the Church *via* Christian communities. Pope St. Paul VI put it this way:

> Take a Christian or a handful of Christians who, in the midst of their own community, show their capacity for understanding and acceptance, their sharing of life and destiny with other people, their solidarity with the efforts of all for whatever is noble and good. Let us suppose that, in addition, they radiate in an altogether simple

and unaffected way their faith in values that go beyond current values, and their hope in something that is not seen and that one would not dare to imagine. Through this wordless witness these Christians stir up irresistible questions in the hearts of those who see how they live: Why are they like this? Why do they live in this way? What or who is it that inspires them? Why are they in our midst? Such a witness is already a silent proclamation of the Good News and a very powerful and effective one. Here we have an initial act of evangelization. The above questions will ask, whether they are people to whom Christ has never been proclaimed, or baptized people who do not practice, or people who live as nominal Christians but according to principles that are in no way Christian, or people who are seeking, and not without suffering, something or someone whom they sense but cannot name.[103]

Christian communities of missionary disciples can create "shallow ends" for people who are not ready to jump into the "deep end" of sacramental parish life. In fact, a 'none' may very happily accept an invitation to a get-together at someone's home when he wouldn't even consider an invitation to come to church. Simply witnessing Catholics who clearly love each other and have a good time in the process can serve as the first step in establishing *trust*, the first threshold of conversion. This can be the first step toward *Alpha* and the path on to deeper levels of conversion.

The make-up of Christian communities can and should vary based on the stage of life and particular circumstances of the missionary disciples. Following are a partial list:

The Evangelizing "Domestic Church" Families that live out their faith are the most natural Christian community and can serve as the initial step for inviting people into a relationship with Jesus. There is absolutely nothing threatening about being invited into a neighbor's home for a beer and barbeque. The beauty of a family gathered around a table holding hands and thanking the Lord has an irresistible appeal to even the most hardened of hearts.

The Community of Families Imagine you are the mother or father of a family with children at home and/or in college. Maybe, your children are still young and have had very little exposure to other Catholic families. A community of Catholic families that meets every month or two in someone's home for a good meal, prayer, and fun can reinforce all the truths, values, and devotions you are teaching them. Your children can grow up knowing that there are others who seriously believe as they do. This early involvement in a group with other Catholic families lays the foundation for a strong, secure identity that will serve them well as they get older and are exposed to ways of life that lure them away from their faith and the Church. Perhaps, your children are older and being exposed to ideas and ways of living that raise doubts about certain aspects of traditional Christian morality. The example and discussions that arise in a community of families can offer good reasons to remain faithful beyond mom and dad "preaching" at them. Not only can the gathering of a community of families serve as a kind of party that helps to evangelize your children at a crucial time in their lives, but it can be a comfortable place for including friends from outside of the "Catholic ghetto". A Catholic Community of Families is good for all involved.

> Christian communities are a critical component of regional evangelization. Sometimes we can accomplish together what we cannot accomplish on our own.

The Community of Singles For a single missionary disciple, it is probably even more important to be part of a Christian community comprised largely of other singles. Since, by definition, singles tend to spend more time alone than couples and families, they are more prone to isolation with all of its attendant problems. Moreover, despite our best intentions, parishes can be off-putting for older singles, and particularly for divorced and separated people, since churches are so often family-oriented. This fact is born-out by the statistics. According to the Pew Forum, 43 percent of married persons attend religious services at least once a week. The comparable number for divorced and separated is 32 percent. Conversely, 25 percent of married persons fall into the "seldom or never" category vs. 33 percent of divorce and separated people.[104] Meeting in coffee shops, bars, and restaurants, a Catholic Community of Singles can serve as the "shallow end" for young missionary disciples to invite friends who are open or actively searching for truth and meaning. They are a natural venue for pre-evangelization and can also be a source of strength for young people striving to remain chaste either as a "straight" or a "gay" person. Once again, a Catholic Community of Singles is good for all involved.

Role of the Diocese in Fostering Community The diocese is naturally suited as the locus for identifying potential leaders of these communities and linking them to prospective members. Most dioceses have the capabilities to assemble a regional database of Catholics by consolidating parish membership and campus ministry files. Aggregating approximate age, location, marital status, and contact information, the diocese is in a unique position to work with the growing number of missionary disciples who can serve as the facilitator to bring people together into communities that fit the circumstances and preferences of their lives. Geographic information systems (GIS) can map out people who live in any given area, making neighborhood-based communities possible. Dioceses should understand this service as a ministry of encouragement and facilitation for missionary disciples that functions on a permanent basis to keep information fresh and permit the continuation of the communities as members move and life circumstances change.

Drilling in to the *Regional Catholics Initiative*

 If it is true that what we cannot do as an individual, we may be able to do as a community, then it is also be true that what we cannot do as a community, we may

Regional Catholics Initiative

Aims:

To evangelize large segments of society through modern means of communication

To "connect" those who respond to the messaging with the local Church

To facilitate public understanding of Church teachings

To involve Catholic institutions located in the diocese in the Regional Catholics Initiative

be able to accomplish as a community of communities; in other words, as the entire diocesan Church working together, possibly even with the participation of other sympathetic Christians. This section takes a look as the fourth of the long-range initiatives in the *Vision Achievement Strategy*. While the specifics of such a strategy will, of course, vary from diocese to diocese, five possibilities are touched on in this section: a media campaign, the occasional "grand event", a "new apologetic", evangelization to the poor and other special populations, and Catholic institutional involvement. The chapter closes with a few words about formation for the *Regional Catholics Initiative*.

Looking Ahead Despite the gloom-and-doom prognostications of social commentators, it is possible to see glimmers of hope even now. If you get the opportunity to attend a SEEK Conference put on by the

Fellowship of Catholic University Students (FOCUS) and you will see what I mean. There is a nascent vibrancy in the Church even now that may be barely perceptible at the average parish Sunday Mass, but soon will be difficult not to notice. It is also happening in Europe. Despite the conventional wisdom of the secular press, the *Federalist* recently published a piece reporting on the signs of a budding new generation of Christianity breaking out all over Europe, even in Sweden, France, and other countries that have been written off. In an article by John D. Martin, a Parisian Catholic by the name of Pascal-Emmanuel Gobrey is quoted:

> On a recent Sunday, my family and I only showed up 10 minutes early for Mass. That meant we had to sit in fold-out chairs in the spillover room, where the Mass is relayed on a large TV screen…. This is business as usual for my church in Paris, France.
>
> I point this out because one of the most familiar tropes in social commentary today is the loss of Christian faith in Europe in general, and France in particular. *The Wall Street Journal* recently fretted about the sale of 'Europe's empty churches.'
>
> Could it be, instead, that France is in the early stages of a Christian revival?[105]

My wife and I recently visited Paris for a couple days and we witnessed just a hint at what Monsieur Gobrey reported. Passing by a Catholic Church at 5:30 on an ordinary Monday afternoon, we stopped in for a visit. As it happened, Mass was beginning in a small chapel in the front of the church, so we decided to stay. To our surprise, there were at least fifty people in attendance, most of them young adults and youth. Make no mistake, Europe is indeed very secular, but as reported by Martin and others, there are significant hints of a revival of faith, not only in the Catholic Church but throughout much of the Protestant world as well.

With the supernatural gifts of faith and hope, it is possible to think in terms of great missionary outreaches breaking out in post-modern, Western society. While we need to resist Pollyannaish forecasts that this revival will take place overnight and without resistance, we should *plan for it as a long-range goal.* Perhaps it will take a couple decades, but with a majority of parishes renewed and functioning purposefully to bring people to Christ and with a growing army of missionary disciples formed and functioning in vibrant communities, the organizational and human infrastructure will be in place for even greater things to happen.

The Media Campaign: Evangelization as Advertising In the context of the *Regional Catholics Initiative* television advertising lends itself as one potentially very important, albeit expensive, element. According to the Nielsen Company, TV commercials reach over 87 percent of individuals aged 18 and over.[106] In 2017, the average American consumer spent three hours and fifty-eight minutes in front of a TV every day.[107] The numbers are higher for adults. According to Nielsen, American adults watch five hours and four minutes per-day.[108] The ministry *Catholics Come Home* (www.catholics come home.org) led by former TV advertising executive Tom Peterson has demonstrated the immense potential of large-scale TV buys to proclaim the Gospel. In the dioceses that have worked with *Catholic Come Home*, the hard-hitting "evangomercials" that were aired have been successful in increasing Mass attendance by as much as 17 percent in six weeks with an average increase over 10 percent.[109] Moreover, most of the are not limited in their impact to the 'inactive Catholic' market.

Some have protested that many of the Catholics who "come home" as a result of these ad campaigns eventually return to their former ways. However, even if that is true, it is not the fault of the TV campaign. If the lives of those who responded to the TV spots were not always changed sufficiently to keep them coming back, the fault for that has to be laid at the feet of the institutional Church for not having previously created purposeful parishes and the army of missionary disciples needed to identify the returnees and accompany them until they have become committed disciples themselves.

Imagine the impact of a professionally-designed 6- to 8-week broadcast and cable TV ad campaign running on the major networks. Imagine commercial radio spots and well-located billboards complementing the television ads. Imagine this whole effort "saturated" in diocese-wide prayer and fasting.

Intentional Connection to Missionary Disciples Further, imagine the campaign being explicitly connected to a committed group of trained missionary disciples staffing a call-in and online response team. Imagine further that these front-line disciples listen to and pray with the responders (even online) and develop a modicum of trust. The missionary disciples would request the first name, home zip code, cell phone number and/or email address of the responders for the purpose of matching each one with a Catholic "welcomer" of the same sex and approximate age from a parish located near the responder's home. Being mature missionary disciples themselves and happy to meet responders before a weekend Mass, these welcomers patiently accompany and lovingly cultivate friendships with the responders; friendships that perdures for the long haul; friendships that give rise to a newly-committed relationship with Jesus and his people manifested in sacramental reconciliations after years away, or receptions into the Church, or even baptisms. All of these musings are actually possible. They have the very real potential produce an immediate 10- to 20-percent increase in weekly Mass attendance that would hold solid over time.

Suppose the campaign is so fruitful that the diocese repeats it every three to four years. Holding everything else constant, a region could reasonably expect a sustained increase in Mass attendance of well over 50 percent in a little over a decade. The key is long-term focus, accompaniment, and perseverance

Coming Together: Evangelization as Great Events Of course, there can be other potential components of the *Regional Catholics Initiative.* Much of what we commonly associate with evangelization historically has taken place through great preaching in the context of large gatherings. After Christ's ascension, the Acts of the Apostles records the first of these gatherings when Peter preached to a crowd in Jerusalem on the Jewish Feast of Pentecost with some three thousand responding and being baptized that very day (cf. 2:14-41). History is replete with the likes of John Chrysostom, Patrick, Peter Chrysologus, Anthony of Padua, Alphonsus Ligouri, Louis de Monfort, Fulton Sheen, and many others who dedicated their lives to converting large groups of people who listened to their compelling preaching.

The huge Protestant revivals of past and present can all be traced to the anointed preaching of committed evangelists. In our own times, the late Billy Graham, now-retired Luis Palau, and numerous others forthrightly invited and led many souls into conscious relationships with God. I myself have had the privilege of being on the floor of the arena at two such "crusades" as a member of the Catholic team designated to receive other Catholics who came forward during the "altar call".

As Catholics, we have a tendency to eschew such events as "too Protestant" for our taste. Because we don't share the "once-saved-always-saved" soteriology that underlies some of these events, we are inclined to dismiss their positive blessings altogether. We would do well to remember that it is not a bad thing for an individual to make a public commitment to Christ. It may not be the *whole* thing, but it is certainly a *good* thing and has been the beginning or re-beginning of many lives lived thereafter in union with our Lord.

Pope St. John Paul's establishment of World Youth Day in 1986 has some of the same overtones as these evangelical Protestant revivals. The scale is massive and the tone joyful. There may not be an altar call *per se*, but the popes have all invited the assembled young people to give their lives to Jesus and the altar call is implicit in their response to the Eucharist. Celebrated every two to three years at a different place around the globe, all of our popes since John Paul have embraced World Youth Days with tremendous enthusiasm.

It is reasonable to expect that well-planned diocesan- or province-sponsored regional youth days could very well have similar benefits. Including an individual public commitment to Christ in the company of missionary disciple-mentor-chaperones could add to their value, especially if follow-up is part of the plan. Great preaching, a plentiful supply of priests for Reconciliation and Anointing of the Sick, Eucharistic Adoration, great music, and small discussion groups could create a moment that reverberates throughout an entire lifetime.

In addition to these large-scale evangelical events, gender-specific gatherings of men and women may be very valuable. In the fictional interlude named *A Bishop's Dream* earlier in this book, Bishop Paul articulates his grand dream for the future of his diocese at an annual Priests Convocation. In his visionary speech he refers to a future moment standing together with his priests in a great sports arena leading all the men there in a solemn vow to honor their wives and future wives by never again using pornography. Combine such a vision with the healing opportunities of Reconciliation and Anointing and prayers for deliverance from demonically-influenced obsessions and, once again, lives can be changed. What a perfect time and place to experience the depths of God's mercy and to begin again on a whole new level!

In all of these initiatives, follow-up is key. This is one of the major reasons why the Church needs an "army" of well-formed missionary disciples. Without these mature Christian mentors (aka, 'Ananiases') who are willing to make friends with and accompany the seekers for the long-haul, even the best planned and executed *great event* will gradually fade in its impact. They must be planned as the *beginning* of something great; not as an end in themselves.

A New Apologetic: Telling our Story Better In bygone days, it was sufficient for priests and religious to teach the commandments without explanation. The population was largely illiterate. So, whatever Father or Sister said was simply received without question. After all, they may have been the only semi-educated people in the village. Hundreds of years have passed since those days, yet we still have a tendency to teach matters of faith and morals by *fiat*, or worse yet, not at all. Many young adult Catholics have not even heard that artificial birth control is morally problematic. The Church just hasn't told them. If by chance they have heard, it's a near certainty that they haven't been taught why.

Many people today have equal or superior educations *vis-à-vis* the clergy and their education has taught them to examine all assertions of truth through a critical lens. Take as an example cohabitation. If the underlying reasons *why* cohabitation are morally wrong are not immediately obvious, people understandably write it off as a remnant of a long-gone, irrelevant "religious society". In this day and age, we owe people: (1) the chance to hear that cohabitation may in fact be morally wrong, and; (2) all the reason why it may in fact be morally wrong. For the most part, they get neither from the Church at the present time.

Since the Church teaches that faith and reason support one another, it is not an affront to our faith to put forward arguments based on reason, logic, biology, sociology, and history, in addition to revelation. They all form a coherent whole. For example, the

315

combined arguments of faith and reason in favor of natural family planning versus artificial birth control are compelling. Yet, very few Catholics – let alone larger secular society – have ever systematically heard these arguments. The same can be said of the Christian understanding of human dignity, the inviolability of human life from conception to natural death, Catholic principles of social justice, the beauty and wonder of monogamous heterosexual marriage, the redemptive value of human suffering, and on and on.

There are many people who reject Christianity out of hand because of a particular moral teaching. Some will refuse to listen for any number of reasons. But some *will* accept it, if we become more intentionally forthcoming with the answers.

It is true that catechesis is not the same thing as evangelization. That said, they are closely related and the Lord sometimes uses those intellectual "aha" moments to remove cultural obstacles to other Christian truth claims. Kimberley Hahn (the wife of Professor Scott Hahn) tells the story of taking a course in college when she was a Protestant Christian in which she researched the teachings of the Catholic Church on artificial birth control. Much to her surprise, the arguments resonated with her and she later reported that this experience was the first serious opening she had ever given to Catholicism. For sincere seekers, commonly held secular beliefs, left unchallenged, can block any consideration of even more central gospel claims.

Accordingly, pastorally sensitive apologetics can play a role in regional evangelization. To this end, possible approaches that dioceses might explore include:

- *Why We Believe* call-in numbers staffed by a team of specially-trained, on-call apologists
- Free webinars focusing on specific "hot button" issues

Aiming at the Poor and the Hurting There is a growing body of research that the poor are being left behind in this country; not just economically, but in many facets of traditional American life. Most alarmingly, the percentage of the population in the bottom third income group that is practicing *any* religion is now so small that – as a group – they are becoming disconnected from even basic moral moorings that are the foundation of any civil society (see Chapter XV). [110] At the same time, the poor are often among the first to respond to proclamations of the Gospel, because – unlike their more prosperous neighbors – they cannot deceive themselves into thinking they can get through life happy and healthy without a Savior. Without an intentionally evangelizing Church, they do find other "saviors".

Measured in terms of social services for low income people, the Catholic Church continues to reach out with many helping hands. Unfortunately, we have tended to compartmentalize our faith from our services. Moreover, our capacity to educate the poor has diminished over the years with the loss of religious communities dedicated to that charism.

Suppose a bishop took it upon himself to address these simultaneous realities in a single, long-range strategy. Whatever that strategy might look like, it is safe to say that it will require *regional resources, purposeful parishes,* and *committed missionary disciples* who are well trained for the task. I can only hope and pray our bishops will take up this challenge with clarity of vision, determination, and great patience.

Needless to say, there are other special populations that may or may not be poor in an economic sense: the mentally ill, the homebound, the incarcerated, the physically disabled, the dying who are cut off from their families. A *Regional Catholics Initiative* that is truly comprehensive will include committed missionary disciples ministering in love to all of these hurting people.

Involving Catholic Institutions I have heard several bishops acknowledge that the largest Catholic institutions in his diocese operate on a day-to-day basis without any reference at all to their Catholic identity. In fact, the local Catholic university or the gigantic Catholic medical center probably answer to independent boards which often do not include the bishop as one of their members. Some seem to have consciously made the decision to exclude him. I don't pretend to have an answer for how to address these situations. In some cases, the *de facto* break between the bishop and the institution may be of long-standing and probably cannot be fixed by a unilateral mandate.

That said, if one contemplates the potential benefits of a reconciliation between bishop and institution, it would certainly be worth the effort from a Catholic evangelical perspective to try to breach the gap. If – over time – a "Board-level" policy directed renegade "Catholic" universities to begin filling vacated faculty chairs with highly-qualified *and* orthodox Catholic professors, there would undoubtedly be a faculty revolt. But after the "dust settled", students would begin to come home still being Catholic rather than freshly-minted secularists. If the "Catholic" hospital integrated authentically Catholic ministry into its palliative care practice, otherwise confused and anxious people could die in peace with their families prepared to make changes in their own lives.

All of this is simply by way of suggesting that the gradual remaking of nominally Catholic institutions into truly Catholic ones should be considered as an element of the long-range *Vision Achievement Strategy.*

Preparation for the *Regional Catholics Initiative* About the only thing that can be said with certainty about the PREPARE step associated with this initiative is that its specifics will depend entirely on the elements included in the *Short-Range Tactical Plan*.

For example, if the *Tactical Plan* includes a major media advertising campaign within the next year or two, then pastors and parish staffs have to be prepared for how to respond effectively to those who respond to the ads. The diocese will need to put in place protocols to graciously introduce inquirers to designated pastors and parish staffs. In turn, the parishes will need to have mechanisms to move the responders to the "right" missionary disciple who will intentionally befriend and take some measure of responsibility for mentoring and guiding them to the next step in their faith life (e.g., Reconciliation, RCIA, etc.). A non-threatening reporting system might be put in place to encourage and assist missionary disciples to follow through and see to it that newly-(re)committed folks get registered in their parishes and their progress tracked.

Similar forms of welcoming and committed accompaniment would need to be in place for those who respond to a diocesan "great event".

A potential resource that holds promise for a "new apologetics" component is a British-based ministry that trains spokespersons in over twenty countries to competently communicate the Catholic message on TV and radio. *Catholic Voices* began in the United Kingdom in 2010 as an emergency response to extremists' efforts to prevent the visit of Pope Benedict to England (see www.catholicvoicese.org.uk). Their immediate 6-month goal was to train twenty-four lay people and a priest "to improve the Church's representation in the media, above all in news programs and debates." Their appearance on over one hundred programs was so successful that they were urged to continue as a permanent ministry after the pope's visit. After a bumpy start in the U.S., *Catholic Voices* is currently planning on restarting training in New York in the near future and subsequently in Chicago and Los Angeles.

If a diocese's *Regional Catholics Initiative* includes (an) element(s) for evangelizing special populations such as poor families, or the mentally ill, the *Tactical Plan* will need to incorporate the expertise of local specialists in the formation of the missionary disciples who will be assisting. Catholic Charities would almost certainly play a role in training and coordination and the expertise of trusted social workers, psychologists, and others may be needed.

* * *

"For Nothing Will Be Impossible for God"

After hearing the stunning news that she was being invited to become the mother of the Son of God, Gabriel's parting message to Mary – a committed virgin – were words of unimaginable hope: "for nothing will be impossible for God" (Lk 1:37).

The aims and the methods associated with building a totally evangelized and converted region may seem about as daunting as Gabriel's announcement to our Lady. But it is "not impossible for God". For our part, it will require some organizational changes, to be sure. More importantly, it calls for a new long-term, results-oriented focus on proclaiming the Gospel and making disciples with a purpose bigger than themselves. But it is possible, "for if God is for us, who can be against us?" (Rom 8:31)

XIII. Interlude: *Heroic Holiness*

"Okay, Bishop, three-two-one, you're on."

"Good morning and thank you for coming. I have called this news conference to make an announcement that has the potential to change the local Church from this moment forward. It will require us to take up an altogether new challenge. This is my greatest hope: that in taking up that challenge, it will change us. If it helps to change our city; if it helps to change the lives of our friends, so much the better.

"I have to start here. St. Paul, St. Peter, St. John… all of them at one time or another wrote something that sounds like this: My life is not my own. My body is not my own. I have been purchased at a price, a very high price, the price of Christ's blood (cf. Rom 8:9, 1 Cor 6:19-20, 1 Cor 7:23, Gal 3:13-15, 1 Peter 1:19, Rev 1:5, Rev 5:7). I think of that often. I believe it, but I do not always live like I believe it. Too often, I forget that I am not my own; that I am a willing indentured servant to the One who bought me at the price of his own life. But, for myself, I am resolved to change. I am resolved to grow as a Christian man and I am asking every Catholic family in this diocese to join me. No, let me restate that. I am inviting every Christian family and even those who may not be Christian to join me.

"Beginning this afternoon, anyone who is hurting, anyone who is scared, anyone who is homeless, anyone who needs a new start in life, anyone who is alone, anyone who is victimized, anyone who simply needs a friend or a ride to the doctor's office… call the number on the bottom of this screen. *Let us become your friends.*

"One afternoon on the way to the Temple Peter and John encountered a disabled man begging for alms. Peter looked at the man and said, 'I have neither silver nor gold, but what I do have I give you: in the name of Jesus, the Nazorean, the Christ, rise and walk.' (Acts 3:6) For myself, I will begin to give what I have. I have a home, a nice home with a lot more room than I need. I have already asked Father John Madison to move in, and together, Father John and I will open our home to someone who needs housing. Maybe we can help someone get back on his feet.

"There are many couples – empty nesters – in the same situation, people who have plenty of room. I expect that some of us will be willing to open our homes to families who are now living in their cars.

"Of course, everyone's situation is different. Many will not be able to open their homes. But everyone can do something: Talk on the phone to someone who is lonely. Be a friend to a cancer patient facing chemo therapy. Adopt a "grandma" in a nursing home. If you live in a nursing home, perhaps you can knit a sweater for a homeless child.

"If you're a student and just learned that you are expecting a baby, we will try to be father or mother, sister or brother, always a friend. If your boyfriend has abandoned you and your parents have thrown you out, you can stay with us. In short, we will be your companions; a shoulder to cry on; a friend to laugh with. We will walk with you, sometimes clothe you, sometimes feed you. We will be there for you both before your baby comes, and after. We will babysit, we will educate and tutor, we will use whatever influence we have to your advantage. Should it happen that you lose your baby – no matter how that happens – we will be there for you then as well. Should you decide to give up your baby for adoption, we will help you find the right home for her. No questions asked. No judgments. No recriminations, no conditions, and no publicity.

"No one will be too low to receive our friendship and no one too high to offer it. Maybe you have a made a serious mistake; maybe you are caught up in drug or alcohol abuse and you need a second or third or fourth chance. If you're willing to try to help yourself, we will be willing to do whatever we can give you that chance.

"At the end of the day, whether you realize it or not, you will be our reward. We will receive from you as well as the other way around. We will learn from you. We will receive *your* friendship as well as you receiving ours. We will laugh together. We will cry together. We will become "we".

We will not be perfect. Life is messy. We won't guarantee "success". All we guarantee is that we will be friends and walk through life together. That's why I've decided to call this initiative *"Friend-to-Friend"*. If you're interested, simply call the number on the bottom of the screen.

"Now, I'm sure you have many questions and I will do my best to answer them."

"Bishop Paul, Bishop Paul...."

"Yes, the woman here in the front row."

"Bishop, I'm sure everyone applauds your good intentions, but how in the world do you propose to do this"? I mean, you could be flooded with requests. How is the Diocese going to pay for all this?"

"Excellent question... The short and utterly truthful answer is: I don't know yet. All I know is that God is big enough to provide it. It is the Lord who will make this happen. Not me. Honestly, I'm not worried about that in the least. Typically, I expect there will be no exchange of money at all. If there is, it will happen indirectly through Catholic Charities or the St. Vincent de Paul Society or any one of several great philanthropic agencies here in town. We will work with all of them to bring all the resources available to help address the needs of our friends.

"Bishop, Bishop, how can you guarantee people won't get hurt? I mean, you're asking people to open their homes to some pretty unsavory and probably unscrupulous people out there."

"Another great question. The short answer is: I can't guarantee anything. There is always risk in following the Lord. If there weren't, we wouldn't call it faith. That said, not everyone is in a position that they can open their homes. Not everyone is called to do that. If you have young children living at home, you're first responsibility is to them. I would never put one of them at risk by asking such a family to open their home to a troubled single man. Perhaps, later in their life, they may be able to. But a young family could very easily befriend a college student who is going through a difficult patch in his life. We can't give what we ourselves do not have. Just as Peter and John said to the disabled man at the Temple, 'I have neither silver nor gold, but what I do have I give you.'"

"Bishop, Bishop…"

"Yes, the gentleman in the back… there."

"Bishop Paul, forgive my saying so, but some people are going to view this announcement as a publicity stunt to cast the Catholic Church in a more positive light than has been in the news lately."

"Oh, heaven forbid." Chuckles were heard throughout the room. Continuing with a twinkle in his eye, "Wouldn't it be a sad thing if the world were to see the loving side of the Church?" More laughter. "Seriously, I will not ignore the sins of the Church. The things that have been done to innocent children by abusive priests have broken my heart and I will never be the same. I can honestly say that I myself – a lifelong Catholic and priest and now bishop – have been sickened

324

that the problem exists at all, let alone by the extent of it. From the bottom of my heart, I am truly sorry.

"Having said that, in the interest of balanced reporting, it would be helpful if the media reported on the progress that has happened since 2002 when the U.S. bishops adopted the *Dallas Charter for the Protection of Children and Young People*. All but a handful of the clergy sex abuse cases reported in the Pennsylvania Grand Jury report happened before 2002. In fact, most of them long before 2002. There have always been bad priests and bishops and even a few popes in the two thousand-year history of the Catholic Church. There is no denying that.

"There is also no denying the Catholic Church has opened and run more hospitals than any nation or other organization in history. We were the first organization to establish orphanages and care for destitute children. To this day, we educate more children than any institution in the world. We founded the university system of higher education and, contrary to popular belief, we developed the scientific method. For centuries, there were very few scientists who were *not* associated with the Church. In fact, this rich tradition of scientific and engineering accomplishments continues right up to the present. Did you know it was a Catholic priest from Belgium – Father Georges Lemaître – who discovered the Big Bang in 1927?" The litany of good that the Church has given to the world doesn't even begin to touch on the countless lives that have been changed and healed and, yes, saved by the love of good Catholics who have always vastly outnumbered those how aren't.

"Please pray for us as we move forward to become better than we have been."

"Bishop, Bishop Paul…

XIV. The Key to Getting It Done

*When he has driven out all his own, he walks ahead of them,
and the sheep follow him, because they recognize his voice.*

John 10:4

*I have become all things to all,
to save at least some.*

1 Cor 9:22

In Chapter XII, we focused on those things we have to *do* in order to evangelize a region. In this chapter, we will focus on *how* to do those things, because *how* we do things is as important as *what* we do. In fact, to a large degree, *how* we do anything, determines the success of *what* we are doing.

Although there is plenty for *everyone* to do, when it comes to evangelization, this chapter has been written mainly with the diocesan clergy in mind – most especially, diocesan bishops. At times, it is even addressed to them in the vocative voice. That is not to say that there isn't a load of content here for the rest of the Church, especially if you're interested in becoming a transformational leader. I sincerely hope that everyone will read it, but ask your indulgence if it doesn't "speak" directly to you.

Let's begin by considering the special gift – the charism – of the diocesan clergy.

The Charism of Diocesan Clergy: *In the World but Not of It*

I first met Father Joe when I was 14 years old. Liked him immediately. Only out of the seminary a few years, Fr. Joe had a winning smile and a kind, winsome way about him that just naturally drew people to him. With a freshly-minted Masters in English from Notre Dame, he taught English at Magister Noster Latin School, a new diocesan high school seminary. He was – and still is – a model priest. As an impressionable kid, I knew I wanted to be like him.

I remember going to him one day and asking him how Jesus, the Son of God, could possibly be the equal of God the Father. After all, Jesus had seemed to correct the man who addressed him as "good teacher" by gently asking him, "Why do you call me good? No one is good but God alone." In response to my early questioning, Father Joe just as gently pointed out that Jesus may have actually been proclaiming his own divinity with that statement (cf. Lk 18:19). He then went on to remind me that Jesus had also said, "the Father and I are one" (Jn 10:30) and that he told Philip, "whoever has seen me has seen the Father" (Jn 14:9). Problem solved.

While it didn't take long to discern that God was calling me to marriage instead of the celibate priesthood, to this day, I still find myself trying to emulate him. After those early high school years, I didn't see Father Joe again until I was a grown man. Our paths crossed and he invited me to be his guest at a civic group luncheon, a civic group where he was president that year! I was surprised, not at his invitation, but rather that he – a priest – was president of a *civic* group that had absolutely nothing to do with the Church. Over the years, it became clear that Father Joe knew practically everyone in town... and they all loved him and he loved them. He had a regular column in the local paper. He routinely played tennis with a group of guys, not all Catholic by any means.

Father Joe was the most caring man I think I ever knew and he still is. When you talk to him, it doesn't matter if there are a hundred other people around, at that moment you are the only person on earth. He is blessed with that remarkable recall that allows him to call people he hasn't seen in years by their first name. When someone dies and he has the funeral, it is commonplace for Father Joe to shed a tear or two right in the middle of his homily, right along with the family.

People just naturally are drawn to him, and over the years more than a few have been drawn into the Church. When that has happened, it was usually after years of friendship. Not just a quick, facile conversion or two. As a friend, he *earned* their trust. He was the *real thing.*

As a deacon who had the privilege of serving with him for several years, I became amazed at his boundless commitment and energy. A part of his weekly routine was to visit parishioners (and others) in the hospital *every Sunday* afternoon. It was not uncommon for him to celebrate and/or preach three Sunday morning masses, grab a bite to eat, go spend a few hours at the hospital, and be back at church in time for 5:30 p.m. Mass. (By comparison, when I preached all the weekend masses, I was usually knapping on Sunday afternoon.)

Another thing I noticed about Father Joe in those years: when a parishioner had a reasonable idea for a ministry, he *always* let them run with the ball. He was an "empowerer" in the best sense of the word. As a result, ministries flourished at St. John the Baptist Church. To this day, St. John is blest with a large thrift store and food bank, founded, managed, and run entirely by parishioners.

Although he would probably wince to read these words: Father Joe did *not* have an open-door policy. In my book, that was to his *credit.* He didn't spend a lot of time in the office. He had a wonderful executive assistant who managed a lot of things for him and did a great job of cleaning up after him. If you wanted to talk to Father Joe for more than 30 seconds, you usually had to make an appointment like anybody else. When he was "in", the door was typically closed, because someone else was in there. The rest of the time, he was "out" attending to the people who couldn't conveniently come to him or he was at a meeting somewhere because, of course, he was constantly in demand.

Father Joe was and still is – even in his so-called retirement – *effective*. He was *affective*. Never without his Roman collar (except on the tennis court), he brought people to Jesus and, by his very presence, he brought Jesus to people.

Underlying all of this activity, Father Joe was a man of great prayer. I remember sitting next to him in a cramped economy seat on a trans-Atlantic flight. After a long, tiring day, he pulled out his breviary, prayed evening and night prayer, put on his neck donut, and peacefully fell asleep.

He is a man of immense *emotional intelligence*. He has the *charism* of the diocesan priesthood. He is "*in* the world, but not *of* it" (cf. Jn 17:15-18).

* * *

On the Call to Universal Holiness

One of the great themes of the Second Vatican Council was the "call to universal holiness" (cf. *Lumen gentium,* II). The council fathers rightly recognized the ubiquitous attitude of the laity that tended to cordon off the clergy and religious from everyone else. If you wanted to be holy, you went into the seminary, or joined a religious community. It was as simple as that. They were the holy ones. They prayed for the rest of us. The priests offered the Sacrifice of the Mass for us. The rest of us were obliged to attend Mass on Sundays, abstain from meat on Fridays, and throw a little something in the collection box. If you were a really *outstanding* lay person, you might pray the rosary, have masses said for dead relatives, make a retreat once in a while, and send money to the missions. Done.

This ecclesiology needed to change. And it did. And we are still reeling from it. It has been a little over a half century since those heady days of Vatican II and I suspect it may take another half century before the Church fully regains the balance and maturity the council fathers were hoping for.

One of the unintended consequences of the Council's "call to universal holiness" was the diminution of the role of the clergy as *leaders*. Even if the ordained were still recognized as *the* leaders, they were no longer expected to *be* leaders. In the efforts of the Church to encourage the laity to step up, many of the clergy stepped down. It was now right and good for ordinary dads and moms to strive for holiness. Simultaneously, it seemed to be okay for priests and religious to become unholy, and even make a point of it.

This was no more evident than in the arena of evangelization. It was up to the laity to become the sole voices of the Gospel. After all, it was the laity that were in the marketplace. They could go places and influence people that priests and nuns (supposedly) couldn't.

> Even if the ordained were still recognized as *the* leaders, they were no longer expected to *be* leaders. In the efforts of the Church to encourage the laity to step up, many of the clergy stepped down.

In order for the New Evangelization to thrive, we need to appropriate a healthy balance here.

Imagine a particular Church in which the bishop is well-known throughout the larger community because of his involvement in activities and events that are not strictly Catholic or even Christian.

How much value might there be if he invested in secular friendships made at, say, *Rotary?* Through those relationships, could he reestablish the Church as a voice worth listening to in the community?

Imagine pastors throughout the diocese training and leading small teams of parishioners in weekend visitation ministries; knocking on doors and asking neighbors if they have prayer needs and agreeing to accompany them if they would like to come to church.

Imagine deacons going with the Men's Club to a soup kitchen and sitting down afterwards for Bible study with their new friends – the street people they had just served.

If our leaders had their proverbial "antennas" extended so as to "pick up signals" about the hurts and concerns of people and recognize the evangelical opportunities right in front of them, how many people might eventually be brought into a relationship with our Lord and mentored, grafted into the Church, and grow into mature disciples? And, how many more ordinary Catholics would broaden their horizons, gain new confidence, and learn to share their faith in altogether new situations?

Imagine the impact that *clerical* leadership of this type would have on laywomen and men who witness this Christ-like example. These kinds of leaders would help to redefine what it means to be a committed Christian. They would bring us out of our exclusive Catholic enclaves and inspire creative new ministries "to the peripheries", as Pope Francis is fond of saying. They would debunk some of the misconceptions and stereotypes about Catholicism that are so common in secular culture. They would expand the horizons of what is possible beyond the four walls of our church buildings.

XIV. The Key to Getting It Done

The Missed Call to Clerical Holiness Something our clergy must learn to do is make the distinction between the respect and even affection the faithful accord them versus a vote of confidence in their leadership. In many cases, the high regard lay people have for the ordained is based on their spiritual grasp of the validity and efficacy of the sacrament of Ordination. This valid spiritual perception does not automatically translate into credibility or confidence.

At the 2018 Fall Meeting of the USCCB, Cardinal William Tobin of Newark commented: "If Catholics' trust in the credibility of our bishops was so easily shattered by the sex-abuse crisis, what was there before? What was our credibility built on, that it could be so swept away?"[111] I must confess being a little surprised by his remark. It suggests a certain clerical naïveté, even in high places. Maybe this disconnect is part-and-parcel of the aura that automatically comes along with ordination to the episcopacy.

The fact is: Our bishops have not had the widespread confidence of the people for decades. Any illusion to the contrary only serves to strengthen the perception that bishops tend to live in a Catholic "bubble". For that matter, many of the "most involved Catholics" do too.

In referring to bishops, an old friend used to quip: "A tree grows from the bottom up and dies from the top down." Not without good reason, he saw whatever was good in the Church coming about from lay movements; certainly not from the "institutional church". That has been the experience of many (if not most) Catholics who grew up during or after Vatican II. If we're lucky, a lay movement may get a nod of approval from the local ordinary. But, enthusiastic support? Well, that only comes about after great circumspection, if at all.

Moreover, the thought that a bishop might demonstrate heroic holiness himself and initiate an inspiring movement of faith is simply not a part of the experience of many U.S. Catholics. The expressions "leading from behind" and "leadership by consensus" come to mind. These modes of leadership are about the best we have come to expect from our bishops. For the most part, the same can be said of our priests and deacons (including myself). As George Weigel has put it: "No one is going to be converted to friendship with Jesus and enflamed with a passion for mission by a discussion-group moderator: not priests, not lay adults, not the young."[112]

Despite Cardinal Tobin's perplexity over how our bishops' credibility could be so easily crushed by the sex-abuse crisis, Archbishop Charles Chaput lays at least some of the problem right back at the feet of our bishops.

> The 'power' of the Church resides not in her public statements or material resources, her structures or social services, but in her ability to form and lead her people – and to be their first loyalty. When Catholics trust their leaders and believe their teaching, the Church is strong. When they don't or when they lose sight of who and what the Church is, she's weak. This is why bishops are so gravely accountable for their actions and inaction. It's also why Catholics who undermine trust in Church teaching sin so the seriously against their own Baptism.[113]

What engenders trust in the Church? The answer is simple: sincere, unabashed holiness. It is not great managerial qualities, nor is it bombastic rhetoric. When we encounter holiness, it is obvious. It stands out against the darkness like "a city set on a mountain that cannot be hidden." It is "a light that shines before others" that is clearly visible to all, "so that they may see your good works and glorify your heavenly Father." (Mt 5:16)

The Missed Call to Lay Holiness Of course, there is room for blame all around. There was a time in U.S. history when Catholics were more "Catholic" than "American". At that time, bishops had great credibility among the faithful. Not so anymore. In our desire to demonstrate what good Americans we could be, the Catholic Faith weakened over the past century and that faith has been replaced with secularization and relativism. Ordinary Catholics have come to view the world through the eyes of ordinary Americans whose beliefs are formed primarily through media opinion-makers and entertainment-elites.

This can be verified by the very fact that, in the aggregate, Catholics' opinions on most issues, as well as our behavior, are indistinguishable from the "average American". Views on abortion are only slightly different. We divorce at about the same rate as the general population; accept non-biblical sexual activities at the same rate; we are evenly divided between Democrats and Republicans just like the rest of America; we attend Mass on Sundays about as often as the population as a whole goes to church. Even some of our theological beliefs have taken on a more Protestant leaning (e.g., widespread disbelief in the true Presence). Belief in a "personal God" as opposed to an "impersonal force stands at only 61 percent of Catholics, a mere 4 percentage points higher than the population as a whole. (Among Christian groups, on this central doctrine of Christianity, Catholics come in dead last.) [114, 115]

So, why would Catholics as a whole find their ordained leaders to be any more credible than say, a congressman or a senator or any other "leader" in the secular sphere? The troubling truth is that most "Catholics" have only a weak Catholic identity; something akin to having Irish ancestry. To this large swath of the American population, bishops are a combination of "figurehead" and bureaucratic "functionary"; not "shepherd", and certainly, not "fisherman". Without a strong Catholic identity, the only source of news about our bishops is the mainstream media. In fact, many Catholics would not recognize their own bishop in a line-up of mug shots.

In an open, pluralistic culture, each individual customizes his own personal identity; nothing is simply inherited anymore. Identity with a group must be earned, not passively assumed. As a starting point for self-identification as a Catholic, an individual must be distinguishable from the typical secularist. Accordingly, if our leaders want credibility, they must first become very public saints; very distinguishable from secular leaders. This is possible, even in modern times. St. Maximilian Kolbe did it. St. Teresa of Calcutta did it. Pope St. John Paul II did it... and many more.

To identity with a group that professes special access to the Truth – especially Truth which proposes norms of behavior that constrain our unconstrained impulses – the Truth must be presented *credibly*. It is not likely to be credible, if its official spokesmen are not heroically holy. Credibility must be earned.

It is also not likely to be credible if its purported followers refuse to follow; if we set our own perceptions and worldviews above those of Christ and the Church that he promised to preserve and lead "into all truth" (cf. Mt 16:18, Jn 16:13).

The Senses of Clericalism

In one sense, "clericalism" is a disease that has afflicted the Catholic Church for centuries. It always starts with the priest, who claims a certain entitlement to special treatment in restaurants and signs of deference at ecclesiastical gatherings. I have even seen it among brother deacons (as low as we are in the clerical pecking order). In any case, by virtue of his special calling, some clerics place themselves above the people they were ordained to love in a special way. They can twist reality into a justification of almost any kind of behavior. While they would never admit it, they are narcissists of the worst kind. They can be predators who will use their position of power to intimidate the weak, even to the point of using them for their basest desires. These are the Pharisaical "blind guides who strain out the gnat and swallow the camel" (Mt 23:24). They are the ones who would be better off "to have a great millstone hung around (their) neck and drowned in the depths of the sea" for having dragged "a little one" into sin (cf. Mt 18:6, Mk 9:42, Lk 17:2).

Now, for comparison, let's go back to Father Joe for a moment. While he is very clearly a Catholic priest, there is nothing about him that is unapproachable or that feigns superiority. In fact, he is the most warm and approachable of men. Little children come up and wrap their arms around his legs. He wants to know how Memorial High School did at Friday night's game. If a person has lost her job, he will pray with her right on the spot. One of the most touching things to witness is Father Joe conferring the Sacrament of Healing in a communal setting. He spends a minute with each person who approaches him in line to quietly find out about the nature of his illness and then he lays his hand on the recipient's shoulder and personally prays with him before anointing his forehead and hands. Sacramental efficacy aside, *everyone* comes away healed by the presence of Christ in this holy, caring man.

This is a very healthy and holy form of clericalism. It is not something that I would look for in a person who has *not* been ordained. We need to face it: It is the *laity* who won't let go of this understanding of clericalism. Why? Because, this is the *sensus fidei* lived out. The Holy Spirit doesn't want them to let go of it. This also accounts for the continuing affection that so many Catholics have for their bishops, despite the very same bishops' bungling mismanagement. It is also the same reason why cases like that of (former Cardinal) Theodore McCarrick engender so much anger. People rightly feel betrayed.

The long-overdue "call to universal holiness" is one of the great gifts to the Church that the Second Vatican Council ushered in. It is right for lay people to pursue holiness, especially a holiness that is appropriate to being a mom or a dad, to being a physician or an ironworker.

This fact does not obviate the need for clerical leadership, even in the work of evangelization. The ascendancy of some does not infer the descent of others. The ordained and those in religious life should not act as if they are no longer needed; as if they should abdicate their own special calling to leadership. In his 1992 Post-Synodal Exhortation *Pastores Dabo Vobis*, Pope St. John Paul offered an insight that pertains directly to the issue of clerical involvement in evangelization.

> Without priests the Church would not be able to live that fundamental obedience which is at the very heart of her existence and her mission in history, an obedience in response to the command of Christ: "Go therefore and make disciples of all nations" (*Mt.* 28:19) and "Do this in remembrance of me" (*Lk.* 22:19; cf. 1 *Cor.* 11.24), i.e., an obedience to the command to announce the Gospel and to renew daily the sacrifice of the giving of his body and the shedding of his blood for the life of the world. (1)

Evangelization and Eucharist – the two enduring jobs of a priest. Without these, the Church will never be able to bring the world to Jesus. Evangelization is *not* the sole preserve of the laity. The fact that so many hierarchs seem to have made that unjustified leap lies at the root of our failures to bring Jesus to our broken world.

The Human Need for Leadership

In the First Book of Samuel, we learn that the Hebrew people desired to have a king – a military leader who would protect them from their enemies in just the same way that the neighboring pagan nations looked to their kings for protection. Samuel was upset with this request. By now, he was an old man and looking back over his life, he had conscientiously tried to judge the people with wisdom and fairness. He knew that his two approbate sons would not do a good job as his successor. Still, it hurt that the people wanted a monarch, a completely different mode of governance than he had provided under the direct counsel of God. Samuel did his best to dissuade the people. He pointed out how a monarch would impose taxes and conscript their sons into military service. It was to no avail. They persisted and when Samuel took the matter to God, the Lord answered him: "Grant the people their every request. It is not you they reject; they are rejecting me as their king (8:7)."

There is something instinctive in the human race that longs for human protection and security beyond that which we are able to provide for ourselves. At its root, I suspect this is a longing for our Creator. It is an innate desire that draws us to him. In the best of worlds, we would rely only on him and on "the work of our hands". But insofar as we are limited in what we can do for ourselves and dependence on God requires a degree of faith that many do not have, we erect governments for protection from adversaries, to mediate justice, to coordinate the provision of common needs, etc. As we can see from the experience of Samuel, God respects these human desires and even blesses them.

What's more, he provided a clear form of governance for his Church that blossomed even within the first century A.D. By the second century, this trifold system of bishop-presbyters-deacons was the norm throughout nascent Christendom.

The point is this: While we may not always be happy with our ecclesial system of governance, until our Lord returns, this is what we've got. It is the system he actually set up (cf. Mt 16:15-1, Mt 18:18, *et al*) and experiments with more democratic modes of governance have not proven any better. He also emphasized the importance of being in agreement and that the Father would grant anything we asked together in his name (cf. Mt 18:19, *et al*). So, the best we can hope for during the foreseeable future is outstanding human leadership from those he has ordained to lead us combined with a common search for and dependence on the providence of God.

People need human leadership and, whether they admit it or not, most actually *want* to be led. At times, this desire for human leadership has given rise to autocrats and demagogues who are more than happy to lead in self-aggrandizing and destructive ways. One need only consider the history of the twentieth century to recognize that tendency. Yet, even after those disastrous experiences, the desire for leadership – even strong, decisive leadership – has not gone away. Consider the attention and exaggerated importance we Americans give to presidential elections. Supporters of whatever political stripe fawn over their candidate as if the outcome will be a coronation rather than a defined term of public service.

It is inevitable that we will always have leaders – good ones and bad ones. The question that remains open is whether or not the Church can raise up leaders – especially ordained leaders – who are capable of leading people into truth. Again, quoting Archbishop Chaput:

> Everyone's grasp of truth rests to some degree on authority. No one is really autonomous. We can't know everything on our own. We need to trust others for guidance. This is normal. But who and what we trust matters greatly.[116]

What might such leaders look like?

On the Call for Transformational Leaders

It goes without saying that leaders come in all shapes and sizes, colors, and (both) genders. Some people are perceived as leaders by virtue of the position they hold. Other leaders may not be formally recognized, but draw many followers by dint of sheer personality or charisma. Assuming we are talking about a well-intentioned leader, it is helpful when formal position and personal leadership traits line up. In virtue of his ordination, an *ordained* leader shares in the leadership of Christ *in persona Christi capitis*. This sacramental grace, however, may or may not line up with his personal attributes. For the church leader who wants to influence the mindset and behavior of the faithful, these attributes become very important. So, what can we say about the attributes of someone who aspires to be a *transformational leader?*

In 2001 a book entitled *Good to Great* was published that sold over three million copies, was translated into 32 languages, and stayed on the *New York Times*, *Wall Street Journal*, and *Business Week* best-sellers lists for months.[117] The author was Jim Collins, arguably the reigning researcher, teacher, and author on great business practices. In one of his earlier books, *Built to Last,* Collins unearthed the qualities of that small list of companies that manage to sustain greatness from one decade to the next. But the question that continued to haunt him was how average or even poor companies *become* great companies. In preparing for *Good to Great,* Collins headed up a team of twenty researchers for over five years to answer that question. What makes some companies ascend to "enduring greatness", while others don't?

Their process was rigorous. The research team started with a *tabula rasa,* developing "all of the concepts in [the] book by making *empirical* deductions *directly from the data.* We did not begin this project with a theory to test or prove. We sought to build a theory from the ground up, derived directly from the evidence (*italics* in original)."[118] Not surprisingly, they found that leadership was one of the key ingredients and not just leadership in general, but a special kind of leadership. Collins rigorously defined the qualities of business leaders and at the top of his taxonomy were a rare group of people he dubbed "Level 5 leaders". These are the leaders who were always at the helm during the transition of companies from being merely good to great. According to Collins, Level-5 leaders…

embody a paradoxical mix of personal humility and professional will. They are ambitious, to be sure, but ambitious first and foremost for the company, not themselves. Level 5 leaders set up their successors for success in the next generation... Level 5 leaders display a compelling modesty, are self-effacing and understated... [They] are fanatically-driven, infected with an incurable need to produce sustained *results*... Level 5 leaders display a workmanlike diligence – more plow horse than show horse. Level 5 leaders look out the window to attribute success to factors other than themselves. When things go poorly, however, they look in the mirror and blame themselves, taking full responsibility (*italics* in original). [119]

Some of these qualities came as a real surprise. They had expected a bit more showmanship, but it was simply not there. Collins ended his discussion of Level 5 leaders saying:

We were not looking for Level 5 leadership in our research, or anything like it, but the data was overwhelming and convincing. It is an empirical, not an ideological, finding.[120]

Level 5 leaders are just as unexpected as our Lord's description of himself, when he said: "For the Son of Man did not come to be served, but to serve and to give his life as a ransom for many" (Mk 10:45). Because the world teaches us to expect aggression and arrogance in our leaders, it comes as a surprise when the *empirically best* <u>*transformational*</u> *leaders* display the humility of the publican *vis-à-vis* the pharisee (cf. Lk 18:9-14), the selflessness of the Good Samaritan (cf. Lk 10:25-37), and the risk-taking spirit of the most profitable servant in the Parable of the Talents (Mt 25:14-30). He is happy to be the first laborer in the vineyard, and just as happy for the extraordinary good fortune of the last man in (cf. Mt 20:1-16). Finally, when all is said and done, the Level 5 leader says, "We are unprofitable servants; we have done what we are obliged to do" (Lk 17:10b). Transformational bishops, priests, and deacons work at cultivating these Christian virtues. Consequently, they have the potential to produce a rich harvest.

Looking over the attributes of Level-5 leaders, important words come to mind, such as:

† **Selflessness and Solidarity** – He stands with his people and looks to give credit to them instead of himself. He is not a "show horse"

† **Diligence and Responsibility** – He is a "work horse" in the trenches and doesn't expect his followers to do anything he won't do himself. If something goes wrong, the leader takes the blame

There is truly good news in this. In my experience, most bishops exhibit these transformational leadership qualities in spades. They are hard workers. They take responsibility and stand in sincere solidarity with their people.

Notwithstanding these positive attributes, in my opinion, there are a few Level-5 attributes that bishops and ecclesiastical leaders, too often lack. As a deacon, I include myself in the following indictment. We lack:

† **Humility** – It is difficult for any of us to admit that we really aren't doing what we need to be doing. With respect to evangelization, we are more than willing to acknowledge that things are not as they should be, but less inclined to focus attention on the ways that we ourselves sometimes create obstacles to it.

† **Modeled Behavior** – While we talk a good show, we are disinclined to speak openly of our own *personal* love for Jesus. If we can't bring ourselves to do this, how can we expect the laity to become missionary disciples themselves? Moreover, our almost exclusive involvement inside the Church restricts

343

our opportunities to make friends with the unchurched, the poor, the broken; in short, to become "fishers of men" as well as "shepherds of the flock". Employees in a *great* company are proud to emulate the priorities and work ethic of their Level-5 CEO. When it comes to modeling evangelization for our parishes, most clergy have a long way to go.

† **Results-Orientation** – Level-5 leaders maintain a laser focus on the outcome of their work. While they work hard, they are equally concerned with working smart. To be blunt, as church leaders, we are awful at this. At the end of a day, we are satisfied if we can say that we have worked hard. We're especially happy if we have accomplished *our* checklist for the day, but rarely do we consider whether or not our checklist is accomplishing what God wants us to do. All too often, the subject of evangelical fruitfulness doesn't enter our minds.

Four Questions for Ecclesial Leaders

---

1 – **What am I doing wrong?**
2 – **What can I do differently?**
3 – **What are my next steps?**
4 – **Where am I going to get the support to make this happen?**

Ron Huntley of the *Divine Renovation Network* offers a few questions to help with the problem of becoming more results-oriented. They begin with a simple self-examination: *What am I doing wrong?* The next question is the logical follow-up: *What can I do differently?* In many cases, the answer to Question #1 has to do with poor time management and the answer to Question #2 has to do with improving time management.

This is a problem that assails most people who carry a load of responsibilities. In a 1954 speech he gave at Northwestern University to the Second Assembly of the World Council of Churches, President Dwight Eisenhower is quoted as having said:

> I have two kinds of problems, the urgent and the important. The urgent are not important, and the important are never urgent.[121]

Eisenhower no doubt used the black-and-white qualifiers "not" and "never" for a touch of rhetorical flourish. Reality is a bit more nuanced. Accordingly, the second sentence in Eisenhower's quote usually reads: "The urgent are rarely important and the important are seldom urgent." Regardless of the wording, no one can dispute the wisdom of his statement. In fact, teachers of management have adapted the statement to a graphic called the "Eisenhower Matrix"

Figure 12
The Eisenhower Matrix

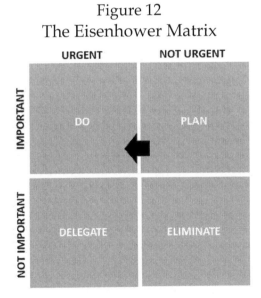

seen in Figure 12, which is used as a kind of decision-making tool for organizing one's time. If something is unimportant and not urgent, we probably shouldn't be doing it all (at least in the context of a work day). If something is unimportant, but urgent, we should do everything possible to delegate it. Herein lies a problem for people without a support staff; they may not have anyone to delegate it to. Hence, something that is honestly important, such as evangelization, may get squeezed out of life altogether because of all the urgent things that simply have to happen (e.g., funerals, paying the bills, doctors' appointments, etc.) This is one reason why it is so important for a diocese to cultivate permanent deacons and lay ecclesial ministers who can step in and provide relief for the bishop when there are urgent, but unimportant jobs to be done.

If you are still reading this book, you would surely agree that evangelization is important. The problem is that most of us have not promoted it from the "not urgent" into the "urgent" category. We have not brought urgency and importance into alignment. Accordingly, it is something that we may *plan*, but hardly ever spend time doing. In fact, many of us don't even know how to spent time evangelizing, which is why the formation of missionary disciples is so important. (A bit of good news is that evangelization can often be done while in the course of doing something else, such as having lunch, talking on the phone, etc.)

> Evangelization has to become urgent or we will never get around to it and, the fact is, the salvation of souls is an urgent matter.

In any event, the reality is that we have to *create urgency*. It is easy to treat the whole subject of evangelization as an important goal to be pursued in the future. If we do nothing to remove it from the future and bring it into the now, it will always be preempted by other "important/urgent needs". Evangelization has to become urgent or we will never get around to it and, the fact is, the salvation of souls *is* an urgent matter.

Returning to Huntley's second question, *what can I do differently*, one great response would be to create time for evangelization by better personal time management; specifically, by moving evangelization from an important/non-urgent need to an important/urgent one.

One's answers to Question #3 – *what are my next steps* – will, of course, depend on where one is in implementing the *Vision Achievement Strategy.* But, suppose you are a bishop or a pastor and would like to get started. Then, I would recommend as the first answer to Question #3: Go on record with a public statement making evangelization your highest priority. If you are "out there" with that kind of statement, you have just created a little forward motion and established a public expectation of things to follow. You may recall from the last chapter that this is exactly the first step for bishops in the *Episcopal Initiative* and the first step for pastors in the *Purposeful Parishes Initiative.* Secondly, having created a little time through better personal time management, *model evangelization* in some way that will permit people to emulate you. Perhaps it will be something as simple as reaching out to a few alienated Catholics and asking others to join you in this effort. Maybe, it will involve joining a St. Paul Street Evangelization team on Saturday mornings or participating in an *Alpha* program.

Your answer to Question #4 – *where am I going to get the support to make this happen* – is partially answered in what you decide to do to model evangelization. The important thing is to invite other leaders to do it with you; people who in turn will recruit other people in their own spheres of influence. All of this will create not only a sense of urgency, but also a sense of excitement "that we're finally doing something". This excitement will engender further forward motion.

In the context of the *Vision Achievement Strategy* a part of the answer to Question #4 involves creating and maintaining the Regional Evangelization Advisory Group (see Chapter XII) and enlisting curial department heads in changing the culture of the diocesan office.

It is critical to recognize the importance of modeling behavior and inviting others to follow you. This has been the path of every founder for every religious order. It has been the gateway to every ecclesiastical reform that has ever succeeded. It is the path of heroic holiness.

Creating a Catholic Evangelical Culture

The renowned business management consultant and author, Peter Drucker is credited with the statement: *Culture eats strategy for breakfast.*[122] This is an unassailable fact. Think of all the times you have watched this reality play out in your own efforts to change something. I recall one time trying to engage parents more fully in an inter-generational Confirmation preparation initiative. The program itself was great, but the culture of the parents just wasn't supportive of the idea. So, the question is: *How can we change the local Church so that our Catholic culture aligns with our strategies for regional evangelization?* As Father Mallon humorously put it, "Running evangelistic, outreach, or renewal programs without addressing the necessary cultural conversion of our parishes will only leave us open to charges of false advertising."[123]

If you are a priest or bishop, by working to take on the qualities of a transformational leader, by exercising improved time management, by announcing your highest priority and modeling evangelization, you have already begun the long-term process of creating a new ecclesial culture. By prioritizing evangelization – both personally and organizationally – you have taken the first steps to *normalize* it in the local Church. That's what creating culture change is all about. But it can't end here and you can't do it by yourself.

Pray, fast, and prepare You're about to embark on something that is probably unlike anything you have ever done before and it is certainly unlike anything the local Church has ever experienced before: the launch of a united, focused work to immerse every person in your part of the world with multiple opportunities to accept Jesus into their lives. This is a spiritual undertaking. The forces of hell will oppose you at every step. So, prepare yourself for battle.

Inspire hope with your *Vision* of a converted society Be counter-cultural and convince people that we are not on a fatalistic trend to oblivion. Comedian and filmmaker, Mel Brooks, coined the saying:

> "Hope for the best. Expect the worst.
> Life is a play. We're unrehearsed."[124]

Unfortunately, this catchy little couplet seems to be the dominant view of the future. From time immemorial, there has been a constant stream of Malthusian prognosticators offering ostensibly compelling evidence that the worst thing imaginable is about to happen... And yet, we are still here.

In fact, by several standards of well-being, life has *improved* markedly throughout the world. The World Bank estimates that "in 2015, ten percent of the world's population lived on less US $1.90 a day... That's down from nearly thirty-six percent in 1990." [125] Between 1990 to 2015, the proportion of hungry people in lower-middle-income countries was almost cut in half: 23.3 percent to 12.9 percent.[126] The same trends hold true in the field of public health. According to the University of Oxford:

> Many of us have not updated our world view. We still tend to think of the world as divided as it was in 1950. But in health — and many other aspects — the world has made rapid progress. Today most people in the world can expect to live as long as those in the very richest countries in 1950. Today's global average life

expectancy of 71 years is higher than that of any country in 1950 with the exception of a handful in Northern Europe.[127]

What's more, in the arena of public health, the gross disparities on a global level that existed only a few decades ago are quickly moving toward parity.

> [T]he world in 1950 was highly unequal in living standards – clearly divided between developed countries and developing countries. This division is ending: Look at the change between 1950 and 2012! Now it is the former developing countries – the countries that were worst off in 1950 – that achieved the fastest progress. While some countries (mostly in Africa) are lacking (sic) behind. But many of the former developing countries have caught up and we achieved a dramatic reduction of global health inequality.[128]

If we believe in a loving God, why do we find it so unbelievable that the future cannot be better than it is today. If we can acknowledge progress in matters of economic justice, health, nutrition and technology, why is it that we have such trouble believing that the Christian faith is inevitably doomed in North America? Some will point to our Lord's enigmatic question: *But when the Son of Man comes, will he find faith on earth?* Fair enough, but who is to say that such a sad future is not thousands of years in the future; that, in the meantime, we cannot experience a dramatic resurgence of Christian faith and praxis? Moreover, St. Paul's understanding of the eschaton prompted him to write about *the mystery of his will… as a plan for the fullness of times, to sum up all things in Christ, in heaven and on earth* (Eph 1:8b-10). In the final analysis: God wins! We need to remind people of that.

In *Evangelii Gaudium*, Pope Francis wrote:

> One of the more serious temptations which stifles boldness and zeal is a defeatism which turns into querulous and disillusioned pessimists, "sourpusses." Nobody can go off to battle unless he is fully convinced of victory beforehand. If we start without confidence, we have already lost half the battle and we bury our

talents. While painfully aware of our own talents we have to march on without giving in, keeping in mind what the Lord said to St. Paul: "My grace is sufficient for you, for my power is made perfect in weakness" (2 Cor 12:9).[129]

Articulate your 'BHAG' In 1994 Jim Collins and his colleague Jerry Porras wrote a book named *Built to Last: Successful Habits of Visionary Companies*. In this book they introduced a concept they called the *"Big Hairy Audacious Goal"* or BHAG, for short. If you Google it, you'll learn that "a true BHAG is clear and compelling, serves as [a] unifying focal point of effort, and acts as a clear catalyst for team spirit." It also "has a clear finish line, so the organization can know when it has achieved the goal." [130] President Kennedy's 1961 challenge to the American people to "commit itself to achieving the goal, before this decade is out, of landing a man on the Moon and returning him safely to the Earth" is sometimes used an illustration of a BHAG.[131], [132]

Now, suppose you are a bishop of a 15-county diocese and you want to spark an unprecedented, regional, evangelistic explosion. Where would you start? You have already tried to exhort your flock to "become missionaries in your own back yard", "to proclaim the Gospel by word and action", "to join the New Evangelization", *ad nauseum*. Nothing changes, RCIA numbers aren't even holding steady. The number of funerals continues to rise, while the number of marriages and baptisms continue to fall.

How about challenging the Church with a completely different vision of the future from the one everyone is expecting? You might try articulating a Big Hairy Audacious Goal like this:

> *Eight out of ten people*
> *in our 15 counties converted to*
> *our risen LORD JESUS*
> *in, by, and through the Church*
> *by 2050*

This encapsulates a *Vision* that is so challenging that it implies a Church with a hope-filled, "let's-get-it-done" outlook . It may prove to be unachievable... but, it may *not* be (cf. Lk 1:37). We will never know, if no one even considers it. To be sure, it is a *challenge* of immense proportion... but it is a challenge that *inspires,* a challenge that will motivate an otherwise moribund flock. You may get egg on your face, but so what? There are far worse fates. By itself, the BHAG won't sustain a 30-year effort. That's okay. It's just the rallying cry to bring the troops together, not the battle itself.

There's your first step. Now, flesh it out. What would a little chunk of the United States look like in three decades if everyone was living for and in Christ? Begin to picture it. How would families be changed? What would crime statistics look like? What would now-moribund neighborhoods look like? What would the Church look like?

Make that your *Vision* and share it with your flock. Then, challenge them with an irresistible BHAG. Do *not* take it to your consultors for approval. Do *not* look for wordsmiths to make it sound better. This is *your Vision* and you're the one who was anointed to lead. Father Mallon righty says: "[It is] the essential untransferable duty of a leader to be a vison caster." In his view, "the primary role of a leader of any organization is to develop and communicate a vision for what can be."[133]

Obviously, this *Vision*/BHAG will not answer many questions. That's okay. It is not meant to. Its purpose is to inspire. It's the view from 50,000'. In time, it will come into sharper focus and you will add specificity to it. You will connect the vision of this great future to the work the Church is going to undertake – *together*. In time, it will take on very practical characteristics with concrete objectives related to clear conversions, Mass attendance, increases in the number of well-prepared missionary disciples and Ananias's, etc. Perhaps, there will be goals for increased foster parenting and mentors for young mothers and on and on. For now, step out in faith and challenge them with the grand *Vision*.

Connect the *Vision* and BHAG to Evangelization (aka 'Greatest Unmet Need') The world needs Jesus. Without our Lord, everything else fails to satisfy. Everything else breaks down – relationships, families, appreciation for the Mass, care for the poor, moral clarity. There's a reason for your *Vision* being the top priority: *Bringing people to God is the greatest unmet need in our society at this point in history.* This doesn't mean that other needs do not exist. But, to the extent that they are clearly unrelated to this greatest unmet need, they can wait for your attention and possibly even get by for a time with fewer resources.

Establish "Priority #1" Let the local Church know that regional evangelization is to become Priority #1 – both for you personally and among all the diocesan pastoral priorities. Of course, such an assertion implies that other goals are *not* Priority #1 and that will *not* make everyone happy. Serious evangelization has been delayed long enough. If everything has equal claim to our attention, we will go through life accomplishing very little. Perhaps you have read Gary Keller's book *The One Thing.* If not, get a copy. It begins with an old Russian proverb: "If you chase two rabbits… you will not catch either one."[134]

Catechize on "Priority #1" From time immemorial the Church has held that an essential part of *accepting* the Gospel is to spread it. After all, it was Jesus who said: *Whoever acknowledges me before others I will acknowledge before my heavenly Father. But whoever denies me before others, I will deny before my heavenly Father* (Mt 10:32-33). This is the very passage that the *Catechism* quotes when it teaches:

> The disciple of Christ must not only keep the faith and live on it, but also profess it, confidently bear witness to it, and spread it... Service of and witness to the faith are necessary for salvation. (*CCC*, 1816)

If our very salvation in some way hinges on whether or not we are willing to evangelize, then it is not too much of a stretch to say that, at least in praxis, the Church herself is not yet a fully Christian community.

As mentioned several times previously, the Church has a "*primary* purpose" which Pope St. Paul VI succinctly summarized in *Evangelii nuntiandi*. At the risk of repeating myself (which isn't always a bad thing), Pope St. Pope Paul said: "... evangelizing all people constitutes the essential mission of the Church... She exists in order to evangelize" (14). Church leaders are not immune to getting this wrong. After all, many - maybe, most – Catholics think the Church is primarily there to meet their "needs" and they're not shy about telling their pastors that. This is part-and-parcel of the American consumer mentality. The first step in the game plan is to correct our misconceptions and make sure everyone understands that to be a Catholic means we have a moral obligation to share the Good News right along with food and shelter and medicine. We need to be crystal clear about this, which will require you to exercise your teaching office with great clarity.

Pursue "Priority #1" relentlessly Make it known you have no intention of being "balanced" about this. *This marks the beginning of something new.* Take control of your calendar like you never have before and apologize in advance for the change that Priority #1 is about to make in your life and in the ordinary operations of your office. Keller's *The One Thing* is not sacred script. It does not allow for the promptings of the Holy Spirit; that there are times when our Lord calls us to interrupt our work to serve the needs of others *right now*. That said, it is all-too-easy to make the moment-to-moment "demands" of life the primary criterion by which we decide how we will spend the next few hours of our day. Any great endeavor requires uncompromising single-mindedness and a degree of personal dedication that squeezes out many other things. In this respect, it is reminiscent of the Parables of the Buried Treasure and the Pearl of Great Price (cf. Mt 13:44-46). Keller writes:

> To achieve an extraordinary result you must choose what matters most and give it all the time it demands. This requires getting extremely out of balance in relation to other work issues, with only infrequent counterbalancing to address it.[135]

Although leading a "balanced life" is touted in contemporary society as the right way to live, if that is our *modus vivendi* we may make the people around us happy, but we may also be disappointing our Lord. I think most would agree that great saints tend to be imbalanced people when it comes to the pursuit of their goals. So be it. We do well to recall the words of our Lord to the Church of Laodicea:

> I know your works; I know that you are neither cold nor hot. I wish you were either cold or hot. So, because you are lukewarm, neither hot nor cold, I will spit you out of my mouth (Rev 3:15-16).

Show some passion Let the people know there is a passionate side of you and show it to them. If the passion is gone, go before our Lord in the Eucharist with a copy of 2 Timothy and read: *For this reason, I remind you to stir into flame the gift of God that you have through the imposition of my hands. For God did not give us a spirit of cowardness but rather of power and love and self-control.* (1:6-7) Pray for a re-kindling of the flame.

Repeat yourself... over and over Repeat your *Vision* and the BHAG. State your top priority and reiterate the greatest unmet need persuasively and often. Remind people over and over and over again. One of the practices of a great teacher is to make the point of the lesson at least three times: Tell them what they're going to hear. Tell them. Then, tell them what they just heard. Father Michael White, the author of *Rebuilt,* relates his experience talking about evangelization to his parish:

> It has been amazing to us how many of our parishioners struggle with the concept of evangelization, and how much of a stretch it is for them culturally and emotionally. That discovery has led us to the conclusion that evangelization has to be presented in a simple, specific, and consistent way. And it must be vigorously maintained as the number one parish priority. We need to teach evangelization in a crystal-clear way and make it a constant theme of our preaching woven throughout the messages throughout the year. And, at least, once a year, we find that we must reintroduce it all over again, as if for the first time. Preaching it once won't work, and preaching it once in a while won't work either. We try to keep evangelization front and center by regularly placing it in the Prayer of the Faithful at Mass and talking about it in the announcements. We plan and rigorously evaluate all our weekend efforts from the perspective and priority of evangelization. And when it comes to Christmas and Easter we turn our preparation and celebrations into church-wide evangelization campaigns.[136]

Lencioni drives home a similar message when he talks about the need to "overcommunicate clarity".

> The point is, people are skeptical about what they are being told unless they hear it consistently over time... The problem is that leaders confuse the mere transfer of information to an audience with the audience's ability to understand, internalize, and embrace the message that is being communicated.[137]

The time for ambiguity is now in the past. Say it over and over and over again. The people will love it, because it takes the guess work out of what is important and gives the entire team a unity of purpose.

Promote the 'Paradigm Shift' This is all about culture change. At the beginning of this book (Chapter II), a *Proposal* for the New Evangelization in the United States was suggested and then described (in Chapter III). This description focuses on ten core attributes and over a dozen changes between the way evangelization happens today and the way it *could* be if we really made it our top priority (i.e., the 'Paradigm Shift'). The bishop must *communicate* this basic content (or something very similar) and commit to it publicly. Take some time to discuss the implications of this commitment throughout the diocese in order to bring some understanding to the local Church concerning what is about to happen.

Invite the people to join you Enthusiasm is contagious. That said, the culture of Catholic laity tends to be passive. We are sheep very much in need of shepherds who will lead us. On the other hand, we are *good* sheep. Catholics do step up when they are asked, but they have to be invited and that's exactly what Jesus did over and over again. He invited. (cf. Jn 1:38-41, Mt 4:19, Mt 9:9, Lk 19:1-6). You have to start the contagion. Invite the people to join you in this great endeavor to bring people to Christ. Point out "the hill we're going to take... together".

In addition to a general, rhetorical "call", identify the most-respected leaders in the parishes. Invite them to make a serious commitment to the *Vision* by entering into a formal process of formation for *missionary discipleship.* (See Chapter XII for more ideas on becoming a missionary disciple). Find these people. Recruit them. Form and train them. Commission them with a specific plan. Then, turn them loose to evangelize with confidence in all their personal environments and in the communal outreaches of the Church.

Keep the Church posted on successes and failures The *Vision Achievement Strategy* (laid out in Chapter XII) serves as the view from 50,000' so to speak. Help the people understand it and let them know what part of the *Strategy* you are focusing on at any given time. But, don't stop there.

Keep the faithful continuously posted on the progress and the setbacks that are being experienced in implementing the *short-range Tactical Plan.* (See pp. 248-249.) This is the view from the 5,000′ level; these are the mundane specifics for the coming months with a horizon no farther out than a year. Share the game plan!

Why is it important to communicate all this detail to the Church? First, they deserve and need to understand that we have moved beyond platitudes and vague exhortations. We actually have a plan for getting it done and we're implementing it. Many faithful Catholics are living without any hope that the trajectory of the Church and the world can still be changed. A powerful way to encourage hope among a disheartened faithful is to let them know that there is a plan for turning things around, as imperfect as it may be. Let the troops on the ground understand just what you are doing and how you intend to win not only the war "in the great by-and-by", but also the battles that are starring us in the face.

The plan will not be perfect. This is also a message the people need to hear; they need to know you are listening and are flexible (up to a point). Regardless of the *Tactical Plan's* shortcomings, it needs to be communicated clearly. Allowing the people to know about the day-to-day nut-and-bolts, the disappointments as well as the victories transforms the *Vision* from an ethereal dream to *something real.* They will come to understand that they are part of a very real movement that just may actually succeed, because its leadership won't be denied.

"Speak so as to be heard" In the Parable of the Dishonest Steward, our Lord commended the embezzler in the story with these words: "[T]he people of this world are more shrewd in dealing with their own kind than are the people of the light" (Lk 16:8, NIV). In the midst of all the distractions and other messages our people are bombarded with all the time, we need to be "shrewd" enough to enculturate the Gospel in a way that can be "heard" above the din. This is exactly what Bishop Barron does when he uses social media to reach secular young people with the message of Christ.

With email blasts, Twitter, routine blogs, tele-messaging, and other forms of social media, we can go to the people directly now. We can compete with all the secular and commercial messages, if we put our mind to it. A bishop does not have to mediate the *Regional Strategy* or *Tactical Plan* exclusively through letters read from the pulpit, and articles in the diocesan paper. While these have a place, modern technology permits pithy, hard-hitting messages that can get through to thousands of people on their cell phones. The same technology can be used as a means of encouraging and keeping your missionary disciples "in the game".

In addition to the obvious practical "shrewdness" of these means of communication, there are good pastoral reasons as well. Pastorally, people need to have a personal bond, a simpatico with their bishop, wherein they feel his love for them and he feels their love for him. This need not be mediated through other people – even pastors. I do not ask my wife to tell my children how much I love them. That's something I do myself.

Moreover, at a practical level, not all pastors can be relied on to communicate your vision and priorities persuasively. Some pastors who are not excited about your priority on evangelization may read the pastoral letter (feeling put upon), but cannot be counted on to communicate any enthusiasm for it. We now have *direct* means for communicating and building unity within the local Church to an extent unprecedented since the ancient Church of one-on-one communication. To be clear, I am *not* advocating going around the pastors, but rather employing *both* indirect *and* direct means of communication.

Many diocesan communications offices are still largely focused on the publication of a regional Catholic newspaper and/or the diocesan website. Newsprint is a means of communication that was on the cutting edge of technology 100+ years ago. And websites are only accessed by those who care enough and are savvy enough to go there. Millennials rarely read newspapers and 'nones' usually don't find themselves with a reason to visit a Catholic website. Again, I am not advocating the elimination of newsprint; rather that we should knock off the cobwebs and begin to deliver our messages in ways that have a reasonable chance of being read or heard by the target audience.

Modern social communication technologies should be considered for purposes such as ...

- Sharing an important aspect of the *Vision Achievement Strategy* that is about to take place

- As a trigger for implementing a specific element of the short-range *Tactical Plan*, e.g.: "Remember, 'Invite-Your-Neighbor-To-Dinner Night' is June 24th, a month away. Won't you make the call today and know that I am praying for you." + Bishop Paul

- Reminding your prayer apostolate to intercede on behalf of the *Vision* and specific projects

- Requesting intercession and volunteers to help on behalf of a regional tragedy or traumatic personal accident

- Providing feedback on opinions and behavior related to evangelization using an electronic survey tool such as SurveyMonkey or similar software

The *judicious* choice of technologies is also important. Middle-age adults rely on email. Younger people are increasingly *not* using email outside of work, preferring text messaging.

Notwithstanding the need for creative and frequent communications, it is possible for *any* means of communication to be overused. If overuse happens, not only will the messages be deleted unread or unheard, but you run the risk of becoming a pariah on a par with robo-callers. *For subscribers only*, frequent, short text messages can be effective. At least one bishop texts a well-received short prayer request to thousands of people every day. On the other hand, a sure recipe for getting ignored or resented is to use technology indiscriminately as a means for general exhortations and platitudes.

The new and largely untested frontier is the use of computer technology as a direct means of on-line evangelization using customized messaging. An example might be individualized, computer-generated messaging aimed at individuals identified by 'artificial intelligence' software as "seekers" and potentially open to the Gospel. It seems to me that there *may* be great potential here when paired with follow-up by a real person, especially as a tool used nationally. At the very least, the development of this technology deserves watching.

Get it in the institutional culture There is a lot of literature on creating culture change in organizations, especially corporations. Here's the problem: The Church is *not* a corporation. A few things map over nicely, but many things do not.

Don't be a corporate copycat A diocese's internal management team has only limited authority outside the chancery office. Administratively speaking, parishes are not branch offices of the diocese and it is precisely in the parishes where the Church lives. Unless you're an Amazon or Walmart, most companies have no desire to influence the world out there, except from the limited perspective of marketing and selling their specific products. The Church, on the other hand, has a direct commission to get out there and convert the world. That simply cannot be done by fiat or "delegation" to aging pastors. Sometimes, this fact escapes outside diocesan consultants.

Corporate management teams are expressly accountable for the profitability, goals, and ethos of a company. Within their respective departments, they have real authority, and collectively, they run the place. No such structure exists in the Church, because if a senior manager (aka, pastor) has a different philosophy from the CEO (aka, bishop), you can't fire him. You only have the power of persuasion and inspiration.

Moreover, outside of the chancery office, you can't incentivize by the threat of job loss or the promise of monetary compensation. Since your goals are spiritual, you wouldn't want to anyway. So, you have essentially no sticks and no carrots. Of course, we want to strive for accountability. But, at the end of the day, it can't be forced.

Moreover, within the Church we are talking about two overlapping cultures, not one. One of these cultures is administrative and highly structured by canon law. The other is the culture of the parishes and the Church at-large. *Both* cultures have to be changed and each has at least a limited influence on the other. One tends to have an administrative focus where the core values are the smooth running of the Church and compliance with canon law. The other has a sacramental focus where the core values are personal sanctification and annual calendar maintenance; maybe doing it slightly better this year than last. Both cultures need to be saturated with the *Vision* and begin to understand that their primary purpose is the conversion of the world, not administrative ease or maintenance of the status quo.

So, be very discriminating in implementing the counsel you receive from corporate consultants and well-intentioned lawyers. Sometimes, important decisions that should be based on pastoral considerations are unduly influenced by mistaken ideas about how the chain of ecclesiastical command functions. Regarding legal counsel, risk aversion is usually priority #1. For the Church, the teachings of Christ may not always line up with self-protection.

Apply great (but appropriate) management practices Having said all that, there is plenty from the management sciences that can and should be embraced: Personal time management, improved routines to enhanced accountability, state-of-the-art practices for information sharing and running efficient, productive meetings. These same practices should all be brought to bear on the subject of regional evangelization.

Build healthy curial and evangelization leadership teams Given the fact that there are two cultures within a particular Church, there need to be two leadership teams: (1) the long-standing "management" structures that are mostly comprised of clergy and guided by canon law (canons 460-572) for the smooth running of diocesan business, and; (2) a leadership team that may be less "organizationally-integrated", but more vital for the planning and implementation of regional evangelization.

There needs to be significant overlap between these two leadership groups, since official diocesan business subsumes *all* pastoral goals, including evangelization. Accordingly, the vicar general(s) and certain other presbyteral consultors need to be part of the bishop's evangelization leadership team. In fact, the diocesan organizational structure may very well have a vicar for evangelization, and another for clergy, and a third for vocations, etc., all of which need to be involved in the regional evangelization process. The Finance Officer should be involved as well.

Having said that, there is so much 'non-official' talent in the local Church – both lay and clerical – who are loaded with creativity and expertise that a second leadership team is warranted. Moreover, the evangelization team will be better equipped for some functions than the diocesan organizational team. (See discussion on the roles of the evangelization leadership team in Chapter XII).

In any event, there should be a team exclusively for evangelization and both teams should be able to function as "organizationally healthy" working groups communicating well and free of turf battles. How well this works out, once again, may depend to a large extent on the emotional intelligence, spiritual leadership, and personal discipline of the bishop.

Operationalize Regional Evangelization Patrick Lencioni's best-seller *The Advantage* was written principally as a resource for engendering organizational health in businesses. As a devout Catholic and a co-founder of *Amazing Parishes*, Lencioni also works hard to apply the principles in *The Advantage* to improve the organizational health of the Church. One of his "Four Disciplines" for organizational health is to *"create clarity"* which may very well be the key to promoting organizational culture change.[138]

The last two questions Lencioni uses for creating clarity are: (1) "what is most important right now?" and; (2) "who must do what?" In other words, culture change must find its way into day-to-day, tactical operational decisions. Otherwise the new culture is nothing more than the new "party line" that doesn't really affect immediate decision-making. At whatever point a diocese is in its *Tactical Plan,* these two questions bring focus to getting the job done in very concrete terms.

In thinking about what is most important right now, I often picture one of those "whac-a-mole" (sic) games you see in arcades. Just when you think you've gotten control of the game, three new "moles" pop up and you have to whack them down. That's a part of deciding "what's most important right now?" Those moles may or may *not* be what's really important. In either case, the bishop and his evangelization leadership team need to be sufficiently on top of the game to make that call; strategic enough to keep their eye on the end game, but tactical enough to recognize and avert potentially serious obstacles. Finally, there needs to be clarity regarding who is going to do what, so that the issue is addressed without confusion or mixed messages being sent.

* * *

Getting Beyond Common Objections

Over time I have heard a number of "objections" to prioritizing evangelization ahead of other pastoral priorities from bishops or people closely associated with them. In this section, I will identify and try to address the most common of these objections.

"I'm just not a transformational leader" Many bishops were chosen for reasons other than a "Type A" personality. Unfortunately, transformational leadership conjures up an image of an aggressive, take-charge "people person". Insofar as a bishop may be more of an introverted or analytical person, he may believe that he is just not up to the challenge of transforming the local Church into an outward-moving band of missionary disciples. He may be a quiet influencer, but not a winsome, charismatic leader that people naturally follow. As a private person, he may have trouble sharing his own faith with others.

At the root of a transformational leader is the *ability to inspire change*. Inspiring change can come about by heartrending pleas, by threats, by manipulation, and even by quiet, reasoned persuasion. Interestingly, Jesus inspired change in people by his selfless love for them. There was never a display of coercion and whatever strength he displayed was always used exclusively at the service of others. He changed people by virtue of his selfless love for

If we are asked to follow a spiritual leader who shows no sign of sharing our own human struggles, our willingness to follow will be ambivalent at best.

them. He made himself vulnerable and weak, rather than strong and imposing.

We would all rather be strong than weak. And yet, our Lord's words to St. Paul conveyed the importance of human weakness and vulnerability: *My grace is sufficient for you, for power is made perfect is weakness* (2 Cor 12:9). Only when we are recognizably weak, can God's power be put on full display.

In 1978 I made a *Cursillo*, which is a retreat that involves numerous lay speakers who witness the personal experience of God's love to the retreatants. Over forty years later, there is only one talk that I still remember clearly from that weekend. The speaker was a young man, who was very unsure of himself. In fact, he was the last person one would choose out of a line up as likely to give a "good talk". In addition to his personal reticence, this man was severely obese. In his talk he shared how he had always been over weight and was unmercifully teased and bullied for it. Although I do not recall the specifics, he relayed how he had a personal encounter with the God who loved him; who felt his embarrassment and rejection right along with him. That encounter changed his life. It also changed mine and those of the other men who heard him. It was just a simple testimony of Jesus' love for him and, in turn, his love for Jesus. Out of his weakness and pain came perhaps the most evangelical talk I have ever heard. It was transformational.

> The bishop who leads out of his own personal strength will have little influence, while the one who operates out of his own need for God will influence all those who will listen to him

If we are asked to believe in a deity who is impervious to our pain, that deity is not God. Similarly, if we are asked to follow a leader who shows no sign of sharing our own human struggles, we have little desire to follow. It is the paradox of the Cross that the bishop who leads out of his own personal strength will have little influence, while the one who operates out of his own need for God will influence all those who listen to him.

Ultimately, the bishop who believes he is just not a transformational leader needs to come to terms with the fact that by virtue of the Sacrament of Orders, he has been "graced" with all that he needs to do what he has been called to do. After all, he serves a God who loves him and, as a man, knows what it is to doubt his own influence.

"I'll never get the presbyterate on-board" This is the elephant in the living room that no one wants to talk about, but in my experience, it is the most common problem raised by bishops. If you are a priest reading this right now, please don't shoot the messenger. I recognize there are always two sides to every human conflict. Often, the bishop is feeling that some of the priests in the diocese are just chronic malcontents and/or need to have a conversion experience of their own. On the flip side of the coin, the priests are thinking: "One more useless 'program'" or "I can't believe he's asking us to do one more thing." God bless the priests and the bishop who can stand in the breach and God bless all who are willing to communicate respectfully and talk their issues through in a spirit of love.

Sometimes, the bishop's concern about "getting the presbyterate on-board" is based on the misapprehension that diocesan evangelization means bringing everybody on-board *at the same time*. They get the idea that serious evangelistic efforts are going to be required of all parishes throughout the diocese on exactly the same schedule. This really is a misconception of the *Vision Achievement Strategy*. The fact is, it is meant to be understood as a new, but *permanent* component of life in the local Church in which various parishes will be going through the reforms of the *Purposeful Parishes Initiative* on a staggered basis over time. Moreover, these reforms are not intended to be just *pro-forma* checkmarks in a to-do box, but rather a deep conversion of the entire parish family that produces real fruits as demonstrated by high retention, growth in members, real commitments to *missionary discipleship,* and community outreach. Realistically, despite these serious expectations, it may very well happen that some parishes will need to re-cycle back through the process after a change of pastors or for some other reason. If every pastor was an "early adopter", few dioceses would have the financial or staff resources to bring along all parishes at the same time anyway.

But even beyond that, there may be compelling reasons for delaying some parishes, even if the pastor is interested in jumping on-board. Pastoral participation needs to be sincere, not a veiled ruse to promote one's favorite subject or ideological agenda. The only agenda allowed is the conversion of sinners to our Lord and ultimately the incorporation of those sinners – be they cradle Catholics, "converts" or "reverts" – as active disciples in the Church. Full – not selective – participation in parish reforms must be articulated up-front as a clear expectation and a prerequisite for participation.

Other reasons may exist for an unenthusiastic pastor:

- **Bad timing** "We just finished our new parish pastoral plan and we have other priorities right now."[139]
- **Congregationalism or pride** "We have been working on evangelization here for years and everything is going just fine. We don't need the diocese's help."
- **Bad theology** Universalism and/or the sin of presumption
- **American non-judgmentalism and relativism** Value judgments – even those based on Scripture and the Magisterium – are verboten in today's society. Unfortunately, some of that thinking has found its way

into the Church. As post-modern Americans, some Catholics misperceive *any* value statement as intolerant or judgmental. Thus, giving evangelization special attention is viewed as "just wrong".

- **Lack of faith or small thinking** These individuals can't conceive that something as large and complex as regional evangelization is even possible.

Each of these reasons requires its own response. But, how does a bishop avoid the larger problem of a presbyterate, a large group of whom feel they are not being consulted and/or they are being railroaded? The hard truth <u>may</u> be that their perception is at least partially accurate and the bishop must claim some responsibility for the disunity. A serious examination of conscience may be called for. But, regardless of the underlying cause, it is up to the bishop as the spiritual father to take the lead in mending the bridges. Healing wounds, whether perceived or real, is *always* important. I know one bishop who regularly schedules afternoon and overnight getaways with small groups of priests. During these getaways, he schedules time expressly for one-on-one visits for any priest who wants to avail himself of it. Not surprisingly, there is growing affection and love for this bishop throughout his diocese. Even those priests who may have had a chip on their shoulder are reappraising their bishop in a whole new light.

In any event, I would offer a three-part response to the generalized problem of a reluctant presbyterate:

(1) Make clear that not everyone is *expected* to participate immediately and that you are willing to be flexible on timing *up to a point*. Clarify that your *Vision* really is for everyone and that a time will come when every parish will eventually be expected to get on-board. That's non-negotiable, but specific timing is.

(2) After serious preparation, *sell* your decision for prioritizing evangelization and pursuing it aggressively. Give them the <u>reasons</u>. Walk them through your discernment and reasoning process dispassionately. Then, reiterate your *Vision* <u>with</u> passion.

(3) Work with the willing. In fact, work with the *most* willing and the best suited for early leadership. In the meantime, woo the rest.

In the final analysis, there is no quick fix for evangelizing a region. Regional evangelization is ultimately a *trans-parochial* proposition and when it is not understood that way, seekers fall through the cracks. It will take time and patience. Even in Jesus' public ministry, not everyone followed him when he called (cf. Mk 10:21-22). The bishop has an obligation to build unity with and among his clergy. Having said that, unity is a two-way street. Bishops have to solicit input and consider it. But, at the end of the day, the presbyterate and diaconate have an obligation in love and obedience to allow the bishop to lead and for them to follow.

Perfect unity may be the goal, but we have to be willing to settle for imperfection. Again, work with the willing. But, don't leave it at that. Inspire the rest.

"What about all our other legitimate needs?" I had one bishop ask me: "What do I say to the people who just made a case last week that we need to devote an all-out effort to marriage and family life?"

Of course, there are any number of legitimate needs. Take any bishop on any given day and any number of problems may bubble to the surface. One might expect to hear…

- "We have major problems with our schools. I have to focus on Catholic Education?"

- "Fifteen percent of our people do all the work and all the giving. So, maybe we should be focusing on stewardship?"

- "Our diocese has had shootings every week this year. As a simple matter of justice issues, we need to delve into this."

- "Until *Roe v. Wade* is reversed, my first priority has to be Right to Life."

Most people in the United States – including many people in our pews – have not fallen in love with our Savior... Fix THAT problem and all the others have a chance of being ameliorated.

None of these are trivial, short-terms matters. That said, they are *all* to one degree or other *symptoms* of a deeper, more fundamental issue. We have to get back to treating the root cause of the issues that plague us and the root cause is this: Most people in the United States – including many people in our pews – have not fallen in love with their Savior. And, even for some who have, they have not moved onto a mature *spousal* relationship with Him. Fix THIS problem and all the others have a chance of being ameliorated. Avoid addressing this problem and many of our other endeavors will amount to putting a band aid on a gunshot wound.

"I can't make this decision by myself" Diocesan bishops are very collaborative leaders. To an extent, they are obliged to be, especially with respect to the priests of their diocese. The Decree on the Pastoral Office of Bishops in the Church (*Christus Dominus*) states:

> "[The diocesan bishop] should regard [his priests] as sons and friends. He should always be ready to listen to them and cultivate an atmosphere of easy familiarity with them, thus facilitating the pastoral work of the entire diocese.[140]

Diocesan bishops usually live by this counsel, sometimes to a fault. I find them to be much better team players than most CEOs, even though they have more unilateral authority than CEOs who are answerable to directors and shareholders. Without prejudice to the previous excerpt, *Christus Dominus* also states:

> To bishops, as the successors of the Apostles, in the dioceses entrusted to them, there belongs per se all ordinary, proper, and immediate authority which is required for the exercise of their pastoral office...

In a certain sense, their "ordinary, proper, and immediate power" is the final word on the subject, as the same document in the next paragraph says:

> The general law of the Church grants the faculty to each diocesan bishop to dispense, in a particular case, the faithful over whom they exercise authority as often as they judge it contributes to their spiritual welfare, except in those cases which have been especially reserved by the supreme authority of the Church.[141]

So, it seems to me that when it comes to the spiritual welfare of his people, the bishop really *can* "make the decision by himself". That's not to say that he should exercise this prerogative willy-nilly, but it does suggest that he need not go to the other extreme of seeking consensus either. In the final analysis, it is the diocesan bishop who holds the *munus regendi* over the diocese and, after seeking counsel, there are times when he needs to exercise it decisively as the shepherd of his flock.

"Our people just don't understand the need This is a common problem throughout the Church, but it begs the question. The fact that people do not understand the need for evangelization really has nothing to do with whether or not it should become Priority #1. Make it top priority and then use your *modus docendi* to teach them *why* there is a need.

"Evangelization is not my primary job" Okay, I confess I've never really heard a bishop say this. But, as the saying goes, "actions speak louder than words." Based on the variety of meetings and events that many bishops attend, it is difficult to get a good sense of what they think their "primary job" is; other than perhaps attending meetings and events. Actually, according to the *Catechism*, evangelization is *supposed to be* their primary job. At the risk of repeating myself, the *Catechism* states: "Bishops, with priests as co-workers, have *as their first task* 'to preach the Gospel of God to all men,'* in keeping with the Lord's command." (888, *Italics* added)

"I'm not going to be a 'sheep thief'" Many in the Catholic community have experienced the wonderful grace of true brotherhood with other Christians; an experience which the Second Vatican Council referred to as "spiritual ecumenism". It is the "change of heart and holiness of life" which derives from our own interior conversion to Christ and puts us in touch with the reality of our common baptism.[142] The desire for and work towards Christian unity is no longer an option for Catholics. However, there is another factor in play. Many priests have felt the sting of some evangelical churches targeting Catholics and sometimes convincing the innocent that their Catholic faith was not even Christian. This has been a bitter pill. Notwithstanding how difficult it is, many priests have tried to rise above the fray by clinging to our Lord's command to "do good to those how hate you". For these priests, the issue is *not* a misplaced belief in universalism. Rather, it is a genuine desire to be faithful to Christ by avoiding retribution.

So, a bishop who finds himself reluctant to prioritize evangelization out of ecumenical respect should be commended... but, the discussion should not end there. Very gently, it needs to be brought around to a consideration of the distinction between evangelizing and proselytizing. As Pope Francis has pointed out:

> [E]vangelization is first and foremost about preaching the Gospel to *those who do not know Jesus Christ or who have rejected him*. Many of them are quietly seeking God, led by a yearning to see his face, even in countries of ancient Christian tradition. All of them have a right to receive the Gospel. Christians have a duty to proclaim the Gospel without excluding anyone. Instead of seeming to impose new obligations, they should appear as people who wish to share their joy, who point to a horizon of beauty and who invite others to a delicious banquet. It is not by proselytizing that the Church grows, but "by attraction".[143] (*italics* in original)

Pope Francis' teaching reiterates what all our popes since Pope St. Paul VI have taught about evangelization. It is *not the same* as proselytism. Moreover, the "*New* Evangelization" as used by the pontiff who popularized the term – St. John Paul II – targets *lapsed* Christians, *plus* the gigantic world of secularists and non-Christian seekers. That leaves an incredibly large number of people to evangelize without becoming overly concerned about sheep stealing.

What's more, as spelled out in canon law, the bishop has an obligation to proclaim Christ to all people without distinction:

> [A] diocesan bishop... is also to extend an apostolic spirit to those who are not able to make sufficient use of ordinary pastoral care because of the condition of their life and to those who no longer practice their religion.

> He is to consider the non-baptized as committed to him in the Lord, so that there shines on them the charity of Christ whose witness a bishop must be before all people.[144]

"I've got to let my Director of Evangelization do her job"

Agreed, but her job is not to *lead* evangelization in the diocese. That is expressly the job of the bishop. In fact, as discussed above, that is arguably his most important job. Delegation has its place, but that does not include usurpation of the leader's primary responsibility.

* * *

'Ten Commandments' for Transformational Leaders

In addition to the grace of the Holy Spirit and the intercession of the saints – living and deceased – the key to achieving widespread conversions throughout a region is transformational leadership. Clearly, the diocesan bishop is the key player for initiating and sustaining regional evangelization over a long period of time. When he has finished his work, one can only hope and pray that his successors will pick up the torch and build on his legacy.

The following "ten commandments for transformational leaders" is an attempt to condense these thoughts into a list of pithy exhortations. As has been the case for this entire chapter, these "ten commandments" are most applicable to diocesan bishops. That said, there is much in here that is transferable to others. In fact, some of it is expressly *for* others. So, here they are, not etched in stone by the finger of God, but offered with the hope that they will be helpful.

1. Be Heroically Holy In spite of your own sinful tendencies, you are called to holiness in the most selfless and humble ways possible. The more singular your office is, the more heroic your life should be. If you are a diocesan bishop, your life should be so radically given to our Lord that it inspires not only the particular Church, but the whole populace to follow you. If you are part of the diocesan clergy, you are a *public person* regardless of your personality or preferences. You are called to heroic leadership which eschews the opinions of men, to integrity of commitment and lifestyle that serves as an inspirational example for the people you have been called to shepherd. So, stand up and shepherd them! Be the kind of leader that people <u>want</u> to follow – sincere, hard-working, winsome, and humble. Recognize that you have been called to be a bright city on the mountainside, a lamp not hidden but placed on the lampstand to bring light to the world. This means your life must stand out and be transparently holy. This is the *only way* to re-build credibility and confidence, so that souls can be won.

If you are religious or lay, your calling may be less public, but it is just as integral for all those the Lord places in your path. You are called to work with others as the salt of the earth and the leaven in the dough, preserving the good, elevating conversations to heavenly things, and enriching all around you.

2. Embrace Uncertainty Leadership is not a comfortable place. As leaders, we must make decisions. We take the risk of doing things knowing that it is possible the decision may not lead to the best possible outcome. This is the cross of leadership. It is also the nexus of the supernatural virtues; faith, hope, and charity are central to risk-taking for the good of the other When we do things, when we make those decisions, we do them in humility and uncertainty. Some will criticize the decision. Misunderstandings will occur. All of this is in the nature of leadership.

So, put yourself out there, just as Jesus did. He too, surely, experienced uncertainty. Remember the occasion when even our Lady and some of Jesus' kin seemed to question his decision to put himself "out there" in the radical ways that he did (cf. Mk 3:21-35).

A transformational leader must put it all on the line for God, his security, his comfort, sometimes even his good name. In uncertainty, this individual must adapt the attitude of King David when he decided to flee Jerusalem in response to an informant's news that his son, Absalom, planned to incite a coup d'état (cf. 2 Sam 15:1-26). David said: *"If I find favor with the Lord, he will bring me back and permit me to see [the Ark of the Covenant] and its lodging. But if he should say, 'I am not pleased with you,' I am ready; let him do to me as he sees fit"* (v 25-26).

The devil sows seeds of doubt and the very nature of hope involves uncertainty. So, pray, seek counsel, discern, then act. Jesus will grant you his gift of peace. Humility will free you from undo anxiety. The Holy Spirit will *teach you everything* and correct your course if you make a misguided decision (cf. Jn 14:26-27). Indeed, *[w]e know that all things work for good for those who love God and are called according to his purpose* (Rom 8:28).

3. Take a Huge Step of Faith Dream a BIG DREAM, step out in faith and publicly share your vision with passion. When the disciples were disappointed in their inability to exorcize a demon, our Lord said: *Amen, I say to you, if you have faith the size of a mustard seed, you will say to this mountain, 'Move from here to there,' and it will move. Nothing will be impossible for you* (Mt 17:20).

In his book *A Purpose-Driven Church*, Rev. Rick Warren recounts the fears he had announcing publicly his dream to build a large evangelical church in southern California. In 1980 he gave his first sermon to a small community that would grow into Saddleback Church. As he approached that auspicious moment, he recounts:

> I was overwhelmed with the fear of failure. What if it doesn't happen? Is this vision really from God, or is it just a wild dream of an idealistic twenty-six-year-old? It was one thing to privately dream of what I expected God to do; it was another matter to publicly state that dream. In my mind, I had now passed the point of no return. In spite of my fears, I now had to move full-speed ahead. Convinced that my dream would give glory to God, I decided to never look back.[145]

In that first sermon, Warren gave voice to a dream that he believed and hoped came from God. A part of that dream back in 1980 included a church family of 20,000 members. According to their website, Saddleback Church now averages 22,000 in weekly attendance.

4. Rely Entirely on the Holy Spirit Ask the Holy Spirit to reveal the best ways and means for proclaiming the *kērygma* to every person in your region. Insist on a significant block of unprogrammed time every day to pray and listen to God; to work through the tough issues with him in a sacred place where interruptions are not allowed. Enlist the prayers of the whole Church for the goal of regional evangelization. God assured Zechariah that "small beginnings" were not to be scorned. He also assured him that the small beginnings would not stay small (cf. Zech 4:8-10). If necessary, be willing to start small and slow. But, be equally willing to end fast and large. In all things, submit yourself to his will.

5. Embrace the Freedom of Your Vocation If you are a bishop, recognize the extraordinary freedom that comes with your position. In fact, you have more freedom than the CEOs of the largest multinational corporations. You do not have a board of directors to second-guess your every judgment. You are not constrained by the profit expectations of shareholders. You are chief executive, legislator, and appellate court judge wrapped in one. In a strictly juridical sense, you are answerable only to the pope. Accordingly, you do *not* have to live up to the expectations of everyone who asks you for a meeting if God is calling you to spend your time more fruitfully. You do *not* have to attend every annual function just because your predecessors did. Take control of your calendar and do not be enslaved by past precedent unless you know the precedent is the best way of serving your Lord and your people. He expects you to use this extraordinary freedom to follow in the paths he shows you; to shepherd his people knowing full-well that someday you will be called to give an account of your stewardship.

If you are a pastor, you too have remarkable freedom. Your pastoral council is there to provide valued counsel. You certainly have the authority to delegate some decision-making to them and others, but you are expected to lead your flock in unity with your bishop, not at the whim of your most demanding parishioners. You do not have the freedom to lead them down the path of narcissism, either your own or theirs. In every way, lead by example.

If you are a single person, you have been given the precious gift of time. You have opportunities to serve the Church and proclaim the Gospel that married people do not have. Thank God for your freedom and don't squander it.

If you are a religious, recognize how easily the evangelical counsels and your particular charisms elicit the question: *why is she different?* Lead your joy-filled lives so as to *always be ready to give an explanation to anyone who asks you for a reason for your hope* (cf. 1 Pt 3:15). You too are *called to be fruitful and multiply* (cf. Gen 1:28, 9:7). Know that our Lord has given you too the gift of freedom. So, in the words of St. Vincent de Paul, if "a needy person requires medicine or other help during prayer time, do whatever has to be done with peace of mind… One of God's works is merely interrupted so that a another can be carried out."[146]

If you are married, God has given you a partner. Take time for each other. *For the unbelieving husband is made holy through his wife, and the unbelieving wife is made holy through the brother… For how do you know, wife, whether you will save your husband; or how do you know, husband, whether you will save your wife?* (1 Cor 7:14,16) Your highest priority is your spouse, your children, your grandchildren. Give yourselves the liberty to invest all you are in your family. Jesus told the Gerasene man whom he had just delivered from demons: <u>Go home and tell them all that the Lord in his pity has done for you</u> (Mk 5:19).

Give yourselves permission to be who God wants you to be, not someone else; not a slave to anyone else's expectations.

6. Move outside the 'Catholic Ghetto' Jesus' last words to his apostles were stunningly challenging. It was one thing to be his witnesses "in Jerusalem and throughout Judea". Familiar territory. They had even had their forays into Samaria and perhaps had made a few disciples among those strange people. But, "to the ends of the earth"? Making "disciples of all nations"? Jesus was talking about a dream that would take his apostles *far outside* their comfort zones. Without the Holy Spirit, it would be nothing short of impossible... Don't forget: He did send them the Holy Spirit and he has done the same for you.

Ghettos are not necessarily bad places. The chancery is a comfortable environment. Our rectories and parish offices? Well, they're home. Our parishioners? They're our family. This is all part-and-parcel of the community of faith, and we have a right to return to them. *But,* we do not have a right to stay there, never venturing out. He called us into mission fields, sometimes even hostile places.

You bishops, how will you convert secular opinion leaders who want nothing to do with the Church? Think about it. Pray about it. Enlist the wisdom of your brothers and sons. Then, do it. Have you ever met a meth head or a drug dealer? Probably not. *Why* not? Jesus made friends with tax collectors and prostitutes. He, himself. He didn't delegate it away. Who are the tax collectors and prostitutes in your life? Find them.

You men, think about how you can reach drunkards and prisoners who live in places you would rather not go. Think about it. Pray about it. Talk to your bishop. With his guidance, he will commission you to go there.

You women, how can you take the message of Jesus' amazing love to high school dropouts and abuse victims? Think about it. Pray about it. Talk to your bishop. He will get you the help you need and even walk alongside you.

Just as the disciples gradually discerned that that the Good News was for everyone – not just the Jews – Catholic leaders must re-learn the same truth. Make friends with "tax collectors, drunkards, and prostitutes". Take the message to the house of the most prominent Pharisee. Be public and personal in describing your love for Jesus. Tell your story. Let the world know what's motivating you.

Make many acquaintances and even a few friends throughout the region with secular leaders and people who are *not* in the pews. Model evangelization for your flock. Expect conversions.

7. Balance your time, not your priorities Become a long-range strategist. Remember the Eisenhower Matrix (Figure 12). Some of what appears to be urgent, really is not. If something is truly important, make it urgent. By prioritizing evangelization, you will be normalizing it. By normalizing evangelization, you will be prioritizing it. What you spend your time on will either divert your focus from the *Vision* or reinforce it. The best way to stay focused is to take control of your calendar, while remaining flexible enough to allow for the unpredictable nature of real (not imagined) human needs. Keep at arm's length anything – however good it may be – that would demand so much of you that it would significantly distract from your #1 Priority. Insist that your long-range goal becomes a part of your daily, short-range work. This may mean telling some good people "no". When this happen, say "no" with grace and a word of explanation.

Transformational leaders are constantly focusing on the big picture by asking strategic questions. How are we doing? Is the last round of *purposeful parishes initiatives* beginning to bear visible fruit? If not, why not? Do our missionary disciples need some kind of further training or encouragement? Will we have enough new *Ananias's* for a regional campaign in three years? What needs to be done that only I can do? What can be done by others? These are the questions that should occupy you and your senior staff. A list of Focus Questions is offered in Figure 13.

Don't let something new divert your attention for more than a very short time from your long-range #1 Priority. Nothing stands still very long these days. New distractions pop up all the time. Some are

Figure 13
Leadership Focus Questions for Regional Evangelization

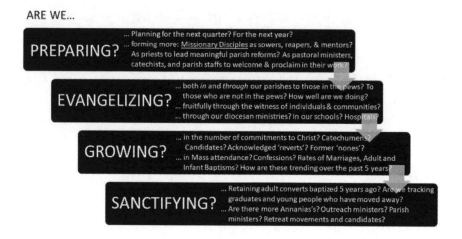

even good ideas. But, unless the latest "opportunity" is of such great importance that it casts serious doubt on the validity of your big-picture decisions (and it rarely does), stay the course and keep your resources focused on what needs to be done. Let others chase after the "second rabbit". You have to give the *Vision Achievement Strategy* and your short-range *Tactical Plan* a chance to make a discernable difference and that won't happen if you divert resources for something that wasn't planned.

8. Lead Alone, Achieve Together Make time for direct leadership of diocesan evangelization. Do NOT delegate away your highest priority. This is what you need to be spending time on. Having said that, be aware that a typical mistake of unusually gifted people is to micromanage. Force yourself to step back from controlling the details, unless a specific detail is a deal breaker. In that case, don't let it slip by without your attention.

Decisions of great importance should not be made by committees. The "big hairy audacious goal", the big-picture *Vision*, adherence to the long-range *Strategy* – these are the non-negotiables. But the *way* you make these decisions is important. Transformational leadership involves great emotional intelligence. So, lead graciously and carefully, knowing that you cannot evangelize a region without a *whole lot of other people,* starting with the people closest to you. An obsession – even a noble one – can morph into idolatry, especially when it becomes detached from prayer. Bring as many people on-board as you can. Turn no one away. Build up your army of missionary disciples and work with them.

9. Communicate with Charity and Clarity Differentiate between those occasions when it is best to communicate privately, one-on-one vs. occasions when the message can be delivered in a meeting or mediated by someone else. If the matter involves strong convictions and/or deep feelings, communicate privately and face-to-face. Maintain the importance that Pat Lencioni places on achieving clarity. Choose your words carefully. Leave as little room for ambiguity or misinterpretation as possible. Be honest and encourage honesty. Quoting Marilyn Chandler McEntyre, Archbishop Chaput wrote:

> "Words are entrusted to us as equipment for our life together, to help us survive, guide and nourish one another." That is why honesty always ranks among the qualities most admired by colleagues. No one wants to hear bad news or criticism. But people consistently prefer the truth to soothing lies that end in bad surprises.[147]

Balance passion with humility and vulnerability. Let everything flow from the center of who you are out to the world. Use emotional intelligence. Communicate <u>directly</u> to the faithful as much as you can, but not so often that it leaves no time for reading and listening.

10. Create a Culture of Accountability Establish goals and benchmarks for yourself with respect to work you have agreed with your Regional Evangelization Leadership Team that *you* will do. Report on your progress to them at every meeting and ask the same of them. Set an example of accountability and, in so doing, you will elevate the accountability of the entire diocesan culture. Don't be outdone in the accountability you place on yourself. This will permit you in turn to ratchet up the expectations you place on your pastors and parishes. Ask the same level of accountability from them as you are willing to render to them.

XV. The 'Catholic Moment' Revisited

*He gives strength to the fainting; for the weak he makes vigor
abound. Though young men faint and grow weary, and
youths stagger and fall, they that hope in the Lord will renew
their strength, they will soar as with eagles' wings. They will
run and not grow weary, walk and not grow faint.*

Isaiah 40:29-31

Evangelizing Nationally

While evangelization carried out by individuals, parishes,
dioceses, ecclesial movements, and special ministries are all central
to the conversion of our country to Christ, it is not all that we can do.
A national evangelistic endeavor developed and executed through
the United States Conference of Catholic Bishops (USCCB) is also
needed. The notion of *national evangelization* is an important element
of the *Proposal* and the central focus of this final chapter.

Despite our current problems, the Roman Catholic Church is
uniquely positioned to lead national evangelization in the United States
in ways that no other ecclesial body or denomination can. We have
at least a minimal presence in all areas of the country, a ubiquitous
and consistent institutional infrastructure, and the potential (if not
reality) for strong inter-diocesan communications in support of a
common goal. Working together to evangelize the United States as a
whole, our bishops may be able to achieve what they cannot hope to
do as individuals. Moreover, as will be explained below, the poor
would likely be the greatest beneficiaries.

There are but three things stopping us from undertaking such an ambitious initiative: a conviction that our credibility is so damaged by recent events that no one will listen to anything sponsored by the U.S. Bishops; a hidebound culture of diocesan autonomy, and; a phlegmatic "maintenance mentality" that inhibits reimagining a creative, united approach to proclaiming Christ to a broken world.

All three of these inhibitions are self-made. We still live in a country where the right of free speech is widely (if not perfectly) respected. Moreover, there are many Christians who long for just such a united evangelical outreach and would be invigorated to new levels of zeal by the hope that such an apostolic initiative would enkindle.

"But haven't we destroyed our credibility?"

As I have talked to people about the idea of a new 'Catholic Moment' of evangelization in the United States, it is often met with a mixture of excitement and skepticism; excitement at the possibilities, but skepticism that the 'moment' still exists. Many Catholics express the feeling that the recent round of sex abuse revelations has so tarnished the credibility of our bishops that they have effectively disqualified themselves as a viable source of evangelization in the United States at this time in history. These are reasonable people who raise a valid question. So, let's probe this matter.

The apostles were also men who were completely without credibility of their own. St. Peter had actually denied even knowing the Lord; not once, but three times. And yet, Peter went on to evangelize fearlessly. St. Paul had self-righteously persecuted the Church, a history that in his own eye's rendered him "the least of the apostles" (1 Cor 15:9a). And yet, Paul evangelized the nations. Sts. John and James shamelessly sought superiority over their fellow disciples. St. Matthew knowingly defrauded his brother Jews. St. Thomas refused to believe because he had "not seen". These were all soiled men. "But by the grace of God," Paul said, "I am what I am" (1 Cor 15:10a). That could have been the epitaph for all of them. They were all acutely aware of the truth in our Lord's words: "The one to whom little is forgiven, loves little" (Lk 7:47b). Through their own missteps, they came to realize that evangelization without love is a sham. Despite all their shortcomings, the Lord specifically chose them and empowered them to proclaim the Good News. After all was said and done, they remained apostles, who were *sent* with the message of salvation.

> They were able to proclaim the Gospel even to their deaths, precisely because they were so badly broken and the risen Lord had loved and forgiven them anyway

They were able to proclaim the Gospel even to their deaths, precisely *because* they were so badly broken and their risen Lord had loved and forgiven them anyway; not because of any outstanding qualities on their part. They did so by proclaiming the One who loved them while they were still sinners, not by proclaiming themselves or even the Church.

We need to follow their example. When we evangelize, we must proclaim Jesus alone and trust the Holy Spirit to lead seekers into the fullness of all truth. As much as we love the Church and understand the desirability of becoming a Catholic, if it should happen that someone responding to an evangelical invitation decides in favor of another Christian denomination or a "non-denominational church", so be it. Rejoice with them. That is a better outcome by far than remaining distant from Christ and the Christian community.

Our willingness to allow that to happen also demonstrates the sincerity of our love for Jesus. First-and-foremost, our evangelical motivation must flow from a desire to bring people to an authentic encounter with the living God, not a reaction to the heartbreaking exodus of so many souls out of the Catholic Church.

So, we need not worry about having lost our credibility. Ironically, by preaching Jesus out of humility and brokenness and repentance for having avoided that proclamation in recent times, we can expect far greater fruitfulness, because, in having lost our own credibility, we may now speak more persuasively of *his*. We can speak of his forgiveness because we have personally experienced it ourselves.

We must all evangelize – including our bishops – in just this way. It is in our weakness that his strength is made perfect. The face of evangelization should include ordinary people who have yielded their lives to Christ. They might also be well-known entertainers, educators, scientists and the like. But they must also be humble, repentant bishops, speaking out of the same weakness and vulnerability as the rest of us.

As St. John Paul II prepared for the advent of the twenty-first century, he made this point loud and clear in his apostolic letter *Tertio millennio adveniente* when he said:

> [T]he Church should become more fully conscious of the sinfulness of her children, recalling all those times in history when they departed from the spirit of Christ and his Gospel and, instead of offering to the world the witness of a life inspired by the values of faith, indulged in ways of thinking and acting which were truly *forms of counter-witness and scandal (Italics* in original)...
>
> She cannot cross the threshold of the new millennium without encouraging her children to purify themselves, through repentance, of past errors and instances of infidelity, inconsistency, and slowness to act. Acknowledging the weaknesses of the past is an act of honesty and courage which helps us to strengthen our faith,

which alerts us to face today's temptations and challenges and prepares us to meet them.

Among the sins which require a greater commitment to repentance and conversion should certainly be counted those which *have been detrimental to the unity willed by God for his People* (*Italics* in original).[148]

The 'Catholic Moment'

In 1987 the late Richard John Neuhaus wrote a book entitled *The Catholic Moment*. In it he argued that the Catholic Church is uniquely situated to lead the proclamation of the Gospel in the world. This book was anything but a return to nineteenth-century Catholic triumphalism. Rather, he saw in the Catholic Church the new standard bearer of authentic ecumenical evangelization, committed to visible unity while uncompromising on the unique identity and salvific work of Jesus.

Neuhaus garnered significant attention at that time, not only because of what the book said, but because of who he was, namely one of the most influential *Protestant* thinkers of the late twentieth-early twenty-first centuries. A few years after the publication of *The Catholic Moment*, Neuhaus requested to be received in the Catholic Church and, given the fact that he was an ordained Lutheran pastor with impressive credentials, a year later was ordained a priest for the Archdiocese of New York, where he faithfully served until his death in 2009.[149]

In having lost our own credibility, we can now speak more persuasively of **his**

I have attempted to synopsize some of his major points in the following excerpts from *The Catholic Moment*.

This, I have argued, is the moment in which the Roman Catholic Church in the world can and should be the lead church in proclaiming and exemplifying the Gospel...[150]

> In the [Second Vatican] Council's further development of the tradition, it is made much clearer than it was before [the Council] that the Roman Catholic Church is vulnerable to the Gospel and to the entire [Christian] community that is claimed by the Gospel... In truth, the Reformation understanding of the Gospel as God's justifying grace centered in the scriptural *kerygma* of cross and resurrection is today more boldly proclaimed by Rome than by many of the churches that lay claim to the Reformation heritage...[151]

Interestingly, Neuhaus argued that Catholicism's unique understanding of episcopal leadership made for a degree of independence from bureaucratic control that he saw taking place in some major non-Catholic denominations; an independence freeing our bishops from ideological agendas that sometimes develop among the "professional" insiders of Protestant church bureaucracies.

> Bishops in other bodies – Methodist, Lutheran, Episcopalian – frequently have as much power, in practice, if not in theory, but are more susceptible to becoming managers of the branch office of the national church. That is not to say that many Roman Catholic bishops are not susceptible to that and other ways of becoming mere functionaries. But the Roman Catholic bishop is somewhat less bureaucratically "capturable" by virtue of having diverse lines of accountability attached to his office. He is pastor of the people, leader of the clergy who exercise their office by his authority, responsible to diverse institutions and religious communities in his diocese, and, very importantly he is accountable to Rome.[152]

Rather than viewing "Romanism" as an obstacle to evangelization, Neuhaus recognized in the papacy a form of internal discipline, holding in check the excesses of those who might stray away from the central truths of the Gospel.

He also noted what he saw as a unique relationship between Catholic bishops and their people. He wrote: "Among major American bodies, the Roman Catholic people's manifest sense of identification with, and usually affection for, their bishop is singular."[153] Despite recent events and the anger it has engendered among rank-and-file Catholics, our anger toward our bishops is more that of a wife upset at the stupidity of her husband. When all is said-and-done, affection has a way of returning (even if grudgingly).

In Neuhaus' view, the unique diversity of the Catholic Church also serves to buttress her potential effectiveness as the leader in "proclaiming and exemplifying the Gospel".

> Pluralism in the Church should not be the result of dissent from the Gospel but of diverse forms of radical obedience to the Gospel. The Roman Catholic Church is by far the most diverse of churches. With its discrete orders of ministry, its monastic communities, its myriad works of mercy, its multifarious national and cultural traditions, its political and ideological inclusiveness, and even its patterns of theological reflection, the Roman Catholic Church is the paradigmatic instance of the unity in diversity that other churches should emulate and to which the world aspires... The future of Christianity in the world will be powerfully influenced by whether Catholicism emerges from the [Second Vatican] Council with a unity that is not uniformity and a diversity that is not division.[154]

The attributes of the Catholic Church noticed by Father Neuhaus in making his case for the 'Catholic Moment' *still exist*: strong adherence to the *kērygma*, relative freedom from hidden bureaucratic agendas, the papacy, a cooperative (if disheartened) laity, widespread diversity, and a respect – albeit wary – for Christocentric ecumenism.

Many of the worst forms of disunity that existed in the wake of Vatican II have dissipated, if not entirely disappeared

Having said that, we are not as united among ourselves as we could and should be. And as noted, many of us are suffering from broken hearts about the clergy sex abuse scandal and often-misguided episcopal reactions to the problem. Notwithstanding this fact, many of the worst forms of disunity that existed in the wake of Vatican II have dissipated, if not entirely disappeared: non-Christocentric universalism, flagrant liturgical abuses, liberation theology, and other forms of anti-authoritarian rebellion. Today, we struggle, but it's a good struggle. We struggle to know how to reach the huge contingent of disaffiliated young adults who have rejected Catholic sexual morality and are suspicious of institutional religion. We struggle about how best we might evangelize and serve the world. But we are less inclined to compromise on the essentials and we are looking for answers in a spirit of humility. God can work with that.

Elements of a National Evangelization Strategy

The aims of the United States Conference of Catholic Bishops have evolved since its inception as the National Catholic War Council a century ago rendering help to servicemen and their families. Today, the USCCB acts collegially on all sorts of matters of widespread importance: the Right to Life, threats to religious freedom, aid to refugees and victims of human trafficking, political positions with moral implications, matters of internal discipline, etc.

There are several ways in which the national bishops working as a group can contribute to the evangelization of the nation. Moreover, there are some distinct advantages of united action on a purely practical level, such as financial economies of scale for widespread evangelistic outreach and related research.

Not intending to replace diocesan or provincial *Regional Vision Achievement Strategies,* a broad consultative process could be initiated to *enhance* them. Bishops could be asked to respond to such questions as:

† How can the USCCB most help you in your apostolate of evangelizing the people and culture of your diocese?

† Could the USCCB mitigate or even eliminate certain obstacles to evangelization you are currently experiencing?

As conceived, the *National Evangelization Strategy* could provide the knowledge base and media resources needed for the particular churches to evangelize better. It would also send out a unified

National Evangelization Strategy

Aims:

Mutual episcopal support and accountability for evangelization

National expertise and possible financial assistance

National Christ-centered media presence coordinated with the local Church

Data informed decision-making

Financial economies of scale

message and afford economies of scale for widespread research and evangelistic outreach. One might expect that national expertise and possible financial resources to assist missionary dioceses would be among the services a *National Evangelization Strategy* might bring.

Mutual Support and Accountability While the almost-sovereign autonomy of bishops is one of the most time-honored practices in the Church, we can no longer ignore the fact that on a human level, it can be conducive to sin. And, even where sin is *not* involved, it encourages irresponsibility and idiosyncratic behavior that can blind a person to the way he is being perceived by others and impede the cause of the Gospel. In bygone years, mutual accountability among brother-bishops was simply not practical due to the exigencies of long-distance communications. Today, no such impediments exist. Moreover, in the contemporary world, peer reviews in many professions are commonplace and job performance reviews are in every industry and for every job, even CEOs.

I would be the last to argue for a radical "pendulum swing" that would replace independent episcopal freedom with a new national "group think". But reasonable requirements of transparency with respect to adherence to basic Christian values has great potential to improve the Church's witness to the world. For example, if a bishop is living in palatial luxury in the midst of a low-income diocese, his brother-bishops should feel free to provide charitable correction and, in grave situations, outright censor. If an influential bishop receives an expensive gift from a brother-bishop whom he hardly even knows, the gift should be returned with comment. If two or three bishops agree that a brother is exhibiting behavior that suggests a moral problem may exist, they should step in; even if the problem turns out not to exist, the *appearance* of a problem is a problem in itself that needs to be addressed.

What about sins of *omission*? These, of course, are much more difficult to recognize and demand sensitive prudential judgments. Notwithstanding, if a bishop is clearly not investing *any* time and energy in, let's say, critical matters of social justice that are particularly relevant in his own diocese, brother-bishops should at least feel free to raise the issue in a non-threatening environment; there may be a very simple explanation that is not immediately obvious. In such cases, the brother-bishops may be able to provide fraternal support by helping the bishop under scrutiny to think through the problem and find a hitherto unthought-of solution.

Because fruitful, unambiguous evangelization is not currently a part of our ecclesial culture or widespread praxis in the United States, mutual accountability and support are needed until it is. Perhaps a semi-decennial peer audit of evangelization in each diocese would make sense. It could very well have far-reaching effects. Just the knowledge that a systematic, but charitable form of scrutiny is going to take place is likely to stimulate some improved apostolic action.

St. Paul wrote: *Therefore, putting away falsehood, speak the truth, each one to his neighbor, for we are members of one another* (Eph 4:25). In our age of hyper-sensitivity where tolerance is exalted as the highest of virtues, speaking the truth to one another can be difficult. But we have a scriptural mandate to do so (cf. Mt 18:15-17, Gal 6:1, 2 Thes 3:15). Moreover, throughout the history of the Church, there have been many examples of mutual correction (e.g., the monastic practice of holding a "chapter of faults") and even correcting those in high places (e.g., St. Catherine of Siena's gentle rebuke of Pope Gregory XI).

The practice of mutual support and accountability in the context of trans-diocesan evangelization has an additional dimension. Some apostolic actions can only become possible when bishops agree to work together. This is especially true in missionary dioceses where financial resources simply do not exist.

May bishops begin to think more collegially, not only regarding matters of discipline and common threats, but also in matters of building up the kingdom of God. (More thoughts on inter-diocesan cooperation and mutual accountability are discussed in Chapter III: *A Paradigm Shift*, pp. 76-83).

National Christ-Centered Media Presence Many have observed that we live in a society full of distractions. Constant auditory and visual stimulation is ubiquitous, serving to distract us from the big questions of life. Unless we are deliberate about tuning it all out, it is easy to go through life skimming along the surface, rarely if ever thinking about the big questions of life: How did we get here? Does my life have a purpose? Do I owe anybody anything beyond "not hurting" them? Is death the end?

Unfortunately, the Church has to become a part of the "noise" just to compete. If the message of Jesus and the wisdom of

Christianity is even to be considered, then the Church has to enter into the noise just to get attention. We must move outward and find ways of insinuating the proclamation of Christ into social circles that normally are not Christian with messages that can hit the mark. One way to do that is through well-produced media that expressly targets "markets" that generally avoid us and that we normally cannot reach.

A bewildering variety of media exist: social media, print media, billboards, TV, radio, direct mail, email, phone messaging, etc. Most dioceses do not have the technical knowhow to enter into this morass. Consequently, we have historically avoided it. This is an area in which the USCCB could serve a vital, centralized role with the potential to provide both professional communications/marketing skills and mass purchasing power.

A new and untested frontier is the use of computer technology as a direct means of on-line evangelization using customized messaging. An example might be individualized, computer-generated messaging aimed at individuals identified by 'artificial intelligence' software as "seekers" and potentially open to the Gospel. It seems to me that there *may* be great potential here when paired with follow-up by a real person, especially as a tool used nationally. At the very least, the development of this technology deserves watching.

Admittedly, undertaking a national Christ-centered media presence would be the boldest and most expensive endeavor the Church in the United States has ever pursued, requiring diverse messaging for different geographies and demographics. But the potential to open up minds, move hearts, and provoke that first responding phone call or text message is immense. The *sine quo non* for making such a strategy truly fruitful includes...

† Unreserved participation of the local churches

† Data-informed decision-making

Participation of the Particular Churches One thing that is certain about national media-based evangelization is that it will *not* "work" in any meaningful sense of the term if the local bishop, parishes, and missionary disciples are not fully prepared for it and have a concrete plan to *complete* the evangelization begun by the media. A person may open herself to the Lord by hearing or reading the message of salvation through the media, but without the Body of Christ embracing her in selfless love and long-term accompaniment, a huge opportunity will have been lost.

Hence, the critical importance of a national system that connects the seeker to a sincere and fully-trained missionary disciple, ideally a member of a parish near the residence of the seeker. The goal here is not to tweak a moment of passing interest, but to enable a lifetime of Christian discipleship.

Any sponsor of a TV commercial automatically tells the prospective buyer where and/or how the product can be purchased. In a similar way, an 800-number or some other simple way of connecting the viewer or Internet user to the local Church *via* a committed disciple *must* be a fully-coordinated partnership.

Data-Informed Decision-Making In order for a national Christ-centered media presence to be effective, it needs to be undergirded by the best social science and marketing research that money can buy. Currently, everything we know about the human process of conversion to Christ is anecdotal. There has been some limited research on the reasons why people *leave* the Catholic Church that reveals the need for far greater pastoral awareness and sensitivity. [155] , [156] However, in reading over the statements of individual respondents, the reasons given for leaving the Church are so varied that one gets the sense many of them are thinly veiled rationalizations. As Father James Mallon has observed: *"The issue is not always the issue"*.[157]

Of far greater value would be research into how to deliver the *positive message* of salvation effectively. This research could inform the national media messaging (and conceivably, even the work of individual evangelizers). Empirically speaking, we know next to nothing about what can spark interest in a relationship with Christ. What helps to sustain it? What diminishes it? What media messages can the Church use to encourage authentic conversions? What messaging would be most effective in "markets" with differing ethnicities and demographics? This is not to suggest that our Lord does not offer his grace in totally unpredictable and serendipitous ways. Absolutely, he does. But, one of our jobs is to proclaim the Good News "on the housetops" and to be "as shrewd as serpents" in how we do it (cf. Mt 10:27, Mt 10:16).

One point is certain: the media message needs to focus on Jesus, not the Church. In time, people will be "loved into" the Church, so long as we lead with Jesus – the reason the Church exists in the first place. Once again, quoting Father Mallon:

> My own experience of being a parish priest for seventeen years tells me that people will live in the tension of conflicted beliefs if they can experience real belonging. As they are loved and cared for – as they come into contact with and grow in Jesus – many of the issues cease to be such. This will happen after loving and accompanying people, we make our primary purpose the person of Jesus Christ and not to preach the Church. If we bring people through an experience of belonging to believing, then behavior will change and the Church will be embraced and eventually understood and loved.[158]

Pre-Evangelization Messaging Having said that, there is another message that needs to be an early part of the national media message – the reasonableness of Christian Faith. A prerequisite for Christian belief is rejection of the widespread myth that *Christian faith and science are in conflict,* a prevarication that many so-call "new atheists" are doing their best to propagate and one that has been uncritically accepted by many young people. As a consequence of this widespread myth, Dr. Mark Grey, a senior research associate at the Center for Applied Research into the Apostolate says: "It's almost a crisis of faith. In the whole concept of faith, [young people are] struggling with faith in ways we haven't seen in previous generations."[159]

Unfortunately, the literal adherence of many fundamentalist Christians to Genesis' creation accounts has been used effectively by a new breed of aggressive atheists to categorize *all* Christians as anti-science "know-nothings". This has been a sad turn of events, since it undercuts an intellectual prerequisite for theism, which must be accepted before the notions of divine revelation, the Incarnation, and *kērygma* can even be considered.

It is problematic that a religion which gave the world the following partial list of groundbreaking *ordained scientists* would be perceived as anti-science, but for many it has, because the following facts of history are largely unknown:[160, 161, 162]

- Bishop Robert Grosseteste († 1253) – Founder of the scientific movement at Oxford
- St. Albert the Great, OP († 1280) – Early practitioner of experimental science
- Canon Nicolaus Copernicus († 1543) – First person to formulate a comprehensive heliocentric cosmology
- Fr. Christoph Scheiner, SJ († 1650) – Invented the pantograph and a telescope strong enough for the first systematic investigation of sun spots

- Fr. Athanasius Kircher, SJ († 1680) – Made the first definite statement of the germ theory of disease
- Fr. Jean-Felix Picard, SJ († 1682) – "Founder of Modern Astronomy"
- Bishop Nicolaus Steno (Niels Stenson) († 1686) – "Father of Geology"
- Abbot Gregor Mendel, OSA († 1884) – "Father of Modern Genetics"
- Fr. José Algue, SJ († 1930) – Inventor of the barocyclonometer
- Fr. Julius Nieuwland, CSC († 1936) – Inventor of synthetic rubber
- Fr. Pierre Teilhard de Chardin, SJ († 1955) – Discoverer of both Piltdown Man and Peking Man
- Fr. Georges Lemaître († 1966) – Discoverer of the Big Bang Theory and Hubble's Law
- Fr. Stanley Jakey, OSB († 2009) – Nuclear physicist and winner of the John Templeton Foundation Award for "writings that "parsed the histories of science and religion and the intertwining of Faith and reason"
- Fr. Michael Heller – Mathematician and astronomer and winner of the John Templeton Foundation Award. Currently researching "the singularity problem in general relativity and the use of non-commutative geometry in seeking the unification of general relativity and quantum mechanics." (I trust you understand that.)

A serious attempt at national evangelization must include the *pre-evangelization* work of debunking anti-Christian myths about science and asserting the fact that there is actually *rigorous and compelling scientific evidence* pointing to the existence of God.[163]

Another pre-evangelistic feature of a national TV campaign could also include short, hard-hitting spots that reveal the most compelling scientific evidence supporting widely-recognized miracles, such as:

- Eucharistic miracles of consecrated Bread and Wine that have transformed into human heart tissue and blood (always with the same blood type) that never decomposes after centuries and even a millennium; miracles that can still be witnessed today

- The unexplained, preserved images of the Shroud of Turin and the Tilma of St. Juan Diego; again, observable today

- Medically inexplicable healings in response to the intercession of the saints and at privileged places, such as Lourdes

- The liquefaction of St. Januarius' blood that continues multiple times a year even after 1,700 years

These are phenomena that the secular media typically avoids; phenomena that the vast majority of the general public has absolutely no awareness of. Revealing them on commercial television has the potential to help debunk the myth of a conflict between science and Christian belief. The spots could clarify that none of these phenomena are required as articles of Catholic faith, but that the best scientific testing cannot explain them in terms of natural causes. They could also provide addresses to credible websites for those who want to learn more; the objective being to document that science can affirmatively support the reality of the supernatural realm.

Re-reading Inter mirifica The Second Vatican Council provided good reasons for national evangelistic initiatives that make innovative use of the media. One of the earliest documents promulgated by Vatican II was the *Decree on the Means of Social Communication (Inter mirifica)* published in December 1963. Only nine pages in length, it is the second-shortest of the major Vatican II documents and well worth re-reading.

Much of its thrust is directed toward the proper use the media, so that it glorifies God rather than sin. However, it also calls for the media to be put at the service of evangelization.

Man's genius has with God's help produced marvelous technical inventions from creation, especially in our own times. The Church, our mother, is particularly interested in those that touch man's spirit and which have opened up new avenues of easy communication which of their nature can reach and influence not merely single individuals but the very masses and even the whole of society…[164]

The Catholic Church was founded by Christ our Lord to bring salvation to all men. It feels obliged, therefore, to preach the gospel. In the same way, it believes that its task involves employing the means of social communication to announce the good news of salvation and to teach men how to use them properly.[165]

Inter mirifica goes on to charge bishops with taking responsibility for this work (cf. 20) and to encourage them to undertake a *unified effort* on social media projects at the national and even international level (cf. 20-21).

Many things have been done within the Church since the 1960s to make apostolic use of the means of social communication. We have the Vatican Dicastery for Communications, which was originally established by *Inter mirifica* for just that purpose. The USCCB has a standing Committee on Communications along with a professional staff. Moreover, the bishops have been very supportive of Church-based media, most especially the *Eternal Word Television Network* (EWTN). The present chair of the USCCB Committee on Evangelization and Catechesis, Bishop Robert Barron, is trailblazing the use of social media, YouTube, TV, and print media to evangelize society through his *Word on Fire* ministry.

Notwithstanding these wonderful initiatives, we have only begun to scratch the surface of the evangelistic potential of the media to "sell God". Much of the current media productions supported by the Church tend to "preach to the choir". As fine as EWTN is, its primary audience is already-committed Catholics; while this is a great service to the Church, and while by the grace of God, a serious sinner may stumble across it once in a while, it is not a channel that a cynic or skeptic would normally search out. To his credit, Bishop Barron is taking bold steps to reach 'nones', but his ministry is only a drop in the bucket needed to reach the millions of American souls who know virtually nothing about God and the truth of the Gospel.

Among its many recommendations, *Inter mirifica* proposes ecclesial initiatives to raise up communications specialists who are committed to the Gospel:

> First, lay people must be given the necessary technical, doctrinal, and moral foundation. To this end, schools, institutes or faculties must be provided in sufficient number, where journalists, writers of films, radio and television, and anyone else concerned, may receive a complete formation, imbued with the Christian spirit and especially with the Church's social teaching. Actors should also be instructed and helped so that their gifts too can benefit society.[166]

It is fairly common at American Catholic universities such as Franciscan University of Steubenville for students to double-major in Theology and Religious Education. Suppose our episcopal leaders initiated the creation of endowed chairs and scholarships in Catholic universities for students who want to study theology/ ministry and simultaneously desire to carry this knowledge beyond catechetical circles into the more worldly careers of journalism and the performing arts? This too could become a part of the long-term *National Evangelization Strategy*.

Funding the Media Component The reason why we don't have empirically-aided support for how to evangelize, and; the reason why we do not have a major presence in the secular commercial media is because such things are extremely expensive, far too expensive for a diocese or even most provinces. On the other hand, what would be prohibitive for one hundred ninety-seven individual dioceses and eparchies in the United States might possibly be achievable with the economies of scale and the national fund-raising capabilities that the USCCB could bring to the table.

Whatever the specific elements of a unified national Catholic evangelical apostolate might be, such an ambitious effort will require an absolutely unprecedented commitment of resources... literally, billions of dollars and numerous creative and research professionals dedicated to the task. Such challenges, however, have never overpowered the missionary impulse of Christians in the past and they should not in the present. To make a point of it, *Inter mirifica* states:

> It would be shameful if by their inactivity Catholics allowed the word of God to be silenced or obstructed by the technical difficulties which these media present and by their admittedly enormous cost.[167]

There is no doubt that the financial cost would be daunting and that it would take time to raise the appropriate resources for such a long-term effort. That said, huge sums of disposable income are available to those who can make a case for the efficacy of their cause.

According to the Center for Responsive Politics, $6.5 billion were raised for the combined presidential and congressional races in the 2016 general election cycle.[168] National Public Radio reported that $4.4 billion in the 2016 federal races went for TV ad buys.[169] Of that total, fully 70 percent came from the donations of individuals. (The other 30 percent came from Super PACs supported largely by corporations.) The point is simply this: Provided people believe the message is important, it is possible to raise very large sums of disposable income with most of it coming from individuals. Large corporations do not have to be the key ingredient to do this. [170]

Is it possible for the bishops of the United States to cooperate sufficiently to conduct a national capital campaign for proclaiming the Gospel and urging watchers/listeners/readers to take a step of faith toward God? Would a few very wealthy Catholics be willing to take personal leaps of faith to help fund something that is not brick-and-mortar, but could change eternal destinies? I believe these are very real possibilities and, if they are, millions of rank-and-file Catholics will follow and provide the remaining capital needed to endow a national fund to keep our Lord in the commercial airwaves, Internet, and print media of the United States, *in perpetuity*.

For more content on the use of the media in the New Evangelization, see the *Paradigm Shift* (pp. 76-82), *A Regional Strategy for Vision Achievement* (pp. 271-275, 313-315), and *The Key to Getting It Done* (pp. 356-359).

Proclaiming the Good News to the Poor

A major Catholic broadcast and cable TV presence combined with missionary disciples' boots on the ground is likely to have a disproportionately positive effect on the poor. As it happens, the poor tend to rely on TV and other forms of media entertainment far more than their more affluent counterparts. As a rule, it is TV and other forms of entertainment that advise their belief systems and values rather than reading and independent research. On the flip side of the coin, when an individual from a different socioeconomic background treats a lower income person as a *friend* and not just as a "client" or a "case" to be dealt with, trust is established. Accordingly, if a national evangelistic campaign is coordinated with a local, face-to-face component, there is the potential for great things to happen.

The poor are particularly susceptible to the call of the Gospel. This is so, because they are aware of their own neediness. They can be brought to the Lord more easily than those who have the circumstantial wherewithal to live as though God doesn't exist. To borrow a phrase that Jorgé Cardinal Bergoglio delivered just before his election as Pope Francis, such an effort will require a willingness on the part of the Church to "come out of herself and to go to the... existential peripheries: those of the mystery of sin, of pain, of ignorance and religious indifference..."[171]

Empirical research bears out the special neediness of the poor to hear the proclamation of the Gospel and their susceptibility to it. In the world of sociology and political science, Charles Murray is simultaneously one of the most loved and hated names on the scene today. Hated, because he has contended that racial prejudice as measured by statistics on race and ethnicity do not account for the widening class differences in American society and loved by others, for exactly the same reason. In 2012, this Harvard-and-MIT-trained scholar published arguably the most unassailable of all his works. In part to demonstrate the truth about his claims that racial prejudice cannot adequately account for American class differences, he conducted a meta-analysis of fifty years of data about "whites only".

His vindication came in the resultant blockbuster book entitled *Coming Apart: The State of White America, 1960-2010* (New York, Random House Crown Forum). In it, Murray documented that *white* American society has been drifting in two polar opposite directions for at least fifty years. Incontestably countering previous criticism, he scrupulously documented the diverging paths of the wealthiest 20 percent of the American *White* population *vis-à-vis* the bottom 30 percent. As he demonstrated, this divergence is not exclusively the problem of Blacks. Regardless of the variable under analysis, the class differences among whites are starkly consistent and the trends are alarming.

Murray refers to the top 20 percent of the income distribution by the name of a fictitious upper-crust neighborhood he calls "Belmont". The bottom 30 percent he dubs "Fishtown". Behaviors and attitudes that have always been associated with high levels of Christian faith shrunk substantially among both groups between 1960 and 2010.

Simultaneously, the differences between Fishtown and Belmont became more extreme almost across-the-board: marriage rates, out-of-wedlock births, children living with both biological parents, education, labor force participation, arrest rates, and on-and-on.

Take marriages for example, Murray reports:

> Starting around 1970, marriage took a nosedive that lasted for nearly twenty years. Among all whites ages 30-49, only 13 percent were not living with spouses as of 1970. Twenty years later, that proportion had doubled, to 27 percent – a change in a core social institution that has few precedents for magnitude and speed...
>
> Then, beginning during the last half of the 1970s, the neighborhoods started to diverge. By the mid-1980s, the decline had stopped in Belmont, and the trendline remained flat thereafter. Marriage in Fishtown kept falling.
>
> The net result: The two neighborhoods, which had been only 11 percentage points apart as late as 1978, were separated by 35 percentage points as of 2010, when only 48 percent of prime-age whites in Fishtown were married, compared to 84 percent in 1960. Furthermore, the slope of the decline in Fishtown after the early 1990s had yet to flatten.[172]

Not surprisingly, the prevalence of divorce throughout the American white population sky-rocketed during the same period, with the same growing differential between the top 20 and the bottom 30 percent. More specifically, "the [divorce] trendline in Belmont flattened in the early 1980s. In Fishtown, the trendline continued steeply upward, with the slope shallowing only a little in the early 2000s." By 2010, a third of Fishtown whites aged 30-49 who had ever married (and were not widowed), had been divorced. By comparison, the same statistic is about 8 percent in Belmont and has held flat for about two decades.[173]

Murray's analysis of illegal drug use was limited due to a lack of data until the late 1970s, although he makes a few anecdotal comments that corroborate the terrible explosion of this problem over the past half-century.[174]

Non-belief skyrocketed in both groups between 1960 and 2010. Murray reports that in 1972 when the General Social Survey (GSS) first asked about religious preference, "only 4 percent" admitted that they had "none".

> But it rose rapidly thereafter. By 1980, 10 percent of the GSS subjects were willing to say they had no religious preference. The trend flattened and even dipped a bit through the 1980s. Then the trend shot upward, and by 2010 stood at 21 percent of all whites ages 30-49. That trend represents a quintupling of the hard-core secular white population since 1972 and a doubling since the early 1990s.[175]

Curiously, by 2010, Fishtown and Belmont had converged to almost identical percentages. However, a slight change in the definition of 'nones' revealed a very different picture.

> Let us look at the trends using a broader definition of *secular,* adding everyone who professes a religion but attends worship services no more than once a year... If we think in terms of disengagement from religion, Fishtown led the way, and the divergence was significant. In the first half of the 1970s, about 10 percentage points separated Belmont from Fishtown. Over the next three decades, disengagement increased in Belmont to 41 percent in the last half of the 2000s. In Fishtown, the religiously disengaged became a majority amounting to 59 percent.[176]

When we consider the other end of the religiosity spectrum, the "religious core", the findings are scary. For purposes of definition, the religious core "report that they attend religious services regularly and have a strong affiliation with their religion." These are "the people who teach in Sunday school, staff booths at the charity fund drives, take the synagogue's youth group on outings, arrange help for bereaved families, and serve as deacons." Belmont's religious core dropped from about 30 percent to 23 percent between the first half of the 1970s to 2010. During the same period, Fishtown's religious core fell from 22 percent to 12 percent. As Murray wrote, such a decline from a *relatively* small proportion to a *very* small proportion...

> ... does seem significant from any perspective. Such a small figure leaves the religious core not as a substantial minority that is still large enough to be a major force in the community, but as a one-out-or-eight group of people who are increasingly seen as oddballs.[177]

The point of all this is *not* that the lower class is becoming less responsible, although that may in fact be happening. Rather, the point that Murray and others such as R.R. Reno make is that the upper classes have abandoned their responsibilities to the less fortunate. This abandonment has given rise to a disproportionate lack of faith among the poor which is leaving more and more people un-moored to objective standards of personal behavior and decision-making.

Opinion leaders – the dominant upper-class minority – are residents of Belmont. As religious faith has declined, "nonjudgmentalism" has become the growing ethos of these opinion makers over the past half-century. It has come to the point that the only judgment of a moral nature that anyone dares make is to render an accusation of "intolerance" when someone else is courageous enough to make a religiously-informed judgment.

As Murray points out, ironically the majority of dominant upper-class minority tend *not* to live by the value-free, anything-goes mores they espouse. They marry more often and divorce far less than the lower classes. They pursue higher education and usually do not engage in blatantly illegal activities (although the recent growth of the 'Me Too' Movement places an important qualifier on this generalization). The upper 20 percent more often form their opinions by reading and critically drawing their own conclusions, which may help to account for a greater degree of diversity of opinion within the upper class. The bottom 30 percent, on the other hand, are more inclined to form their opinions through visual media and entertainment, products of Belmont, even though the top 20 percent may not always choose to consume their own products.

The proclamation the Gospel to the poor is a very real *matter of social justice* that we have not yet recognized. Everyone has a human right to hear the Good News. It turns out that one very good way to do this is through commercial media.

* * *

A Rising Tide Lifts All Boats

As we look to the future, one of President Kennedy's favorite sayings comes to mind: "A rising tide lifts all boats." Kennedy was referring to the national benefits of an improvement in the economy. But the *real tide* that will lift all boats is a new surge of Catholic evangelization. Every bishop and all the bishops together should give serious thought to investing human and financial capital (and raising a lot more of both) into this greatest of all causes.

There is literally nothing that can bring about greater good than the proclamation of the Gospel of Christ, since He alone is the ultimate desire of all human longings and the ultimate source of freedom from all disordered proclivities.

Serious sociological research consistently bears out this fact. Patrick Fagan, Ph.D. (research fellow for the Heritage Foundation and senior fellow and director of the Marriage and Religion Research Institute) has copiously catalogued all of the research studies on the relationship between social dysfunction and religious faith over many years. A summary of his findings states:

> Strong and repeated evidence indicates that regular practice of religion has beneficial effects in nearly every aspect of social concern and policy. The evidence shows that religious practice protects against disorder and dysfunction... No other dimension of life in

410

America – with the exception of stable marriages and families, which are strongly tied to religious practice – does more to promote the well-being and soundness of the nation's civil society than citizens' religious observance.[178]

To be more specific, Fagan cites a markedly positive association between religious practice and higher levels of marital stability; lower divorce rates; lower co-habitation rates; lower rates of out-of-wedlock births; lower rates of teen sexual activity; less abuse of alcohol and drugs; lower rates of suicide, depression, and suicide ideation; lower rates of many infectious diseases; less juvenile crime; less violent crime; less domestic crime; stronger parent-child relations; greater educational aspirations and attainment, especially among the poor; higher levels of good work habits; greater longevity and physical health; higher recovery rates from addictions to alcohol and drugs; higher levels of self-control, self-esteem, and coping skills; higher rates of charitable donations and volunteering, and; higher levels of community cohesion and social support for those in need.

So…

† Concerned about the eternal destiny of loved ones? Introduce them to the love of Jesus and one-by-one watch the trajectory of their lives change.

† Concerned about the decline in Christian faith among Millennials? Proclaim Jesus as God incarnate breaking into this world to demonstrate his love and, over time, watch the change in the very course of their future.

† Concerned about the tyranny of relativism and evil in the world? Proclaim the Gospel and objective standards of right and wrong are learned.

† Concerned about the breakdown of the family? Turn a man's heart to Christ, and he will become a better husband and father.

† Concerned about poverty and a culture of drug addiction? Introduce the mercy of Jesus and liberation from sin, and observe the quality of marriages improve and divorce rates fall with fewer single moms desperately struggling to make ends meet.

† Concerned about pornography? Introduce a young man to Christ and his grace will bring about repentance and liberation. Again, more successful marriages.

These are all **_facts_** that we know, either from our own experience or the credible witness of others. The Gospel alone has the cascading power to ameliorate every social pathology. Until our Lord returns, we cannot expect a utopia. Notwithstanding this fact, the Gospel alone re-directs the soul to right-thinking, which eventually *affects everything* – civil discourse, public policy, even church revenue. Most importantly, it will affect eternal destinies. If there were no collateral benefits at all, the salvation of souls would justify all our efforts, and more.

Lost ground can be won back and the future dramatically improved if we consciously raise the cause of proclaiming the Gospel of Jesus – publicly and privately – to the highest priority "whether convenient or inconvenient" (cf. 2 Timothy 4:2).

At this point in history we may be inclined to despair before even trying the actions suggested in these pages. The recent scandals and the longer-term trajectory of history may convince us that "the voice of one crying out in the wilderness" can no longer be heard above the din.

* * *

May the words of Nehemiah and Ezra ring fresh in our ears: "'Today is holy to the Lord your God. Do not be sad, and do not weep' – for all the people were weeping as they heard the words of the law." (Neh 8:9) After hearing the law of the Lord, the people were overwhelmed with how badly they and their parents and their children had failed. They were convicted of their own sinfulness and collectively experienced the grace of repentance. But even repentance was not the final word. Nehemiah went on: "'Go, eat rich foods, and drink sweet drinks, and allot portions to those who had nothing prepared; for today is holy to the LORD. Do not be saddened this day, for rejoicing in the LORD must be your strength!'" (8:10)

In the final analysis, we have been forgiven. The LORD actually loves us even in our rebellion and spiritual blindness. By the miracle of his love, "… the LORD takes delight in his people." (Ps 149:4) May we internalize this fact and share his love with everyone.

Acknowledgments

This book simply could not have been written without the amazing patience and support of Mary, my beloved wife, constant companion (and diving buddy).

As my special friend and co-founder of the St. Paul Evangelization Society (SPES), George Witwer personifies transformational leadership and has provided brilliant ideas that have helped make this book what it is. He has also been an ebullient source of encouragement and kept me going when I was ready to move onto something else. Zane Williamson, SPES' former content manager, also provided a great perspective that kept me on point.

Two other close friends, Deacon Dave Rice and Rev. Bill Conard read chapters, offered invaluable insights, and prayed with me these many months. As a retired executive of the Billy Graham Evangelistic Association, Bill's support and encouragement has meant more than I can say.

Special thanks to Archbishop Charles Thompson of Indianapolis, who in his previous capacity as Bishop of Evansville gave me the time off from my parish diaconal assignment to work on this project. Following his lead, Bishop Joseph Siegel has gone out of his way to help me out on multiple occasions. Without their combined help, this book would have been literally impossible.

Finally, the friendship, encouragement, and prayers of several bishops whom I have come to know and love through SPES helped me believe that this project may, in the end, be a worthwhile contribution to the cause of the New Evangelization. I am indebted most especially to Bishops Philip Egan of Portsmouth UK, Jeffrey Monforton of Steubenville, OH, Donald Hying of Madison, WI, and Sam Jacobs (emeritus) of Houma-Thibadaux, LA.

Notes

The Greatest Unmet Need

1 http://www.fides.org/ en / news/ 63340-VATICAN _Pope_Francis_ the_ proclamation_ of _the _Gospel _is _not _proselytism _Only _ the _ Holy _ Spirit _attracts_and_converts_hearts

2 Pope St. Paul VI, *Evangelii Nuntiandi* (14)

3 *Catechism of the Catholic Church* (1)

A Paradigm Shift

4 Raymond de Thomas de Saint-Laurent, *St. Thérèse of the Child Jesus* (Spring Grove, PA: The American Society of the Defense of Traditions, Family, and Property, English ed., 2018), 76-77

5 Ibid, Pope St. Paul VI, (80)

6 Michael White and Tom Corcoran, *Rebuilt: Awakening the Faithful, Reaching the Lost, Making Church Matter* (Notre Dame IN: Ave Maria Press, 2013), xviii.

7 Second Vatican Council, Dogmatic Constitution on the Church, *Lumen Gentium* (20)

8 St. Clement of Rome, *Epistle of St. Clement to the Corinthians* Chapter 42:1-4

9 Ibid, Chapter 44:1-2

10 *Lumen Gentium,* Ibid, 24

11 Ibid, 25

12 Philp Kosloski, Whatever Happened to the Twelve Apostles? July 21, 2017, https://aleteia.org/2017/07/21/whatever-happened-to-the-twelve-apostles/

13 Tony Mariot, Where did each of the apostles travel after Christ's ascension, November 22, 2017, https://www.quora.com/Where-did-each-of-the-apostles-travel-after-Christs-ascension

14 St. Ignatius of Antioch, *Epistle to the Ephesians* (III), https://www. ewtn.com/ library/PATRISTC/ignatius_ephesians.htm

15 Ibid, *Epistle to the Magnesians* (IV)

16 Ibid, *Epistle to the Trallians* (VIII)

17 Lydia Saad, "Confidence in Religion at New Low, but Not Among Catholics", June 17, 2015, https://news.gallup.com/poll/183674/confidence-religion-new-low-not-among-catholics.aspx (Note: The findings with respect to Catholics in this article do not capture attitudes since the summer of 2018)

18 Rodney Stark, *The Triumph of Faith: Why the World Is More Religious Than Ever* (ISI Books, 2015)

[19] Charles J. Chaput, *Strangers in a Strange Land: Living the Catholic Faith in a Post-Christian World* (New York: Henry Holt and Company, 2017) 186

[20] Melvin M. Webber, *Explorations into Urban Structure,* (Philadelphia, Pa.: University of Pennsylvania Press, [2016] ©1964)

[21] Mark Gray, "Young People are Leaving the Faith: Here's Why", OSV Newsweekly, 2016 https://www.osv.com/ OSVNewsweekly/ Story/ TabId/ 2672/ ArtMID/ 13567/ArticleID/ 20512/Young-people-are-leaving-the-faith-Heres-why.aspx

[22] Julie Bourbon, "Study asks: Why are young Catholics going, going, gone?", NCROnline, 2018, https://www.ncronline.org/news/parish/study-asks-why-are-young-catholics-going-going-gone

[23] United States Conference of Catholic Bishops, *Go and Make Disciples: A National Plan and Strategy for Catholic Evangelization in the United States* (GMD, 133)

[24] Ibid, GMD, 136

[25] Rodney Stark, *The Rise of Christianity: A Sociologist Reconsiders History* (Princeton, NJ: Princeton University Press, 1996) 7

[26] Malcolm Gladwell, *The Tipping Point: How Little Things Make a Big Difference* (New York: Back Bay Books, 2002)

[27] NCR Staff, Catholic dioceses and orders that filed for bankruptcy and other major settlements, May 2018 https://www.ncronline.org/news/accountability/catholic-dioceses-and-orders-filed-bankruptcy-and-other-major-settlements

[28] While religious education can be understood as evangelization, it ordinarily takes the form of formal catechesis that is not aimed at personal conversion

[29] Canon 1267 §3: "Offerings given by the faithful for a specific purpose can be applied only for that purpose."

A Bishop's Dream

[30] Canon. 528 §1 Excerpt: "With the collaboration of the faithful, [the pastor] is to make every effort to bring the gospel message to those also who have given up religious practice or who do not profess the true faith."

Finding Forgiveness

[31] "Catholicism after 2018", R.R. Reno, *First Things,* October 2018, Number 286, 69

[32] https://en.wikipedia.org/wiki/Catholic_Church_sexual_abuse_cases#United_States

[33] https://www.foxnews.com/story/catholic-priest-attended-first-man-boy-love-meeting-documents-show

[34] James Hitchcock, *History of the Catholic Church,* (San Francisco: Ignatius Press, 2012), 69

[35] Second Vatican Council, Decree on the Pastoral Office of Bishops, *Christus Dominus* (16)

[36] St. John Chrysostom, *Office of Readings* for September 13. *Ante exilium*

[37] Raniero Cantalamessa, OFM Cap, *Staying with Jesus Means Going Through a Radical Conversion,* Second meditation to the U.S. bishops retreat, Mundelein Seminary, January 2019, https://drive.google.com/file/d/1psS0uMxScLIH7JGE1ZDbJ Dre2zmC7hGT/view

Rediscovering the Pearl of Great Price

[38] See *Symbolon: The Catholic Faith Explained* (A DVD series used for RCIA produced by Edward Sri, Ph.D. of the Augustine Institute, 2014)

[39] Second Vatican Council's Decree on Ecumenism *Unitatis redintegratio,* 11

[40] Pope Francis I, The Joy of the Gospel, *Evangelii Gaudium* (35)

Servants Who Will Lead

[41] Louis J. Cameli, *Church, Faith, Future: What We Face, What We Can Do,* (Collegeville MN: Liturgical Press, 2017), 44

[42] St. Augustine, excerpt from the beginning of a sermon on pastors, (Sermo 46, 1-2: CCL 41, 529-530) as quoted in the Office of Readings from the Twenty-Fourth Sunday in Ordinary Time.

Attitudes about Evangelization

[43] Nancy T. Ammerman, *Pillars of Faith* (Berkeley: University of California Press, 2005) 117, 134. Cited in *The Urgency of the New Evangelization: Answering the Call* by Ralph Martin (Huntington: Our Sunday Visitor Publishing Division, 2013) 19.

[44] *Catechism of the Catholic Church,* (2093)

[45] http://www.pewforum.org/2015/11/03/ chapter-1- importance -of – religion - and- religious-beliefs/

[46] Pope Francis, op. cit. (3)

[47] See Gavin DeCosta, "Karl Rahner's Anonymous Christian: A Reappraisal". *Modern Theology.* 1(2): 131–148. doi:10.1111/j.1468-0025.1985.tb00013.x. ISSN 0266-7177

[48] Second Vatican Council, Dogmatic Constitution on the Church, *Lumen Gentium* (16)

[49] Ibid

---

[50] Vincent L. Bernardin, Sr., *Survey of Registered Parishioners concerning Evangelization,* Diocesan Evangelization Team, Diocese of Evansville, 2013. This Internet survey was conducted through a controlled email methodology with a total random sample size of 2,309. The sample yielded 608 responses (or 26%).

[51] St. John Paul II, *Novo Millennio Ineuente* (40)

[52] Ibid, Pope Francis (110)

[53] Pope Benedict XVI, *Verbum Domini* (96)

[54] Ralph Martin, *The Urgency of the New Evangelization: Answering the Call* (Huntington: Our Sunday Visitor Publishing Division, 2013), 107

Sharing Our Faith Openly... Really?

[55] Ibid, Pope Francis I (264)

[56] The figure of 21 percent assumes that one is Catholic if registered in a parish. The figure of 25% assumes that anyone who responds "Catholic" in self-identification surveys is really Catholic.

[57] The Pew Research Center, In U.S., Decline of Christianity Continues at Rapid Pace, October 17, 2019. See https://www.pewforum.org/2019/10/17/in-u-s-decline-of-christianity-continues-at-rapid-pace/

[58] The Pew Research Center, *U.S. Religious Landscape Survey*

[59] The Pew Research Center, *America's Changing Religious Landscape,* May 2015. See http://www.pewforum.org/2015/05/12/chapter-2-religious-switching-and-intermarriage/

[60] Ibid

[61] Ibid

[62] *Official Catholic Directory* annual statistics obtained in digital form the Center for Applied Research in the Apostolate. Percentage declines reported in the text are computed from the linear trend line values. Given the high correlations between "year" and "sacramental rate", the trend lines provide a better idea of actual change over time than specific data observations

[63] The U.S. fertility rate (births per 1,000 women aged 15-44) was 63.6 in 1997. It then climbed to 69.3 in 2008 and has since fallen to 62.5 in 2013. See http://www.cdc.gov/nchs/ data/ncsr64/nvsr64_01.pdf

[64] http://dynamiccatholic.com/confirmation/faqs/

[65] Pope St. John Paul II, *Redemptoris missio,* 2-3

[66] Pope Benedict XVI, Synod of Bishops XIII Ordinary General Assembly, *The New Evangelization for the Transmission of the Christian Faith,* Lineamenta (I,10)

[67] Ibid, Pope Francis I (27)

---

[68] Raniero Cantalamessa, OFM Cap., *Remember Jesus Christ: Responding to the Challenges of Faith in Our Time* (Frederick: The Word Among Us Press, 2007) 22-23

Purposeful Parishes

[69] Second Vatican Council, *Decree on the Pastoral Office of Bishops in the Church, (Christus Dominus)*, 30

[70] Michael White and Tom Corcoran, *Rebuilt: Awakening the Faithful, Reaching the Lost, Making Church Matter* (Notre Dame IN: Ave Maria Press, 2013), 37

[71] http://en.radiovaticana.va/storico/2013/03/27/bergoglios_intervention_a _diagnosis_ of_the_problems_in_the_church/en1-677269

[72] Ibid, xviii

[73] Ibid, 47

[74] Rick Warrren, *The Purpose Driven Church: Growth Without Compromising Your Message and Mission* (Grand Rapids MI: Zondervan Press, 1995), 77-79

[75] Ibid, 103-107

[76] https://www.mayoclinic.org/diseases-conditions/depression/ symptoms-causes/syc-20356007

[77] Viktor E. Frankl and Simon Vance, *Man's Search for Meaning: An Introduction to Logotherapy*, (Originally written and published in German,1942)

A Regional Strategy for Vision Achievement

[78] PERT is an acronym for "Program Evaluation and Review Technique".

[79] Sherry Weddell, *Forming Intentional Disciples: The Path to Knowing and Following Jesus* (Huntingdon, IN: Our Sunday Visitor Publishing Division, 2012), 237

[80] Ibid, Warren, 59.

[81] Ibid, Cantalamessa, 22-23.

[82] http://books.google.com/books?id = Fwtjf64nn6AC&pg = PA45&lpg=A45&dq =number+of+baptisms+following+the+apparition+of+our+Lady+of+Guadalupe &source=bl&ots = DDuZZ5rivo&sig = CZK-STgSrZSay RF7Gj0hOa0XUM&hl = en&sa=X&ei=Oii0U4uXGMqSqAbovIHYDg&ved=0CEMQ6AEwBg#v=onepage &q=number%20of%20baptisms%20following%20the%20apparition%20of%20our %20Lady%20of%20Guadalupe&f=false

[83] Stephen R. Covey, *The 7 Habits of Highly Effective People*, (New York: Simon & Schuster, 2013 edition), 102.

[84] Robert Spitzer, SJ, *New Evidence for the Existence of God from Physics and Philosophy*, (Grand Rapids MI: Eerdmans Publishing, 2010))

[85] http://sphweb.bumc.bu.edu/otlt/MPH-Modules/SB/Behavioral Change Theories/ BehavioralChangeTheories4.html

[86] https://link.springer.com/referenceworkentry/10.1007%2F1-4020-0612-8_721

[87] Ibid, Pope Francis, (120)

[88] Ibid, (121)

[89] Such surveys can be conducted by non-professionals very inexpensively these days using online tools such as Survey Monkey.

[90] Ibid, Weddell, 245

[91] St. Paul Evangelization Society, unpublished 2019 study.

[92] Everett Fritz, *The Art of Forming Young Disciples: Why Youth Ministries Aren't Working and What To Do About It* (Manchester NH, Sophia Institute Press, 2018)

[93] https://dwightlongenecker.com

[94] Allen Vigneron, Archbishop of Detroit, Pastoral Letter *Unleash the Gospel*, 2017, 43 https://www.unleashthegospel.org/the-letter/

[95] Ibid, White and Corcoran, 90

[96] Ibid, 91

[97] https://mcgrathblog.nd.edu/category/essays/author/most-rev-michael-j-byrnes

[98] "Why They Left: Exit interviews shed light on empty pews", William J. Byron and Charles Zech, *America,* April 30, 2012

[99] Mark Giszczak, Ph.D., "The Strange Myths of the New Evangelization", published in the Journal of the McGrath Institute for Church Life, May 7, 2018

[100] CARA, "How Many Catholic Converts Stay? A Quick Back of the Envelope Reality Check", *Nineteen sixty-four* blog, February 26, 2016, http://nineteensixty-four.blogspot.com/ 2016/02/how-many-catholic-converts-stay-quick.html

[101] Ibid, Bernardin

[102] Ibid, Weddell, 97-184

[103] Ibid, Pope St. Paul VI, (21)

[104] https:// www.pewforum.org/ religious - landscape - study/ marital - status/ divorced - separated/

[105] John D. Martin, "Reports of Christianity's Death in Europe Have Been Greatly Exaggerated" published in *The Federalist*, March 23, 2018, https://thefederalist.com/2018/03/23/reports-christianitys-death-europe-greatly-exaggerated/

[106] https://www.nytimes.com/2015/07/01/upshot/ why – television – is – still – king - for-campaign-spending.html?abt=0002&abg=1

[107] https://www.npr.org/ sections/ itsallpolitics/2015/08/19/ 432759311/2016-campaign-tv-ad-spending

108 John Koblin (30 June 2016). "How Much Do We Love TV? Let Us Count the Ways". *NY Times*.

109 https://catnolicscomehome.org/ Catholics Come Home, see *Diocesan Partner Highlights*

110 Charles Murray, *Coming Apart: The State of White America, 1960-2010* (New York: Random House Crowne Forum, 2012), 220 *et seq*

The Key to Getting It Done

111 https://www.catholicworldreport.com/ 2018/ 11/ 13/intense-debate-over-handling-of-abuse-scandal-ensues-at-usccb-meeting/

112 George Weigel, *Evangelical Catholicism: Deep Reform in the 21st Century Church* (New York: Basic Books, 2013) 121

113 Ibid, Chaput, 188-189

114 https://www.pewresearch.org/ fact-tank/ 2019/ 01/ 24/ like-americans-overall-u-s-catholics-are-sharply-divided-by-party/

115 http:// www.perforum.org/ 2015/ 11/ 03/ chapter- 1- importance- of- religion-and- religious-beliefs/

116 Ibid, Chaput, 108

117 https://en.wikipedia.org/wiki/James_C._Collins

118 Jim Collins, *Good to Great: Why Some Companies Make the Leap and Others Don't*, (New York: HarperCollins Publishers, 2001), 10

119 Ibid, Collins, 39-40.

120 Ibid, 40

121 As a matter of minutia, a frequently quoted variant of this saying reads: "I have two kinds of problems: the urgent and the important. The urgent are seldom important, and the important are seldom urgent." My source, however claims that Eisenhower used the more categorical qualifiers "not" and "never" as quoted in the text, versus the softer adverb "seldom." https://quoteinvestigator.com/2014/05/09/urgent/

122 Torben Rich, December 16, 2014, https://www.supplychain247.com/article/ organizational_culture_eats_strategy_for_breakfast_lunch_and_dinner/legacy_s upply_chain_services

123 James Mallon, *Divine Renovation: Bringing Your Parish from Maintenance to Mission*, (New London CT: Twenty-Third Publications, 2014) 94

124 https:// www.goodreads.com/ quotes/ 133920-hope-for-the-best-expect-the-worst-life-is-a

125 https://www.worldbank.org/en/topic/poverty/overview

126 https://worldhunger.org/world-hunger-and-poverty-facts-and-statistics

127 https://ourworldindata.org/life-expectancy

128 Ibid

129 Ibid, Pope Francis I (85)

130 Jim Collins and Jerry Porras, *Built to Last: Successful Habits of a Visionary Company* (New York: HarperCollins Publishers, 1994), 113

131 John F. Kennedy, Excerpt from his *Special Message to the Congress on Urgent Needs*, NASA, May 24, 2004

132 https://www.jimcollins.com/article_topics/articles/BHAG.html

133 Ibid, Mallon, 244

134 Gary Keller, *The One Thing: The Surprisingly Simple Truth Behind Extraordinary Results* (Austin TX: Bard Press, 2013)

135 Ibid, 81

136 Ibid, White and Corcoran, 75

137 Ibid, Lencioni, 141-142

138 Patrick Lencioni, *The Advantage* (San Francisco: Jossey-Bass, 2012), 77-78

139 In my opinion, there is a role for pastors and parishes to have their own parish-specific-plan, but it is far more limited than current practice would suggest. In fairness to parishes, one of the reasons why it happens with some regularity is because of the void left by the bishop in articulating a vision and a reasonable pastoral plan for the whole diocese. As a *part* of the local Church, parish plans should be established in light of regional pastoral objectives in ways that build on the parishes' peculiar "strengths" and "opportunities". These are the "S" and the "O" in a commonly-used planning tool known as 'SWOT analysis'. In my view, a parish's particular weaknesses ("W") and threats ("T") of SWOT analysis should be recognized in a joint, collaborative effort with the diocese in the hope that resources can be brought to bear to help shore them up.

140 Second Vatican Council, Decree on the Pastoral Office of Bishops in the Church, *Christus Dominus*, 16

141 Ibid, 8 (a), 8 (b)

142 Second Vatican Council, Decree on Ecumenism, *Unitatis redintegratio*, 7-8

143 Ibid, Pope Francis (14)

144 Code of Canon Law Article 2, Canon 383 §1 and §4

145 Ibid, Warren, 42-44

146 St. Vincent de Paul, Office of Readings for September 27

147 Ibid, Chaput, 120

The 'Catholic Moment' Revisited

148 St. John Paul II, *Tertio millennio adveniente*, 1994, (33-34)

149 Richard John Neuhaus, *The Catholic Moment: The Paradox of the Church in the Post-Modern World* (New York, Harper and Row, 1987). Neuhaus was always an outspoken opinion-leader. As a Lutheran minister and social activist during the turbulent 60s and 70s, Pastor Neuhaus spoke out in defense of the civil rights movement and against the Vietnam Was along with notables such as Father Daniel Berrigan, SJ, and the influential Jewish theologian, Rabbi Abraham Heschel. When the landmark Supreme Court case *Row v Wade* was decided, Neuhaus' passions turned to the defense of pre-born children. He declared the pro-life cause as the new civil rights movement of the times and he remained committed to this struggle the rest of his life. Beginning with the Second Vatican Council in the 60s, certain key features of Catholicism caught Neuhaus' attention and sparked a nascent respect for the Catholic Church. He was deeply impressed by the internally consistent and growing corpus of Catholic social doctrine. Over time, his respect for Catholicism grew, especially under the papacy of St. John Paul II, whom he regarded as one of the great prophetic Christian leaders in the history of Christianity. In 1981, he founded the Institute on Religion and Democracy and its journal *First Things*, which remains one of the most respected intellectual journals on religion and social philosophy to this day. Among his most significant achievements was the co-founding of *Evangelicals and Catholics Together* (or ECT) with his friend, Chuck Colson, former Watergate insider turned born-again Christian and prison reform advocate. ECT might best be described as an eclectic fellowship of conservative theologians and ecclesial leaders within the evangelical world and Catholicism committed to the responsible proclamation of the Gospel... together. Since their inception in 1994, the members of ECT have published in *First Things* a total of nine joint statements addressing theological and contemporary points of unity on such diverse subjects as Justification, Unity, Scripture, Saints, Holiness, Abortion, Freedom, Marriage, and even Mary. At the same time, the statements are all completely and respectfully candid about the numerous points of disagreement that remain.

150 Ibid, 283

151 Ibid, 284

152 Ibid, 264

153 Ibid, 284

154 Ibid, 285

155 William J. Byron and Charles Zech, "Why they left: Interviews shed light on empty pews", America, April 30, 2012, https://www.americamagazine.org/issue/5138/article/why-they-left

[156] Stephen Bullivant, Catherine Knowles, Hannah Vaughn-Spruce, and Bernadette Durcan, *Why Catholics Leave, What They Miss, and How They Might Return* (New York, Paulist Press, 2019)

[157] Ibid., Stephen Bullivant *et al*, 128

[158] Ibid, 128

[159] Matt Hadro, "Why Catholics are leaving the faith by age 10 – and what parents can do about it", CNA/EWTN News, December 17, 2016. https://www.catholicnewsagency.com/news/why-catholics-are-leaving-the-faith-by-age-10-and-what-parents-can-do-about-it-48918

[160] https://epicpew.com/11-amazing-catholic-scientists-you-should-know/

[161] https://aleteia.org/2018/05/25/these-5-catholic-scientists-shaped-our-understanding-of-the-world/

[162] https://www.catholic.com/magazine/print-edition/fathers-of-science

[163] This evidence for God points to a creation event (aka, the Big Bang) and demonstrates the virtual statistical impossibility of the fine-tuned universe we "just happen" to live in with the exact "cosmic constants" that permit the formation of stars and planets in the first place. The odds of any life existing, let alone intelligent life are infinitesimally small. The work of Father Robert Spitzer, SJ and his *Magis Center* (https://www.magiscenter.com/) can be a valuable resource of such a *pre-evangelization* campaign. Father Spitzers's book *New Proofs for the Existence of God: Contributions from Contemporary Physics and Philosophy* (Grand Rapids MI: Eerdmans Publishing, 2010) is highly recommended.

[164] Second Vatican Council, Decree on the Means of Social Communication (*Inter mirifica*), (1)

[165] Ibid, (3)

[166] Ibid, (16)

[167] Ibid, (17)

[168] Center for Responsive Politics, https://www.opensecrests.org/pres16

[169] Ibid

[170] Ibid

[171] Jorge Mario Cardinal Bergoglio, excerpt from his intervention at the pre-conclave gathering of cardinal-elector, March 2013

[172] Ibid, Charles Murray, 154-155

[173] Ibid, Murray, 156

[174] Ibid, 218-220

[175] Ibid, 202-203

[176] Ibid, 204

[177] Ibid, 208

[178] Patrick Fagan, Ph.D., *Why Religion Matters Even More: The Impact of Religious Practice on Social Stability.* See http://www.heritage.org/research/reports/2006/12/why-religion-matters-even-more-the-impact-of-religious-practice-on-social-stability

Made in the USA
Columbia, SC
10 March 2020